Inspiration

After studies at the University of Melbourne and at the University of Cambridge, where he was a research fellow of Pembroke College, Gerald O'Collins taught at the Gregorian University, Rome from 1973 to 2006 and was also Dean of the Theology Faculty 1985–91. Known around the world as a lecturer and visiting professor, he has authored or co-authored seventy-six books. As well as receiving many honorary doctorates and other awards, in 2006 he was created a Companion of the General Division of the Order of Australia (AC), the highest civil honour granted through the Australian government.

T0352680

Praise for *Inspiration*

'an up-to-date, constructive account'

David R. Nienhuis, *Scottish Journal of Theology*

'this masterly treatment... brings together a lifetime of learning in biblical and systematic theology. The style is elegant and economic... This is interdisciplinary theology at its best... a real gem, which deserves to have a significant impact in the Church, and especially in the scholarly community'

Peter Forster, *Church Times*

'a penetrating and stimulating account of the Christian doctrine that the Bible is inspired by the Holy Spirit'

Joseph K. Gordon, *Reading Religion*

Inspiration

Towards a Christian Interpretation of Biblical Inspiration

GERALD O'COLLINS, SJ

OXFORD
UNIVERSITY PRESS

OXFORD
UNIVERSITY PRESS

Great Clarendon Street, Oxford, OX2 6DP,
United Kingdom

Oxford University Press is a department of the University of Oxford.
It furthers the University's objective of excellence in research, scholarship,
and education by publishing worldwide. Oxford is a registered trade mark of
Oxford University Press in the UK and in certain other countries

© Gerald O'Collins, SJ 2018

First published 2018
First published in paperback 2021

Published in the United States of America by Oxford University Press
198 Madison Avenue, New York, NY 10016, United States of America

British Library Cataloguing in Publication Data
Data available

Library of Congress Cataloging in Publication Data
Data available

ISBN 978–0–19–882418–3 (Hbk.)
ISBN 978–0–19–883677–3 (Pbk.)

Preface

Oh Book! Infinite sweetness! Let my heart
Suck every letter and a honey gain
Precious for any grief in any part;
To clear the breast, to mollify the pain.

George Herbert

Within this ample volume lies
The mystery of mysteries.
Happiest they of human race
To whom their God has given grace
To read, to fear, to hope, to pray,
To lift the latch, to force the way.

Sir Walter Scott

Christians everywhere look to the Bible as *the* book which is essential for creating and sustaining their identity. Christianity and Christian life are unthinkable without this volume which binds together the Scriptures of the Old Testament and the New Testament. In various ways, all Christians expect the Bible to guide them in what they believe and do and in how they pray together or alone. They draw from this book the basic narrative for explaining who they are and what they are about in the world. They accept the Bible as centrally authoritative for their faith and practice.

Christian believers attribute such importance to the Bible because they hold that in some real sense God was uniquely involved in producing, over many centuries, the particular books that make it up. Since they speak of the Holy Spirit inspiring its writing, they call it 'Holy Scripture', 'the Sacred Scriptures', 'the Word of God', or 'the Word of the Lord'.

All of this makes it surprising how, for decades now, scholarly works have marginalized or simply neglected the question of biblical inspiration. Before the Second World War, as we shall see in Chapter 1, Karl Barth dedicated many pages of his *Church Dogmatics* to this question.

After the Second World War, another outstanding theologian, Karl Rahner, thought it worth his while to compose *Inspiration in the Bible* (New York: Herder & Herder, 1961; German original 1958). A notable scripture scholar, Bruce Vawter, wrote *Biblical Inspiration* (London: Hutchinson, 1972). A few years later another scripture scholar, Paul Achtemeier, published *The Inspiration of Scripture* (Philadelphia: Westminster Press, 1980; rev. 1999). But in more recent years, theologians and scripture scholars seem to have lost interest in the topic. To talk merely of a diminished interest would seem an understatement.

The six-volume *Anchor Bible Dictionary* edited by David Noel Freedman (New York: Doubleday, 1992) includes a long entry on 'Scriptural Authority' (v, 1017–56) but no entry on 'Inspiration'. But surely the authority of the Scriptures depends on their having been inspired by the Holy Spirit? The *Oxford Handbook of Biblical Studies* (Oxford: Oxford University Press, 2006), a work of over 900 pages edited by J. W. Rogerson and J. M. Lieu, does not even have an entry on 'inspiration' in the index. The *Cambridge Companion to the Hebrew Bible/ Old Testament* (New York: Cambridge University Press, 2016), edited by S. B. Chapman and M. A. Sweeney, likewise has no entry on 'inspiration' in the index. Volume one of *The New Cambridge History of the Bible* (Cambridge: Cambridge University Press, 2012) covers from 'the beginnings to 600', contains much on the formation of the biblical canons, but ignores 'inspiration', which again fails to find a place in the index. The two-volume *Oxford Encyclopedia of the Bible* (New York: Oxford University Press, 2015), edited by Samuel E. Balentine, contains no entry on 'inspiration', and dedicates to this theme barely more than a page within an entry on 'Scripture' (ii, 272–3). The *Oxford Handbook of Theology and Modern European Thought*, edited by Nicholas Adams, George Pattison, and Graham Ward (Oxford: Oxford University Press, 2013), runs to over 700 pages, includes chapters on the Bible and tradition, but has no chapter on scriptural inspiration; and yet again, it does not list 'inspiration' in the index.

There are a few exceptions. John Webster's *Holy Scripture: A Dogmatic Sketch* (Cambridge: Cambridge University Press, 2003) discusses inspiration at length, especially in Chapter 1. In *Beloved Community: Critical Dogmatics after Christendom* (Grand Rapids, MI: Eerdmans, 2015), Paul Hinlicky has a certain amount on 'inspiration', but a great deal more on biblical authority. The same holds true of Don Carson (ed.), *The Enduring Authority of the Christian Scriptures* (Grand Rapids, MI: Eerdmans, 2016); this 1256-page volume deals extensively with the authority of the Bible but much less with its divine inspiration, which provides the grounds for this authority.

Normally theology in the twenty-first century has left the theme of biblical inspiration out in the cold. Hence Chapter 1 of this book goes back behind recent literature, and initiates its discussion of biblical inspiration by entering into dialogue with what Karl Barth wrote in the 1930s and what an American exegete, Raymond Collins, published in 1989. Convinced that any adequate study of inspiration must be firmly anchored in the Scriptures themselves, I then take up several books of the Old Testament (Genesis, Psalms, Isaiah, and Sirach) to examine something of the inspired origin and inspiring impact of these texts (Chapter 2).

The twenty-seven books of the New Testament cite and echo most frequently the Psalms and Isaiah, with Deuteronomy, Exodus, and Genesis ranking next. Chapter 3 examines the inspiring influence of Old Testament Scriptures on the New Testament authors and on the One who provided their central focus, Jesus himself.

Chapter 4 moves to the story of Christianity and investigates the enduring and worldwide influence of the Scriptures, both Old and New Testaments. The inspiring impact of the Bible shows up everywhere: in the worship, preaching, official teaching, hymns, visual arts, and life of Christians. The illuminating and nourishing force of the Scriptures can be documented abundantly.

Before directly examining the characteristics of biblical inspiration, we need to clarify the interrelationship between revelation, tradition, and inspiration itself (Chapter 5). An account of the formation and content of Scriptures lays the ground for expounding five characteristics of inspiration (Chapter 6). Chapter 7 adds five further characteristics, with a special emphasis on the inspiring quality of the Bible (its tenth and crowning characteristic).

Chapter 8 will discuss (a) one major consequence of biblical inspiration, the truth that guides Christian faith, worship and action, and (b) the post-New Testament 'canonization' of the Scriptures that formally recognized their decisive authority for the Church. A ninth chapter will spell out three approaches to biblical interpretation, and a final chapter will set out ten principles for theological engagement with the

Scriptures. The book ends with an epilogue that will highlight the major conclusions to be drawn from this study of inspiration.

For the sake of clarity, two major themes of this book should be stated in advance. First, close attention to the Scriptures themselves and to their reception yields much more insight into inspiration and its workings than abstract theorizing about its nature. Second, even if the study of the Scriptures provides only a limited amount of knowledge about the divine causality involved in their writing (and reading), we enjoy abundant information about the impact of the inspired Scriptures. As is very often the case, *effects* (here the ongoing, inspiring effects) are much more visible than their *cause* and its inner working (here the original inspiration by the Holy Spirit of the Scriptures in the past *and* the continuing impact of the same Spirit on the readers, hearers, and interpreters of the Scriptures).

A double causality must be reckoned with: (a) the original impact of the Holy Spirit on those involved, directly or indirectly, in *writing* the sacred texts; and (b) the Spirit's continuing influence on those who have subsequently *read* these texts and found in them 'saving truth', or enlightenment that promotes their salvation. As regards (b), the readers (and hearers) of the sacred texts must be divided into two classes: (i) those who before the apostolic age ended (roughly speaking, around AD 100) contributed to the writing of the Bible; and (ii) the innumerable Christians and others later influenced by the Scriptures (which were gathered into a closed canon by the fourth century). Earlier scriptural texts influenced many in class (i), not only all the authors of the New Testament but also later writers of the Old Testament. In a coming chapter, we will cite William A. Tooman's *Gog of Magog: Reuse of Scripture and Compositional Technique in Ezekiel 38–39* (Tübingen: Mohr Siebeck, 2011), who shows how earlier sacred texts influenced the composition of those two chapters. The inspiring impact of what we know as the Old Testament Scriptures on the writers of the New Testament is huge, and sometimes involved a radically free rereading, as we will see (e.g. in the case of Paul and Hebrews).

To return to class (ii), the Bible provided their central *language* for liturgy and life. It *informed* them about their basic situation before God; that information helped *form/shape* their Christian existence. The Bible supplied *norms* and principles governing their belief and behaviour. What the Bible does as informing, forming/shaping, language- and norm-supplying, and—above all—revealing God and humanity's situation before God can be gathered together as its inspiring influence. More precisely, we can speak of the inspiring influence of the Holy Spirit that continues to cause its effects through the channel of the Scriptures which the same Spirit originally brought into existence. The inspiring Scriptures are one major and essential mode through which the Spirit of truth remains present and continues to 'guide' Christ's followers 'into all truth' (John 16: 13).

Nearly forty years ago, in *La Parola di Dio alle Origini della Chiesa* (Rome: Biblical Institute Press, 1980), Carlo Maria Martini noted that, while an adequate treatise on biblical inspiration was highly desirable, none was available (42). May this book go some distance towards meeting this need.

When quoting the Bible, I normally follow the New Revised Standard Version (NRSV) but sometimes prefer my own translation. As a Christian, I use the terminology of the 'Old Testament', rather than the 'Tanakh' or Hebrew Bible as in the Jewish tradition. Here 'old' is understood as good and does not imply 'supersessionism', the view that the New Testament has rendered obsolete the Old Testament and so superseded it.

Let me warmly thank Brendan Byrne, Joshua Choong, Marianne Fisher, George Hunsinger, Robin Koning, Tom Perridge, Anne Steinemann, Denis White, Christopher Willcock, and two anonymous readers for Oxford University Press; in different and generous ways, they contributed to the making of this work. I dedicate it with great esteem and affection to the late Fra' Richard Divall, AO, OBE.

Gerald O'Collins, SJ, AC

Australian Catholic University and
University of Divinity (Melbourne)
13 October 2017

Note for Paperback Edition

For this paperback edition, in which a few errata have been corrected, I am grateful to Oxford University Press. I wish to thank also the following reviewers:

Peter Adam, *The Melbourne Anglican*, 9 September 2019.

Tony Clark, *Theology* 122 (2019), 221–22.

Peter Forster, *Church Times*, 7 December 2018, 22.

Joseph K. Gordon, *Reading Religion*, 25 June 2019, 2–3.

Andrew Hamilton, *Jesuit News*, 6 June 2018.

Nicholas King, *The Tablet*, 13 October 2018, 20.

Ela Lazarewicz-Wyrzykowska, *Journal for the Study of the Old Testament* 43 (2019), 176.

Nathan Lefler, *Irish Theological Quarterly* 84 (2019), 434–39.

David R. Nienhuis, *Scottish Journal of Theology* 73 (2020), 172–74.

Henry Wansbrough, *Reviews in Religion and Theology* 26 (2019), 308–09.

Ronald D. Witherup, *Theological Studies* 80 (2019), pp. 449–50.

In the *Irish Theological Quarterly* 85 (2020), 105–06, I have already responded to the review by Nathan Lefler; in a forthcoming article for the same journal, I have an article ('Biblical Inspiration Revisited') entering into dialogue with all the reviewers.

G. O'C

17 March 2021

Contents

List of Abbreviations

ABD   D. N. Freedman (ed.), *Anchor Bible Dictionary*, 6 vols (New York: Doubleday, 1992).

DzH   H. Denzinger and P. Hünermann (eds), *Enchiridion symbolorum, definitionum et declarationum*, English trans. of 43rd edn (San Francisco: Ignatius Press, 2012).

ND   J. Neuner and J. Dupuis (eds), *The Christian Faith*, 7th edn (Bangalore: Theological Publications in India, 2001).

OEBA   T. K. Beal (ed.), *The Oxford Encyclopedia of the Bible and the Arts*, 2 vols (New York: Oxford University Press, 2015).

OEBI   S. L. McKenzie (ed.), *The Oxford Encyclopedia of Biblical Interpretation*, 2 vols (New York: Oxford University Press, 2013).

par. parr.   Parallel passage(s) in Synoptic Gospels.

PL   *Patrologia Latina*, J. P. Migne (ed.), 221 vols (Paris, 1844–64).

TRE   H. Krause and G. Müller (eds), *Theologische Realenzylopädie*, 36 vols (Berlin: Walter de Gruyter, 1977–2004).

1

The Inspiration of the Bible

Two Accounts

Before expounding the (inspired) nature and (inspiring) function of biblical inspiration, I want to recall and evaluate two accounts of inspiration: one by a Protestant theologian, Karl Barth (1886–1968),[1] and the other by a Roman Catholic scripture scholar, Raymond F. Collins (b. 1935). There is a lucid eloquence to what each says, and together they open up issues about biblical inspiration.

Dissatisfied with the optimistic humanism of prevailing Liberal Protestantism, the Swiss-born Barth aimed to recover the central insights of the Reformation and stressed the revealing and judging Word of God that calls forth faith. The monumental exposition of Barth's Word of God theology, the *Church Dogmatics*, was still incomplete at his death. An American exegete, Collins represents the new wave of Catholic biblical scholars, whose work had been hugely encouraged by the 1943 encyclical of Pius XII, *Divino afflante spiritu* (the Divine Spirit Inspiring), and by the Constitution on Divine Revelation (*Dei Verbum*, the Word of God) of the Second Vatican Council (1962–5).

Karl Barth: *Church Dogmatics* I/1

In the preface to the first edition (1918) of *The Epistle to the Romans*, Barth wrote: 'Were I driven to choose between [the historical-critical

[1] See David Gibson, 'The Answering Speech of Men: Karl Barth on Holy Scripture', in D. A. Carson (ed.), *The Enduring Authority of the Christian Scriptures* (Grand Rapids, MI: Eerdmans, 2016), 266–91; George Hunsinger (ed.), *Thy Word is Truth: Barth on Scripture* (Grand Rapids, MI: Eerdmans, 2012); and T. Work, *Living and Active: Scripture in the Economy of Salvation* (Grand Rapids, MI: Eerdmans, 2003), 67–88.

method] and the venerable doctrine of inspiration, I should without hesitation adopt the latter, which has a broader, deeper, more important justification.'[2] One might query the proposed alternative: historical-critical research practised by human beings versus the inspiration of biblical authors coming from the Holy Spirit. Did Barth simply pit human against divine causality, the human causality that expounds the Bible against the divine causality that produced the Bible? Rather it seems that Barth wanted to respect the Bible as being the written Word of God, which provides *the* deep and important justification for being engaged with it. Primarily, one should read the Holy Scripture biblically and not exegetically. Let us begin with Barth's major treatment of this question at the start of his *Dogmatics*.

In part one of the opening volume of *Church Dogmatics*: *The Doctrine of the Word of God*, Barth dedicated a long section to 'The Word of God in its Threefold Form' (as preached, written, and revealed).[3] In treating 'the Word of God Written' (99–111), Barth did not directly examine biblical inspiration, its nature, and function, but unravelled the authority of what he called 'the book of Christ' (109), 'the word of the prophets and apostles', the specific texts which constitute 'the working instructions or marching orders by which not just the Church's proclamation but the very Church itself stands or falls' (101).[4]

The Church's proclamation *recollects* past revelation and *expects* coming revelation, with the object of recollection (essentially Jesus Christ himself) providing the grounds for this expectation. Thus

---

[2] Trans. E. C. Hoskyns (London: Oxford University Press, 1933), 1.

[3] K. Barth, *Church Dogmatics*, I/1, trans. G. W. Bromiley (Edinburgh: T. & T. Clark, 1975), 88–120. Hereafter references will be given within the text.

[4] Here Barth recognized that the life of the Church ('the very Church') goes beyond 'the Church's proclamation', with both depending radically on the witness of the Bible. In the second chapter of its 1965 Dogmatic Constitution on Divine Revelation (*Dei Verbum* ('the Word of God'), art. 7–10), the Second Vatican Council pictured how the Scriptures function as the Book of the Church, with the official magisterium being 'the Servant of the Word' (art. 10). In a concluding chapter, *Dei Verbum* portrays 'the Sacred Scripture in the Life of the Church' (art. 21–6), saying that 'the entire preaching of the Church, like the Christian religion itself, should be nourished and ruled by Sacred Scripture' (art. 21); I translate for myself from *Sacrosanctum Oecumenicum Concilium Vaticanum II: Constitutiones, Decreta, Declarationes* (Vatican City: Typis Polyglottis Vaticanis, 1966).

proclamation takes place now 'on the basis that God's Word has already been spoken, that revelation has taken place' (99). Barth understood 'revelation' as pre-eminently God's Word or the *locutio Dei* (the speaking of God), rather than as God's saving and revealing acts in history (see Oscar Cullmann, Wolfhart Pannenberg, and G. E. Wright),[5] or as a 'sacramental' blending of both the speaking and acting of God (Second Vatican Council (1962–5), Constitution on Divine Revelation, *Dei Verbum* (the Word of God), art. 2, 4, 14).

Proclamation in the Church, Barth declared, 'is confronted by a factor' that is 'superior to it', the Holy Scripture, which 'is there and tells us what is the past revelation of God that we have to recollect'.[6] While the Canon is simply 'there' (as something given by God), 'the list of biblical books' has been 'recognized as normative, because apostolic' by the Church. In acknowledging the Canon to be 'identical with the Bible of the Old and New Testaments', the Church expresses the fact that 'it is not left to itself in its proclamation': the object which it proclaims comes from elsewhere as—here Barth borrowed a classical expression from Immanuel Kant—'a categorical imperative' (101).

Barth called the Holy Scripture 'the deposit of what was once proclaimed by human lips', 'a Church document' that takes the form of 'written proclamation'. He compared the preaching of Jeremiah and Paul with 'present-day preaching'. Yet he also insisted on 'the absolutely constitutive significance of the former [preaching] for the latter [preaching], the determination of [...] present-day proclamation by its foundation upon Holy Scripture', or 'the basic singling out of the written word of the prophets and apostles over all the later words of men which have been spoken and are to be spoken today in the Church' (102). The prophets and apostles authoritatively stand over the Church. The office of apostles, in particular, is unique and unrepeatable.

[5] See G. O'Collins, *Revelation: Towards a Christian Interpretation of God's Self-revelation in Jesus Christ* (Oxford: Oxford University Press, 2016), 54–5.

[6] As Barth put it, 'the Church's recollection of God's past revelation has the Bible specifically as its object, because in fact this object and no other [*sola Scriptura*?] is the promise of future divine revelation which can make proclamation a duty for the Church and which can give it joy and courage for this duty' (107).

Noting that 'apostolicity' is 'one of the decisive notes of the true Church', Barth observed that it is 'also the decisive mark of true Church proclamation' (103). In other words, since apostolicity identifies the true Church, it must also identify true proclamation. For the Church and its proclamation, apostolicity is a 'divine gift' that becomes a 'human task' (104). The apostolic identity of the Church is revealed when true proclamation renews the apostolic witness of Scripture.

This understanding of apostolicity shaped Barth's interpretation of apostolic succession: 'the apostolic succession of the Church must mean that it is guided by the Canon, that is, by the prophetic and apostolic word as the *necessary rule of every word* that is valid in the Church' (104; emphasis added). This '*norm* magisterially confronts the Church', and its correct exposition does not depend 'on the judgment of a definitive and decisive teaching office in the Church or on the judgment of a historical-critical scholarship which comports itself with equal infallibility' (106; emphasis added). Barth left open here several questions: is the prophetic and apostolic word the necessary rule not just of every word but also of *every action* that is valid, life-giving, and virtuous in the Church, and how can it be such a rule for every such action—a theme with which Christian ethicists continue to struggle?[7] Moreover, if the 'correct exposition' of the prophetic (Old Testament) and apostolic (New Testament) word does not depend on teaching authority in the Church or on scholarship, what does it depend on? Perhaps such 'correct' exposition is found when the word of the preacher becomes an event of God's addressing us in 'real proclamation' (see below) or, as one could say, when the preacher allows the inspired Scriptures to prove themselves inspiring. For Barth the 'correct' exposition of Scripture proves itself as something more charismatic than institutionalized or institutionally safeguarded.

Looking back at the history of Christianity, Barth recognized the effective authority of the biblical '*text itself*'. It has 'always succeeded' in 'maintaining its own life against the encroachments of [...] periods and tendencies in the Church, victoriously asserting this life in ever new developments, and thus creating recognition for itself as a norm'

---

[7] William C. Spohn summarizes well the complex and challenging task of using the Scriptures as a source for Christian ethics (*What are they Saying about Scripture and Ethics?*, rev. edn (New York: Paulist Press, 1995), 5–20).

(106; emphasis added). 'As a text, the canonical text has the character of a free power.' Even when the Church enjoys 'the very best' exegesis, it always has 'to realize afresh the distinction between text and commentary' and 'let the text speak again without let or hindrance, so that it will experience the lordship of this free power' (107). Barth insisted on the Bible's 'supremacy and freedom over against the Church' (109). Without rejecting the value of scholarly exegesis and commentaries, Barth appealed here to the life-giving power we can observe when biblical texts directly confront individuals and communities.[8]

In language that explained what he meant by 'a categorical imperative', Barth wrote of 'the Bible constituting itself the Canon', because 'it imposed itself upon the Church as such, and continually does so'. He repeated the point: 'the Bible is the Canon because it is so. It is so by imposing itself as such' (107). Like others, I have pointed to three criteria that guided the Church in receiving into the canon of inspired books these and not those books: some kind of apostolic origin, orthodox teaching or 'the rule of faith', and consistent usage in the Church's liturgy and catechesis.[9] For these reasons, to use Barth's words (see above), the 'list of biblical books' was 'recognized as normative' by the Church. But this recognition might also be characterized as the Canon imposing itself, like a kind of 'categorical imperative'.

This brought Barth to 'the content of Holy Scripture' and his reason for naming the Bible 'the book of Christ'. 'The prophetic and apostolic word is the word, witness, proclamation and preaching

---

[8] In *Church Dogmatics* I/2, trans. G. T. Thomson and H. Knight (Edinburgh: T. & T. Clark, 1956), Barth remarked that 'the Church has become increasingly strong and self-conscious and bold [. . .] and been able to establish comfort and hope for all people, not only within but also without its walls [. . .] when it has had a humble mind, and been prepared to live not above or alongside but under the Word' (502); this work will also be cited within our text. In *Church Dogmatics* II/1, trans. T. H. L. Parker et al. (Edinburgh: T. & T. Clark, 1957), Barth recalled the 1933 *Theological Declaration* of the Synod of Barmen, in which 'Jesus Christ as attested to us in Holy Scripture was designated as the one Word of God in whom we have to trust and to obey in life and death' (175). It was this Word that provided truth and vitality for the struggle against the National Socialism of Adolf Hitler; see ibid. 172–8.

[9] O'Collins, *Revelation*, 170–3.

of Jesus Christ.' At once Barth introduced the saving power of past revelation which prophets and apostles proclaimed. 'The promise given to the Church in his Word is the promise of God's mercy which is uttered in the person of Him who is very God and very Man[10] and which takes up our cause when we could not help ourselves at all because of our enmity against God' (107; see Rom. 5: 10). Thus the revelation of God which is Christ himself is firmly identified as 'the power of God for salvation' (Rom. 1: 16).

Barth turned then to the human response. 'Holy Scripture', he wrote, 'is *the word of men* who yearned, waited and hoped for this Immanuel and finally saw, heard, and handled it in Jesus Christ. Holy Scripture declares, attests, and proclaims' this word, and thus 'promises that it applies to us also'. Anyone who 'so hears this word that he grasps and accepts its promise, believes' (108; emphasis added).

Barth explained further that 'this grasping and accepting' the promise conveyed 'in the word of the prophets and apostles' is 'the faith of the Church'. It is 'in this faith' that the Church 'recollects the past revelation of God and in this faith it expects the future revelation that is yet to come'. Barth firmly anchored in Christ the already of this past and the not yet of this future revelation. The Church 'recollects the incarnation of the eternal Word and the reconciliation accomplished in him, and it expects the future of Jesus Christ and its own redemption from the power of evil' (108).

In passing, one should note how Barth's view seems to rule out the possibility of faith for those who do not hear the Church proclaiming this recollection and expectation. In 'The Faith of Others: A Biblical Possibility',[11] I have challenged this view. But in a private communication, George Hunsinger has responded that Barth dealt 'in different terms' with those who are not, or are not yet, believers. Through 'an incognito operation of grace in the world', so Barth held, such people 'can be and are used by the Holy Spirit as unwitting instruments of grace'. Recently Hunsinger himself, in the spirit of Barth, has written: 'the merciful whom Jesus blesses extend beyond the circle of his disciples'. He adds: 'where works of mercy are performed, Jesus

---

[10] The language of 'person' and 'very God and very Man' is taken from the definition of the Council of Chalcedon held in AD 451 (DzH 301–2; ND 614–15).

[11] *Irish Theological Quarterly* 80 (2015), 313–26.

himself is present in the power of the Spirit, regardless of whether he is known for who he is or not yet known'. He concludes: 'whether the genuinely merciful who do not yet know Jesus are the adherents of a particular religion or of no religion, they are nonetheless being moved by his Spirit in their mercy, and they will one day know whose Spirit it is'.[12]

Apropos of Christian believers, Barth seemed slow to write of a present event of faith responding to the event of *present revelation*. 'The human, prophetic and apostolic word' represents 'God's Word in the same way as the word of the modern preacher'. 'In the event of real proclamation', a 'human word' in which God addresses us 'is an event'.[13] Thus 'the Bible is God's Word [. . .] to the extent that He speaks through it'. (Presumably, if God does not speak through contemporary proclamation, because it fails to bear witness to God's revelation, it cannot be deemed 'real proclamation', or 'correct' exposition of the Scriptures.) 'God's grace and gift' actualize contemporary proclamation and make the word of the preacher an event of God's addressing us (109). Did Barth call this contemporary 'address' an event of present revelation? Commenting on the way the Bible 'grasps at' us, he did write of this 'event': the Bible becomes 'God's Word', because 'it becomes revelation to us' (110). Nevertheless, Barth attended primarily, at least as far as terminology was concerned, to the 'past' and 'future' revelation. The very next page speaks explicitly ten times of past and future revelation but never once of 'present' revelation (111).[14]

---

[12] G. Hunsinger, *The Beatitudes* (Mahwah, NJ: Paulist Press, 2015), 63. For a similar reflection on 'blessed are those who hunger and thirst for righteousness', see ibid. 58.

[13] This high view of preaching sees modern preachers representing God's Word 'in the same way' as the prophets and apostles—a view that seems ruled out by what Barth had already said. Modern preachers cannot do what the prophets and apostles did; the prophetic and apostolic 'word' constituted 'the working instructions' by which 'the very Church itself stands or falls' (see above).

[14] However, in his next volume Barth expounded 'the subjective reality' and 'the subjective possibility of revelation', through which the Holy Spirit actualizes revelation in us (*Church Dogmatics* I/2, 203–79); in this section Barth deftly showed how revelation entails the power of God for salvation: 'in revelation, the whole man is addressed and challenged, judged and pardoned by God' (267). The event

Here he affirmed significantly: 'the Bible is not in itself and as such God's past revelation [. . .] it *bears witness to* God's past revelation, and it is God's past revelation in the form of attestation' (111). As Barth put it later, 'we distinguish the Bible as such from revelation. A witness is not absolutely identical with that to which it witnesses.'[15]

Before moving to a second major section in the *Church Dogmatics* where Barth expounded the 'Holy Scripture' and examined biblical 'inspiration', we can engage in some preliminary stocktaking of the relevant positions that he stated or at least implied in *Church Dogmatics* I/1. Six points invite attention.

First, Barth endorsed a distinction between God's revelation and the inspired Bible. The Holy Scripture 'bears witness' to past revelation, gives the grounds for expecting future revelation, and 'becomes revelation to us' when it 'grasps at us' and becomes God's Word to us. But as such 'the written word of the prophets and apostles' is not revelation.

Second, 'the list of biblical books' that constitute the normative canon have emerged from the Church's foundation in the prophetic (Old Testament) period and apostolic (New Testament) period. Apostolicity, a multifaceted characteristic of the Church, also implies the conviction that the biblical books were all written by the time the apostolic age (conceived as lasting until around AD 100) came to a close. Later Christians are called to proclaim and obey 'the working instructions and marching orders' of these books but not to add to the list of inspired, canonical works.[16]

Third, Barth's high doctrine of proclamation led him to call the Holy Scripture 'the [written] deposit of what was once proclaimed by

---

of revelation is inseparable from the event of salvation or reconciliation. On the actualizing of revelation for what Barth called 'the fulfilment of the revelation of His [God's] Word by the Holy Spirit', see also *Church Dogmatics* II/1, 3–6, and G. Hunsinger, 'The Mediator of Communion: Karl Barth's Doctrine of the Holy Spirit', in J. Webster (ed.), *The Cambridge Companion to Karl Barth* (Cambridge: Cambridge University Press, 2000), 177–94.

[15] *Church Dogmatics* I/2, 463.

[16] On the full import of 'apostolicity', see the Lutheran-Roman Catholic Commission on Unity, *The Apostolicity of the Church: Study Document of the Lutheran-Roman Catholic Commission on Unity* (Minneapolis: Lutheran University, 2006).

human lips'. Unquestionably, the preaching of the prophets, Jesus himself, and the apostle Paul have taken the form of 'written proclamation' in the Bible. Much of the Bible can be called 'written proclamation'. But it is equally true that imposing that label does violence to much in the Bible. The psalms, for instance, were prayed and sung, rather than preached, by human lips. We would misrepresent much of wisdom literature and the apocalyptic books by identifying them as forms of proclamation. To be sure, the Old Testament Scriptures, through entering into the church services of Christians, become texts for proclamation. But Barth's emphasis on proclamation led him to give that name to texts which originally did not have that characteristic.

Fourth, describing the Old Testament Scriptures as 'the word of men who yearned, waited, and hoped for' Jesus Christ seems to force those Scriptures into a straitjacket. Beyond question, messianic promise and expectation shape much of what we read in prophetic and apocalyptic books. But such promise and expectation are normally absent from wisdom literature, for example. Has Barth's Christocentrism led him astray here? In later volumes of *Church Dogmatics*, he was to write of Job, Ecclesiastes (Qoheleth), the Song of Songs, and various psalms.[17] But he tended to read it all 'backwards' from a centre in Christ, without first allowing the Old Testament texts to stand in their own right.

Fifth, if the Scriptures are also 'the word of men', what forms of writing did this word take? Letters, gospels, psalms, popular history, proverbs, and so forth? Did their role in fashioning 'the deposit' of 'written proclamation' enhance the writing talents of these authors when using their different literary genres? We need to look elsewhere for possible answers.

Sixth, there was obviously a heavy stress on what we might call 'the inspiring event', when Barth affirmed that 'the Bible is God's Word [...] to the extent that he speaks through it'. Did this imply that when God does not speak through the Bible, it ceases to be God's Word or

---

[17] On the Song of Songs see *Church Dogmatics* III/1, trans. J. W. Edwards et al. (Edinburgh: T. & T. Clark, 1958), 313–15. The index volume to *Church Dogmatics* (Edinburgh: T. & T. Clark, 1977) lists references to or citations of Job (37–42), Psalms (42–54), Song of Songs (57), and Ecclesiastes (56–7).

what others call an inspired and inspiring text? What Barth wrote in *Church Dogmatics* I/2 may provide answers to this and further questions that we have just outlined.[18]

Karl Barth: *Church Dogmatics* I/2

In part two of volume one of his *Church Dogmatics*, Barth dedicated Chapter 3 to 'Holy Scripture' (457–740); the opening section of this chapter, 'The Word of God for the Church' (457–537) reinforces what Barth wrote in part one and also contains new material relevant to the question of biblical inspiration.

Barth insists again on the priority of divine revelation (point one above), which has 'superior authority' and 'precedes both [prophetic and apostolic] proclamation and Holy Scripture' (457). He reiterates the distinction between revelation and the Bible. Scripture is distinct 'from revelation, insofar as it is only a human word about it, and its unity with it, insofar as revelation is the basis, object and content of this word' (463).

Yes, revelation is frequently the 'object and content' of the biblical word: for instance, the message of Second Isaiah and the preaching of Jesus. But the content of the Bible also frequently extends to other matters that have at best a loose or indirect connection with the revealing Word of God: for instance, the genealogies that fill the first nine chapters of 1 Chronicles. We will come back to this question. Here let me simply remark that it forces matters if we limit, in an unqualified fashion, the Bible's 'object and content' to revelation. While agreeing with Barth about the 'witness' function of the Scriptures, we should recognize that they can *also* witness to matters that are only indirectly connected with the divine self-revelation.

The prophetic and apostolic origin of the Holy Scripture attracts further attention from Barth. He names the prophets and apostles as 'the immediate and direct recipients of the one revelation' (413). These 'eyewitnesses and ear-witnesses' (505) enjoyed 'a singular and unique position and significance', being 'singled out and appointed to

[18] K. Barth, 'Holy Scripture', 457–740, in *Church Dogmatics* I/2; hereafter references will be given in the text.

a role and dignity peculiar to themselves alone' (495). A consequence follows for the writing of the Scriptures. The function of being human authors of the Bible ended with the apostolic age, since, with the resurrection and ascension of Jesus Christ, there could be no further 'immediate and direct recipients of the one revelation'.

Barth modifies his earlier reduction of the Holy Scripture to forms of *proclamation*. He allows, for instance, that the written Word of God can meet us 'in the form of what we think must be called saga or legend' (509). He no longer insists on interpreting the entire Bible as written proclamation.

Barth's Christocentric understanding of the Scriptures surfaces again in *Church Dogmatics* I/2. The Old Testament 'attests' 'the Messiah who is to come', while the New Testament attests 'the Messiah who has already come' (481). Barth even claims: 'the understanding of the Old Testament as a witness to Christ' is 'an understanding of its *original and only legitimate sense*' (489; emphasis added).

A Christocentric interpretation of the Bible can claim many exponents. A twelfth-century Augustinian canon, Hugh of Saint-Victor, wrote of the Bible being united in Christ: 'all divine Scripture speaks of Christ and all divine Scripture finds its fulfilment in Christ, because all divine Scripture forms one book, which is the book of life'.[19] In the sixteenth century William Tyndale expressed the same conviction: 'the scriptures spring out of God, and flow into Christ, and were given to lead us to Christ. Thou must therefore go along by the scripture as by a line, until thou come to Christ, which is the way's end and resting place.'[20] However, Barth goes beyond such Christian interpretation of the Old Testament's books by claiming not simply that a fuller and further sense of these books (which emerged with the coming of the Church) bears witness to Christ, but even that such witness to Christ is 'the original and only legitimate' sense of these books. That view fails to allow for the original and legitimate meaning which the Old Testament texts enjoyed in their Jewish context.

In *Church Dogmatics* I/2, Barth makes room for a historical understanding of the Bible that takes it for 'what it undoubtedly is and is

---

[19] *De Arca Noe Morali*, 2. 8–9; *PL* 176, cols 642–3.

[20] *The Work of William Tyndale*, ed. G. E. Duffield (Philadelphia: Fortress Press, 1965), 353.

meant to be: the human speech uttered by specific men at specific times in a specific situation, in a specific language and with a specific intention' (464). Hence the Bible was 'historically a very human literary document' (501). The human authors were genuine authors who 'made full use of their human capacities' (see point five above). At the same time, the Holy Spirit is 'the real author of what is written or stated in Scripture' (505).

Here Barth introduces something new: the role of the Holy Spirit. 'Scripture is holy and the Word of God, because by the Holy Spirit it became and will become for the Church a witness to divine revelation' (457). It is due to the Spirit that through the written word God speaks as Lord to the Church. The Holy Spirit figures prominently when Barth expounds the 'divinity' of Holy Writ over against its 'humanity'. The 'divinity' inspires and prompts obedience to the lordship of the tripersonal God who speaks through the Bible. It is sharing in the Holy Spirit by the biblical witnesses that 'makes their writing Holy Scripture' (520).

In *Church Dogmatics* I/2, Barth adds an ample section on 'inspiration' (514–26). Here he notes how from the early centuries of Christianity there existed 'a striking inclination to concentrate interest in the inspiration of Scripture upon one particular point', by limiting interest 'to the work of the Spirit in the emergence of the spoken or written, prophetic and apostolic word as such' (517). Barth regrets a tendency to compromise the humanity of the Bible by 'a foolish conception of its divinity', which reduces inspiration to its being dictated by Christ or the Holy Spirit. This was to forget that 'the real human word' is 'the real Word of God' (518).

What Barth calls 'the real miracle' of the Bible is an 'event': in this book we hear and shall hear the Word of God. Hence 'we cannot regard the presence of God's Word in the Bible as an attribute inhering once and for all in this book as such' (530). The Bible is the place of an 'act', 'the actualisation of the act of God which took place once and for all in Jesus Christ' (531). 'The miracle of God', Barth declares, 'takes place in this text formed of human words' (532). Since 'the fallible and faulty human word is used as such by God', it 'has to be received and heard in spite of its human fallibility'. 'The inspiration of the Bible' is knowing God's 'grace and truth' (see John 1: 14, 17) and doing 'the will of God' (533–4). This then is the heart of the matter for Barth when he expounds 'the inspiration of the Bible' or, equivalently, 'the [powerful] presence of God in the Bible'.

Raymond F. Collins on Biblical Inspiration

Whereas Barth developed his reflections on biblical inspiration at leisurely length in two opening parts of his *Church Dogmatics*, considerations of space constrained Raymond Collins in his contribution to a volume in collaboration.[21] Six sections structured his dense account: 'Vatican Council II', 'Early Christian and Jewish Tradition', 'The Prophetic Model of Inspiration', 'The Tract on Inspiration', 'Contemporary Approaches to Inspiration', and 'Corollaries to the Doctrine of Inspiration'. We take up in turn these six sections.

(1) Vatican II's 'Dogmatic Constitution on Divine Revelation (*Dei Verbum*)' included a third chapter, 'the Divine Inspiration and Interpretation of Sacred Scripture' (DV 11–13). Collins summed up the thrust of this key chapter: 'inspiration is a specific way of speaking about the unique sacred character of the Scriptures, having important implications for the way in which the Old Testament and New Testament books are to be regarded by believers'. Following the teaching of the Second Vatican Council, Collins differs from Barth: inspiration is an intrinsic property or character of the Bible.[22] But there are also points of convergence with Barth in what Collins quotes from *Dei Verbum* 11: for instance, revelation precedes the writing of

---

[21] R. F. Collins, 'Inspiration', in R. E. Brown, J. A. Fitzmyer, and R. E. Murphy (eds), *The New Jerome Biblical Commentary* (London: Geoffrey Chapman, 1989), 1023–33; references to this article will be given in the text.

[22] On this issue John Webster puts matters with characteristic precision: 'inspiration is not *primarily* a textual property but a divine movement' (*Holy Scripture: A Dogmatic Sketch* (Cambridge: Cambridge University Press, 2003), 36; emphasis added). This implies that inspiration *is* a textual property, albeit not primarily so. Without reference to Barth, Stephen Davis argues that inspiration is a 'property' or 'special intrinsic character of the Bible' ('Revelation and Inspiration', in T. P. Flint and M. C. Rea (eds), *The Oxford Handbook of Philosophical Theology* (Oxford: Oxford University Press, 2009), 45–6). This opens up the question, to be dealt with later: is the property or character of inspiration actively present in somewhat different forms and with differing degrees of intensity?

the Scriptures; the books of both the Old Testament and the New Testament were written 'under the inspiration of the Holy Spirit'; the human authors 'made use of their powers and abilities'; and God was involved in the composition of the Scriptures 'for the sake of our salvation'. Like Barth,[23] Collins (and before him the Second Vatican Council) takes up two key biblical passages: 2 Timothy 3: 16–17 and 2 Peter 1: 19–21. They 'provide key witnesses as to how inspiration is to be understood and enunciated' (1024).

The relevant words in the first passage refer to the Jewish Scriptures, which Christians would later call the Old Testament: 'all scripture is inspired by God (God-breathed), and is useful for teaching, for reproof, for correction, and for training in righteousness, so that everyone who belongs to God may be proficient and equipped for every good work'. This was a way of expressing the revelatory and salvific function of inspired Scripture. The key affirmation in the second passage explains that 'no prophecy of scripture is a matter of one's own interpretation', because 'no prophecy ever came by human will, but human beings moved by the Holy Spirit spoke from God'. Since the primary cause of what prophets said (to be recorded by the subsequent writers of Scripture) was the Holy Spirit, the conclusion would also be drawn that the sacred authors were primarily moved by the Holy Spirit to write 'from God'.

(2) Collins dedicates several pages to early Christian and Jewish tradition on the nature and function of biblical inspiration (1024–8), citing Barth twice on the question of God as the primary 'author' of the Bible (1027). Collins and Barth both discuss much the same list of Church fathers on the Holy Spirit's role in forming the Scriptures (Athenagoras, Augustine, Gregory of Nazianzus, and Irenaeus).[24] Where only Barth cites Gregory the Great, only Collins brings in the significant contribution of Origen and, even more importantly, Philo of Alexandria. As a contemporary of Jesus and Paul, Philo illustrates the Jewish traditions about the inspiration of prophets and the inspiration of the Scriptures that helped fashion what we read on those themes in 2 Timothy and 2 Peter.

---

[23] Barth, *Church Dogmatics* I/2, 504–6.   [24] Ibid. 517–19.

Both Barth[25] and Collins discuss naming God as 'author' of the Bible, a question that emerged in fifth-century controversies. But only Collins takes time out to note that the Latin *auctor* meant 'producer or source', and so had 'a much broader range of meaning than the English author', at least in the literary sense of 'author' (1027–8). But neither Collins nor Barth pauses to address the broader sense of the Latin *dictare*, a term that surfaced in their accounts of tendencies to understand biblical inspiration as the Holy Spirit dictating to human scribes.

(3) Collins devotes a third section to the prophetic model of biblical inspiration, adding that this model dominated from the time of the New Testament until the sixteenth century: 'the inspiration of the Scriptures was considered analogous to (and dependent on) the inspiration of the prophets'. Thus Thomas Aquinas, Collins recalls, considered inspiration 'within the genus of prophecy'. He used categories of Aristotelian philosophy and, in particular, that of efficient causality, distinguishing God or the Holy Spirit as the *principal* efficient cause from the human authors as the *instrumental* efficient cause. God and the human authors join together in composing the Scriptures, just as a carpenter (the principal cause) and a saw (the instrumental cause) together shape a piece of timber. Aquinas, as reported by Collins, understood prophecy to be 'a gift given by God to a prophet on a temporary basis for a specific function', and 'for the sake of the community'. As we shall see later, both of these views apply happily to the gift of biblical inspiration (1028).

On the same page Collins describes the view of plenary (verbal) inspiration, according to which God simply dictates divine oracles and other words to the sacred authors, who then seem more like copyists than authors. Noting how widely this view was held, he might have mentioned the role of Christian artists in spreading and supporting this reduction of the inspired writer to the role of mere stenographer. In the Pazzi chapel in the Basilica of Santa Croce in Florence, for example, Luca della Robbia represents the evangelists in terracotta. An eagle has arrived from heaven to hold the text for John to copy down. A lion performs the same service for Mark.

[25] Ibid. 520, 523.

Collins summarizes some of the major objections to the 'dictation' view inherent in the theory of plenary (verbal) inspiration. For instance, Ezra names as the source for 7: 11–26 a letter of King Artaxerxes (which authorizes Israelites to return to Jerusalem and to receive a royal subsidy for the Temple) and not some oracle dictated by God. Likewise, in the prologue to his Gospel (1: 1–4), Luke does not claim that what he is about to write comes as a verbal message from God. Rather he reports that he has examined accounts already written about Jesus and taken information from 'eyewitnesses and ministers of the word'.

(4) Under the heading of 'The Tract on Inspiration' Collins shows how the emergence of modern biblical scholarship affected official teaching on and scholarly interpretations of inspiration (1028–31). It became clear, for example, that the first five books of the Bible, the Pentateuch, drew on previously existing traditions and were not simply a matter of God having dictated what we read. Likewise, regardless of the particular theory one produced, scholars came to recognize that the four Gospels relied on earlier sources and documents, including eyewitness testimony.[26] God did not first create the Gospels and then have them transcribed by the four evangelists, as the artistic works of Luca della Robbia and others would suggest.

Collins cites interesting reflections from John Henry Newman (1801–90): for instance, that biblical inspiration 'admits degrees'. He also attends to the outstanding biblical scholar M.-J. Lagrange (1855–1938). When stating that 'the Scriptures were totally the work of God and totally the work of the human author', Lagrange maintained the language of Aquinas: 'God was the principal efficient cause, the human author the instrumental efficient cause' (1030).

(5) The section on 'Contemporary Approaches to Inspiration' naturally includes a paragraph on Barth. Collins sums up his view of inspiration: 'inspiration is not a quality of the scriptural text itself, but an affirmation of divine ability to use the Scriptures to communicate revelation to human beings, either individually or in groups' (1031).

---

[26] See Richard Bauckham, *Jesus and the Eyewitnesses: The Gospels as Eyewitness Testimony*, 2nd edn (Grand Rapids, MI: Eerdmans, 2017).

Like Barth, Pierre Benoit (1906–87), an influential Catholic writer and director of the École Biblique (Jerusalem), understood inspiration to be 'logically consequent to revelation' and interpreted it as a special 'impulse to write and produce a book'. Remarking that 'Benoit's emphasis is essentially on the individual biblical authors', Collins insists that, 'to a large extent, biblical books cannot simply be considered the literary production of isolated individuals, as modern books are'. He adds: 'the individual writers were members of faith communities, which had more than a passing influence on the formation of the biblical literature itself'. This brings Collins to recall 'social theories' of inspiration, including that of Karl Rahner (1032), to which we return later.

Literary approaches remind Collins that texts 'derive part of their meaning from the larger textual unit to which they belong'. He argues that 'the Bible as a whole is inspired and so by implication the parts are inspired'. Such a 'holistic understanding of textuality has no small bearing on an adequate understanding on the notion of biblical truth' (1032). If the meaning of the inspired Scriptures is primarily in the whole, so too is the truth.

(6) Collins concludes by sketching four 'corollaries to the doctrine of inspiration'. As a primary consequence of their being inspired by the Holy Spirit, the Scriptures have a unique *authority* for the Church, Christians, and their liturgical worship. Inasmuch as they originate in God and enjoy a multifaceted religious impact, they may be called *the Word of God*. Collins reflects also on the truth of the Scriptures, reminding readers that *biblical truth* is, first and foremost, a matter of God manifesting 'his fidelity to his people, bringing them into loving union with himself'. Finally, Collins firmly states that 'any adequate treatment of inspiration should begin with the *reality of the Scriptures* themselves' (1033).

Some Conclusions

These eminent, twentieth-century visions of biblical inspiration point the way to major principles that should form and fashion any treatise on this theme. Let me name five such principles. First, revelation precedes and extends beyond biblical inspiration. Hence revelation and inspiration should not be identified. The consequence of this priority of revelation for theology is expressed by John Webster: 'theological talk of the inspiration of Scripture needs to be strictly subordinate to and dependent upon the broader concept of revelation'.[27] The Second Vatican Council drew attention to this subordination and dependence by treating revelation in the opening chapter of *Dei Verbum* before coming to the inspired Scriptures in four subsequent chapters.

Second, the inspired Scriptures bear witness to words and episodes of revelation. But, we should add, they *also* bear witness to other matters that may be only loosely connected with events of revelation. Third, given the unique, unrepeatable function of the prophets and the apostles in the divine scheme of revelation and salvation, the formation of the inspired Scriptures came to end with the close of the apostolic age. Along with what we can call 'foundational' revelation, the gift of biblical inspiration also ended. There could be no more writing of inspired books.

Fourth, as the Word of God or divine message formulated in human words, the Bible involved genuinely human authors, who made full use of their capacities. At the same time the Holy Spirit proved the primary 'author' whose involvement produced the *Sacred* Scriptures and the *Holy* Bible. Fifth, the activity of the Spirit also ensures that the inspired Scriptures have remained inspiring—in the proclamation and public worship of the Church and in the individual lives of men and women.

Collins rightly points to the direction this book should now take. We begin with the reality of the Scriptures themselves, a richly variegated reality that modern biblical scholarship has investigated and illuminated.

---

[27] Webster, *Holy Scripture*, 31.

2

Four Old Testament Books
as Inspired and Inspiring

Any adequate study of biblical inspiration needs to be anchored in the Scriptures and what we know about the human side of their composition. A familiarity with the texts of the Old Testament and the New Testament and with what widely accepted scholarship has concluded about their formation is indispensable. Otherwise our vision of inspiration can be fired by ideas and enthusiasms that, while attractive in themselves, may have little to do with the origins and impact of the actual texts. We begin with the Book of Genesis, recalling significant features in its inspired composition and in its subsequent inspiring impact.[1]

Genesis

The Book of Genesis (or 'book of origins') presents primeval stories that focus on the coming into existence of the world and all humanity (Chs 1–11), and then turns to ancestral, legendary stories of Abraham, Sarah, and their descendants (Chs 12–50).[2]

(1) The first eleven chapters embody elements that bear similarities to ancient, Middle Eastern myths about the creation of the world, a catastrophic flood, and a vow of 'gods' not to destroy life again. Formed

---

[1] For what counts for biblical texts enjoying subsequent quotations, allusions, echoes, and influences, see W. A. Tooman, *Gog of Magog: Reuse of Scripture and Compositional Technique in Ezechiel 38–9* (Tübingen: Mohr Siebeck, 2011), 4–10.

[2] For contemporary scholarship on the Book of Genesis and a select bibliography, see D. M. Carr, 'Genesis', in M. D. Coogan (ed.), *The Oxford Encyclopedia of the Books of the Bible*, i (New York: Oxford University Press, 2011), 316–34.

over many centuries, these chapters draw on oral and written traditions. While it seems relatively uncontroversial to affirm what have been called 'Priestly' and 'non-Priestly' sources,[3] scholars continue to debate further details about the particular traditions from which Genesis 1–11 emerged. But clearly these chapters resulted from 'team-work' that extended over centuries, and involved experiences of God, recital, writing, borrowing, editing, prayerful reflection, and community inter-action. What James Barr observed about biblical inspiration applies particularly to the composition of Genesis 1–11:

> If there is inspiration at all, then it must extend over the entire process of production that has led to the final text. Inspiration therefore must attach not to a small number of exceptional persons [. . .] It must extend over a large number of anonymous persons [. . .] It must be considered to belong more to the community as a whole.[4]

Inspired texts came from many anonymous persons, both as contribu-tors and final authors (e.g. Genesis), as well as from exceptional (and known) individuals like St Paul. In both cases the Holy Spirit directed and affected the contributions to and the writing of the final texts, without prejudice to the abilities of the human beings involved in producing those texts.

We should *also* pay homage to the 'inspiring' work of the Spirit that continues within the Christian Church and beyond, and has affected believers, artists, writers, official teachers, theologians, and others. The richly symbolic story of Adam and Eve brilliantly presents, for example, what everyman and everywoman do: their instinct is to put the blame on someone else. The man blames the woman and even God: 'the woman whom you gave to me, she gave me fruit from the tree' (Gen. 3: 11). The woman blames the crafty serpent who has tempted her: 'the serpent tricked me and I ate' (Gen. 3: 13). But the man and the woman have deliberately disobeyed the divine will and must suffer the consequences. In language that is as fresh as ever, the

---

[3] See J. Schaper, 'The Literary History of the Hebrew Bible', in J. C. Paget and J. Schaper (eds), *The New Cambridge History of the Bible*, i (Cambridge: Cambridge University Press, 2012), 105–44, at 130–1.

[4] J. Barr, *Holy Scripture: Canon, Authority, Criticism* (Philadelphia: Westminster, 1983), 27.

Genesis story drives home the point: far from enhancing their lives, sin leaves the man and the woman less than they should really be and ushers in destructive consequences. The opening chapters of Genesis, read within the context of community worship or beyond, have inspired innumerable insights into the human condition and our relationship with God.[5]

Adam and Eve also prefigure all human families which, while seldom including one son (Cain) who murders another (Abel), are always in various ways dysfunctional and in need of redemption. The future of the human race depends on the health of marriage and the family. The Book of Genesis pictures marriage and the family as coming from the creative hand of God but also as needing redemption from sin and evil.

The inspired text of Genesis led to Adam and Eve being understood to foreshadow Christ, *the* corporate figure par excellence, whose work of redemption impacts on the entire human race and the cosmos. Through the sequence of his frescoes in the Brancacci Chapel (Florence), Masaccio (1401–28) pointed Adam and Eve in the direction of Christ, the Second Adam. Driven from the Garden of Eden, they are in despair. Weeping and weighed down with terrible pain and loss, they move along a path of sorrows. But the same path brings them to the next scene: Christ on the shores of Lake Galilee surrounded by his disciples.

As was the case with fathers of the Church, Eastern icons, numerous Christian artists and writers, and important documents of official teaching, the figure of Christ came into play to enrich the meaning of the opening chapters of Genesis and be enriched by it. The *tree* from which Adam and Eve took the forbidden fruit was coupled with another tree, the *cross* on which Christ hung and died. The victorious tree of Calvary more than recompensed the loss suffered through the tree in the Garden of Eden. Through her part in reversing the harm done by our 'first parents', the Virgin Mary was set over against Eve by St Irenaeus in the second century, St Hildegard of Bingen in the twelfth century, and numerous others.

---

[5] See R. Havrelock, 'Genesis', in M. Lieb, E. Mason, and J. Roberts (eds), *The Oxford Handbook of the Reception History of the Bible* (Oxford: Oxford University Press, 2011), 11–24.

In connecting Adam and Christ, no poem has surpassed 'Hymn to God my God in my Sickness' by John Donne (1572–1631).[6] Another classical account of the Second Adam appeared several decades later in *Paradise Regained* by John Milton (1608–74). After expanding the story of Adam and Eve into the twelve books of *Paradise Lost*, Milton focused the four-book sequel entirely on the temptation in the wilderness. Unlike Adam and Eve, Jesus, the Second Adam, succeeds in resisting temptation. This is an eminent example of how Milton constantly turned to the Bible for inspiration and literary themes.[7]

Often enough what I have ascribed to the ongoing, inspiring work of the Holy Spirit is classified under the 'reception history' of the Scriptures. Many commentators detect places where this reception history takes the form of rereading the sacred texts. Yet, theologically speaking, the term *Wirkungsgeschichte* (effective history or history of effects) deserves our preference. It focuses attention more on the (objective) inspiring power of the Spirit coming through the biblical texts than on the (subjective) reception of these texts by human readers or hearers. *Wirkungsgeschichte* should remind us that the original inspiration of the Scriptures by the Holy Spirit is followed up by the Spirit's 'inspiring' impact on readers and hearers.[8] The powerful inspiration of the Holy Spirit affects both the writers *and the readers* (and hearers) of the Scriptures, or at least those readers open to the Spirit's presence and power.

Moreover, apropos of the 'reception history' of the Scriptures, we should recognize that it does not embody *tout court* the inspiring effect of the Spirit. At times biblical texts, and not least those of the Book of Genesis, have been taken up in harmful and even sinful ways that we may not ascribe to the Holy Spirit. Thus the creation of human beings to have 'dominion' over everything on earth (Gen. 1: 26, 28) calls for

---

[6] 'We think that Paradise and Calvary, / Christ's cross and Adam's tree stood in one place; / Look, Lord, and find both Adams met in me; / As the first Adam's sweat surrounds my face, / May the last Adam's blood my soul embrace.'

[7] See B. Cummings, 'The Bible and Literature in the European Renaissance', in E. Cameron (ed.), *The New Cambridge History of the Bible: From 1450 to 1750*, iii (Cambridge: Cambridge University Press, 2012), 686–717, at 709–17; R. M. Schwartz, 'Milton, John', *OEBA*, ii, 94–104.

[8] See J. Boxall, 'Reception History of the Bible', *New Cambridge History of the Bible*, iii, 172–83, at 175–7.

responsible stewardship, but has too often been misrepresented as a licence to exploit and squander natural resources.[9] Nevertheless, we have many examples of passages from Genesis 1–11 inspiring life-giving insights that have benefited individuals and the wider community. We do not have to look hard to tell the true from the bogus. The Bible itself offers many such positive examples.

Paul drew on Genesis and Jewish traditions to develop in his own striking way a picture of the 'New' or 'Last' Adam to be found in 1 Corinthians 15 and Romans 5. Joseph Fitzmyer gathered the evidence to show that 'the incorporation of all human beings in Adam' is an idea that 'seems to appear for the first time in 1 Corinthians 15: 22'. He likewise produces evidence that allows him to describe as 'novel teaching' Paul's argument in Romans 5 about the way in which the sin of Adam had a 'maleficent influence on all human beings'.[10] But the blessings brought by Jesus Christ, the man foreshadowed by Adam, went far beyond the measure of Adam's wrong-doing (Rom. 5: 15–17). Inspired in large part by what he read in the opening chapters of Genesis, Paul wove the patterns of his permanently successful, 'Last Adam' view of Christ's saving work.

We remain uncertain about the identity of the author of the book with which the Bible closes, Revelation.[11] But this astonishing, apocalyptic work revisits many passages from the Old Testament in its vivid visions of God's whole plan of judgement and salvation being consummated. Revelation ends with a scene of a river, the tree of life, and the garden of the new Jerusalem (Rev. 22: 1–5), a scene which evokes the original picture of Eden (Gen. 2: 8–10). Through the inspiring work of the Holy Spirit, the visionary has reread in counterpoint the picture of the first Eden.

[9] See G. O'Collins and M. Farrugia, *Catholicism: The Story of Catholic Christianity*, 2nd edn (Oxford: Oxford University Press, 2015), 183–8.

[10] J. A. Fitzmyer, *Romans* (New York: Doubleday, 1993), 136, 406, 412.

[11] The author describes himself as 'your brother' who shares persecution with his audience; he seems to have exercised a prophetic ministry among them (Rev. 22: 9). He refers to the twelve apostles as figures from the past (Rev. 21: 14) and does not claim to be one of them. This renders dubious the traditional identification of the author of Revelation, 'John' (Rev. 1: 1, 9; 22: 8), with the apostle of the same name.

To sum up: we lack any detailed knowledge of the ways in which the Holy Spirit inspired the production by many anonymous persons of the first eleven chapters of Genesis. But we have an enormous amount of material if we set ourselves to study how those chapters inspired subsequent readers, both in biblical times and right down to the present day. Such readers as Paul and the author of Revelation helped fill out the meaning of the original texts by completing the biblical pictures of the First Adam and the original Eden. The full meaning of Adam and the first Eden emerges only with the production of the whole Bible. We need to look for meaning and, hence, truth in the whole.

(2) Over the centuries all manner of oral folklore helped forge and shape a contentious story of family life fashioned from accounts of Abraham, Sarah, and their descendants (Gen. 12–50). Many anonymous persons, inspired by the Holy Spirit, remembered, transmitted, borrowed, and edited what we now read in the second part of Genesis. On the one hand, the identity and activity of these sacred authors remain shrouded in mystery. On the other hand, the stories they told of Abraham, Sarah, and their family contain some historical elements and fit into things we know about the history of the ancient Middle East. It is at our peril that we dismiss as mere myths and unfounded legends all that we read in those chapters.

Obviously long-standing traditions from a section of Middle Eastern history fed into the final composition of Genesis 12–50. But did any revelations of God trigger or help trigger those traditions? In three episodes, God is represented as conveying a command and promise to Abram and Sarai (Gen. 12: 1–3), to their son Isaac (Gen. 26: 2–5), and to their grandson Jacob (Gen. 46: 1–4).[12] The patriarchs, their wives, and their families receive from the Lord travel directions and the promise of blessings that will come from obediently fulfilling the divine command. The first such encounter, with Abram (whose name has not yet been changed to Abraham), marks a major shift in Genesis—away from the primeval story to the half light of patriarchal history:

---

[12] See also other episodes, like the first covenant with Abraham (Gen. 15: 1–21), the parallel covenant from the Priestly tradition (Gen. 17: 1–27), and the Lord's visit to Abraham and Sarah (Gen. 18: 1–15), as well as God's command and promise to Jacob in Gen. 31: 3, 13.

Now the Lord said to Abram, 'Go from your kindred and your father's
house to the land that I will show you. I will make of you a great nation,
and I will bless you, and make your name great, so that you will be a
blessing. I will bless those who bless you, and the one who curses you
I will curse, and in you all the families of the earth will be blessed.

(Gen. 12: 1–3)

Abram's first journey took him at once to Shechem in the land of
Canaan. There 'the Lord appeared to Abram and said, "To your
offspring I will give this land." So he built there an altar to the Lord,
who had appeared to him' (Gen. 12: 7).

Do Abraham and Sarah belong to human history, and did they
somehow experience God conveying to them a command and a
promise which were recorded by inspired authors? Did God appear
to Abraham at Shechem? It is hard to hazard any firm answers. But
we have abundant testimony to ways in which these inspired accounts
proved inspiring for later readers. St Paul took up the language of 'all
the families of the earth' being blessed, and understood the divine
blessing to come to the Gentiles through Abraham (Gal. 3: 8). The
Genesis texts about Abraham and Sarah were to prove richly fruitful
in the teaching of the apostle. Paul used Abraham as an outstanding
example of those 'reckoned righteous' by God on the basis of their
faithfulness. Jews and Gentiles both inherit the promise of God when
they share the faith of Abraham (Rom. 4: 1–25).

The subsequent history of Christianity yields examples of people
whose lives were radically changed through the story of the faithful
obedience of Abraham and Sarah. Girolamo Savonarola, for instance,
on 1 May 1474 heard an Augustinian friar proclaim God's word to
Abraham: 'go forth from your country (*egredere de terra tua*) and your
kindred and your father's house' (Gen. 12: 1). The call to '*egredere de terra
tua*' gave Savonarola no peace; he heard it everywhere and it kept
disturbing him. Before a year had passed, the young man made up his
mind and set out to join religious life. Whatever we hold about the
subsequent life and death of Savonarola, what God said to Abraham
inspired a radical, religious decision.[13]

---

[13] See further G. O'Collins, 'The Inspiring Power of Scripture', *Revelation:
Towards a Christian Interpretation of God's Self-Revelation in Jesus Christ* (Oxford: Oxford
University Press, 2016), 207–14, at 212–14.

Talk of 'the Lord [who] appeared' in Genesis 12: 7 (see also e.g. 17: 1) has led many commentators to speak of such encounters as 'theophanies'. The verb used here in the Septuagint (the second or third century BC, Greek translation of the Old Testament) was *ōphthē* ('he showed himself' or 'he appeared'). This same verb provided the vocabulary for Paul (and the traditions he cited) in 1 Corinthians 15: 5–8 and others (e.g. Luke 24: 34), when they witnessed to the appearances of the risen Christ, often called 'Christophanies'. The inspired language used by the anonymous authors of Genesis enjoyed its *Wirkungsgeschichte* in the terminology used by Paul and other inspired authors of the New Testament. But, unlike the theophanies to Abraham, we can say much more about the Christophanies to which Paul and other New Testament writers bear witness.[14]

Before leaving Abraham and Sarah, we should recall that the theme of visitors who turn out to be angelic or heavenly was widespread in the folklore of the ancient Middle East. Three such divine visitors are entertained by Abraham (Gen. 18: 1–15). They speak as a group (vs. 9) and also as 'the Lord' speaking alone (vs. 13) in conveying the promise that, despite being advanced in years, Sarah will conceive and bear a son. We do not know anything specific about the formation of this inspired passage and what lay behind it. But we do know how the story of three mysterious visitors who also speak and act as one produced images of lasting impact—in the icons of the 'Old Testament Trinity'.

The Trinitarian icons based on the heavenly visitors locate faith firmly in the unfolding history of salvation. The famous icon, created by St Andrew Roublev and found in the Tretiakov Gallery in Moscow, expresses the majestic beauty and grace of the tripersonal God. A divine unity and harmony pervade the composition, in which the three figures sit around one table and are entirely referred to each other in mutual self-gift. Through the table, the chalice, and the tree in the background, the icon hints at the climax of the divine self-communication that will come with the passion, death, and resurrection of Jesus. Other icons of the divine visitors bring out more emphatically

---

[14] On these Christophanies, see G. O'Collins, *Christology: Origins, Developments, Debates* (Waco, TX; Baylor University Press, 2015), 54–60.

this story of salvation. They introduce the figures of Abraham and Sarah, as well as that of a servant who prefigures the death of Jesus by slaying a tender calf. These and innumerable other icons have proved integral to the devotion and worship of Eastern Christians.

The Psalms

The Book of the Psalms, which includes 150 psalms in the Hebrew Bible and 151 in the Greek (Septuagint) translation, is the longest and, in some ways, the most complex book in the entire Bible.[15] Poetic texts of various kinds, prayer (especially lamentation),[16] praise (especially thanksgiving), and instruction, the psalms were composed, revised, and edited over five centuries. Psalm 29, a hymn to the God of the storm, seems to be pre-monarchical and may have been a Canaanite hymn of praise—that is to say, non-Israelite in its origin. It appears to have been appropriated as a prayer for rain in the context of the autumn feast of Tabernacles. Many other psalms emerged within the Jewish people during the monarchical period (e.g. Ps. 2). Subsequently the psalms drew their authority from a widespread belief that King David was their author. He may have composed a few of them (e.g. Pss 2, 10, and 18). Some psalms came, however, from exilic (e.g. Ps. 137) and even post-exilic times (e.g. Ps. 1), well after the reign of David.

Various techniques fashion the psalms, especially the use of parallelism, whether synonymous, antithetical, or synthetic, which frequently binds together whole verses or parts of verses. The second segment fills out, intensifies, or modifies the first. Thus in the first two verses of Psalm 142, the second line more or less repeats the first: 'With my voice I cry to the Lord; with my voice I make supplication to the Lord. / I pour out my complaints before him; I tell my troubles before him.'[17] Developing images supply another way of unifying psalms: for instance, Psalm 23 expands the metaphor of God as shepherd-king

---

[15] See K. J. Dell, 'Psalms', *Oxford Handbook of the Reception History of the Bible*, 37–51.

[16] See C. Mandolfo, 'Language of Lament in the Psalms', in W. P. Brown (ed.), *Oxford Handbook of the Psalms* (Oxford: Oxford University Press, 2014), 114–30. The psalms of lament can be individual (e.g. Ps. 3) or communal (e.g. Ps. 44).

[17] See F. W. Dobbs-Allsopp, 'Poetry of the Psalms', ibid. 79–98, at 87–9.

and host. 'Elegant variations' provide a further technique. A grateful meditation on God's law, Psalm 119 runs to 176 verses and is the longest of the psalms. To avoid monotony, it uses various alternatives for 'law': for example, in the New Revised Standard Version translation of the Hebrew terms as 'commandments', 'decrees', 'ordinances', precepts', 'statutes', 'will', and 'words'. Some psalms were obviously written to be accompanied by stringed instruments, along with trumpets and clashing cymbals (e.g. Ps. 150).

Traditional language and techniques have produced the psalms. But, for all that, they witness candidly and vividly to deep religious feeling: anguish, disappointment, amazement, joy, gratitude, and the rest.[18] They make visible in prayer the invisible drama of the self and the community when face-to-face with God. Going to the heart of who we are as human beings, they enjoy the immediacy and power of personal testimony.

Where the Mosaic Torah (Genesis to Deuteronomy) has been understood as the Word of God 'from on high', the Psalms form a response to this revelation and take the form of prayer, praise, and instruction. Occasionally the psalms witness to divine discourse (*locutio Dei*),[19] but human speaking (*locutio hominis*) predominates. The psalms 'consist primarily of human words either uttered to God, whether in petition or praise, or proclaimed about God for worship or instruction'.[20] These poetic prayers record a range of ways in which human beings received, responded to, and interpreted the divine revelation that came through history, creation, and wisdom thought. They can focus on God as creator (e.g. Pss 8, 19, and 104) or as victorious warrior (e.g. Pss 66, 92, and 98). At the heart of the psalms is the loving faithfulness of God that the Israelites experienced in events of history and works of creation. The psalmists felt guarded against despair by the powerful kindness of their God.

After the Babylonian captivity, the psalms formed a kind of hymn book for the Second Temple (AD 520) and a prayer book (and instruction book) for individuals (eventually for Jesus himself). The functions

---

[18] See W. Brueggemann, 'On "Being Human" in the Psalms', ibid. 515–28.

[19] In 'The Psalms: An Overview', ibid. 20, Brown provides a list of the relatively few passages featuring divine discourse.

[20] Ibid. 2.

of the psalms complemented each other, as they served public worship (in the Temple), individual prayer, and teaching. These three functions have been widely and fruitfully maintained in the Christian Church,[21] and not least in monasticism and the life of consecrated men and women living in religious community.[22] With his commentary on the psalms in nine books and seventy-four homilies on the psalms, Origen (d. around 254) led the way in Christian appropriation of the psalms. Augustine lent his enormous authority to this reception with *Expositions of the Psalms*, his longest work and the first complete commentary on the psalms. He expounded the psalms as the *vox ad Christum* (the word addressed to Christ), the *vox de Christo* (the word spoken about Christ), and the *vox Christi* (the word spoken by Christ).

All in all, views about the specific origins of the psalms can often aspire only to be sensible guesses. We can say, in general, that numerous, anonymous Israelites and, in the case of Psalm 29, some non-Israelites were involved in differing ways, under the impact of divine inspiration, in producing our psalms over numerous generations. While mainly originating before the sixth-century Babylonian exile, the psalms took many centuries to be gathered in the collection that we now have in the canonical Old Testament.

The Qumran community of disaffected Jews (about 150 BC–AD 70), for example, produced the library known as Dead Sea Scrolls, in which the psalms are more widely represented than any other book of the Bible. The Great Psalms Scroll, dated to AD 30–50, contains all or parts of thirty-nine canonical psalms. But 'the overall sequence is markedly different from what is found in the Hebrew canon'. It appears 'that the last third of the Psalter [. . .] was still very much in flux'.[23] The evidence from Qumran shows how long it took for the inspired psalms to be recognized as such and gathered

---

[21] See K. B. Long, 'The Psalms in Christian Worship', ibid. 545–56.

[22] J. McKinnon has written of 'an unprecedented wave of enthusiasm for the singing of the psalms that swept from the east to the west in the closing decades of the fourth century' ('Desert Monasticism and the Late Fourth-Century Monastic Movement', *Music and Letters* 75 (1994), 502–21, at 506). See also E. Kingsmill, 'The Psalms: A Monastic Perspective', *Oxford Handbook of the Psalms*, 596–607.

[23] See Brown, 'The Psalms: An Overview', *Oxford Handbook of the Psalms*, 7.

into a canonically authoritative collection—finally, only in the second century AD.[24]

The Dead Sea Scrolls, which contain entire psalms, fragments of psalms, four (fragmentary) commentaries on particular psalms, and twenty-five 'Thanksgiving Hymns' composed under the influence of the Psalms, illustrate the inspiring impact of these texts upon the members of a particular Jewish sect.[25] The community that left us the Dead Sea Scrolls was a dissident sect. But in their own way they anticipated the future, inspiring impact of the psalms in monastic and other Christian communities, as well as in Jewish and other communities.[26] Settings of the psalms have continued to be composed, as much as ever: Ralph Vaughan Williams's *O Clap your Hands* (Ps. 47), Edward Elgar's dramatic settings *Give unto the Lord* (Ps. 29) and *Great is the Lord* (Ps. 48), Gustav Holst's moving setting of Psalm 86, Igor Stravinsky's dramatic *Symphony of Psalms* (Pss 30, 40, and 150), and Leonard Bernstein's *Chichester Psalms* (Pss 108, 100, 23, 2, 131, and 133).

The New Testament cited 129 psalms out of the 150 that constitute the complete psalter. A royal psalm focused the messianic lordship of Jesus—to him the Lord said: 'You are my son; today I have begotten you' (Ps. 2: 7).[27] Along with this verse, Psalm 110: 1 proved the other most widely cited verse that illuminated the status of Jesus: 'The Lord says to my lord, "Sit at my right hand until I make your enemies your footstool".' Various psalms of lament were pressed into service to elucidate the suffering and death of Jesus, especially Psalm 22. He was remembered as having on the cross prayed its opening words: 'My God, my God, why have you forsaken me?' (Ps. 22: 1; see Mark 15: 34; Matt. 27: 46).[28]

[24] Eugene Ulrich uses evidence from Qumran to illustrate how the transmission of sacred texts continued to overlap with the formation of these texts: 'The Old Testament Text and its Transmission', *New Cambridge History of the Bible*, i, 84–104.

[25] See P. W. Flint, 'Unrolling the Dead Sea Psalms', *Oxford Handbook of Psalms*, 229–50.

[26] See A. Cooper, 'Some Aspects of the Traditional Jewish Psalms Interpretation', ibid. 253–68; M. Z. Brettler, 'Jewish Theology of the Psalms', ibid. 485–98.

[27] S. P. Ahearne-Kroll, 'Psalms in the New Testament', ibid. 269–80, at 273–7. See also S. Moyise and M. J. J. Menken (eds), *The Psalms in the New Testament* (London: T. & T. Clark, 2004).

[28] On Psalm 22, see G. O'Collins, *Jesus Our Redeemer: A Christian Approach to Salvation* (Oxford: Oxford University Press, 2007), 140–8; on Mark 15: 34, see

Richard Hays has studied the impact of the Psalms and other Old Testament Scripture on the Gospels and the letters of Paul.[29] The New Testament abounds in citations of and allusions to the Psalms. A remarkable example comes in the Letter to the Hebrews and concerns the tripersonal God, now revealed in the story of Jesus and the coming of the Holy Spirit. First, the voice of the psalmist is identified with God the Father, who speaks in Hebrews 1: 5 (using the words of Ps. 2: 7), in Hebrews 6: 10–12 (using the words of Ps. 102: 25–7), and in Hebrews 7: 17, 21 (using the words of Ps. 110: 4). Second, the voice of the psalmist is identified with that of the Son, who speaks in Hebrews 2: 12 (using the words of Ps. 22: 22) and in Hebrews 10: 5–7 (using the words of Ps. 40: 6–8). Third, the Holy Spirit speaks in Hebrews 3: 7–11 (using the words of Ps. 95: 7–11). It is difficult to imagine a higher tribute to the sacred and divinely authoritative quality of the Psalms.[30]

Over and over again, the Gospels, the letters of Paul, and other books of the New Testament illustrate how the inherited Scriptures, and, in particular, the Psalms, were received as authoritative and used to interpret the revelation of God conveyed through the missions of the Son and the Holy Spirit. We know little about the specific work of the Spirit in forming the Psalms. But in the history of the New Testament and in later history, we know a very great deal about the inspiring impact of the Psalms on the communal and individual life of Christians, Jews, and others.[31] The Psalms feature centrally in the

---

J. Marcus, *Mark 9–16* (New Haven, CT: Yale University Press, 2009), 1054–5, 1063–4.

[29] R. B. Hays, *Echoes of the Scriptures in the Gospels* (Waco, TX: Baylor University Press, 2016); Hays, *The Conversion of the Imagination: Paul as Interpreter of Israel's Scripture* (Grand Rapids, MI: Eerdmans, 2005).

[30] See, in general, S. E. Docherty, *The Use of the Old Testament in Hebrews* (Tübingen: Mohr Siebeck, 2010).

[31] See B. Breed, 'Reception of the Psalms: The Example of Psalm 91', *Oxford Handbook of the Psalms*, 297–310; W. A. Saleh, 'The Psalms in the Qur'an and in the Islamic Religious Imagination', ibid. 281–96; and B. E. Daley and P. R. Kolbet (eds), *The Harp of Prophecy: Early Christian Interpretation of the Psalms* (Notre Dame, IN: University of Notre Dame Press, 2015); S. E. Gillingham, *Journey of Two Psalms: The Reception of Psalm 1 and 2 in Christian and Jewish Tradition* (Oxford: Oxford University Press, 2013); Gillingham, *Psalms through the Centuries*, i (Malden, MA: Blackwell,

liturgy of Orthodox Christians and, specifically, at Vespers and Matins; in the course of a week the whole psalter is sung or read. That also happens in the divine office for the Western Catholic Church but over the course of four weeks.

The impact of the psalter also features one word *halelu-jah*, or *hallelujah* (praise the Lord), found twenty-four times in the Psalms (Pss 103–4, 106, 111–13, 115–17, 135, 141–50) but nowhere else in the Hebrew Bible. In the Greek form *Allēlouia*, the Book of Revelation uses the word four times (Rev. 19: 1, 3, 4, 6). As a joyful praise of God, Alleluia or Hallelujah has been picked up in Christian liturgy, especially Catholic and Orthodox, and beyond (e.g. in the Hallelujah Chorus in Handel's *Messiah*).[32] Even at the level of a single word, the Psalms continue to enjoy a widespread and inspiring impact.[33]

That inspiring impact deserves to be investigated widely in different cultures and countries. Let me cite only one example, that of Tom Greggs, now Marischal Professor of Divinity at the University of Aberdeen. He recalls how his earliest memories of finding 'his heart "strangely warmed" (as [John] Wesley put it) revolved around the reading of scripture', specifically, Psalm 119: 105: 'Your word is a lamp to my feet and a light for my path.' That verse from a psalm helped to make scripture 'the text from which I have sought to hear God speak and to discern God's guiding path'.[34]

2008); S. Greidanus, *Preaching Christ from Psalms* (Grand Rapids, MI: Eerdmans, 2016); W. L. Holladay, *The Psalms through Three Thousand Years: Prayerbook of a Cloud of Witnesses* (Minneapolis: Augsburg Fortress, 1993).

[32] See J. Butt, 'George Friedric Handel and *The Messiah*', *Oxford Handbook of the Reception History of the Bible*, 294–306.

[33] The uniquely important biblical word is, of course, the name of 'Jesus'. Used 993 times in the New Testament, this name became all-pervasive in the faith, worship, and life of the Christian Church.

[34] T. Greggs, '*Sola Scriptura*, the Community of the Church in a Pluralist Age: A Methodist Theologian Seeking to Read Scripture in and for the World', in A. Paddison (ed.), *Theologians on Scripture* (London/New York: Bloomsbury/ T. & T. Clark, 2016), 79–92, at 79–80.

The Prophets

In the case of the Psalms, with the probable exception of King David, we know nothing about *specific authors*, and we know little about the composition of particular psalms guided by the Holy Spirit.[35] We do, however, have extensive information about the activity of some who gave their names to the prophetic books. Yet God's self-communication to the prophets, right down to John the Baptist, meant that they were inspired *to speak and to act*, but not—in general—to write. The God-given impulse to collect, edit, and expand what the prophets had said and done, before eventually distributing in writing what had become the final form, belonged rather to their disciples and others. In short, prophetic inspiration preceded and was distinct from biblical inspiration.[36]

The same conclusion emerges from the picturesque descriptions that Isaiah, Jeremiah, and Ezekiel are remembered as having given of their vocation: they were called to speak (and act).[37] The lips of Isaiah were consecrated for that mission (Isa. 6: 6–7), while Jeremiah received the Word of God in his mouth (Jer. 1: 9). Ezekiel, admittedly, had to eat a scroll that was to fill his stomach (Ezek. 2: 8–3: 3).[38] This detail might suggest writing. But even in his case speaking remained the predominant task. In sending the prophet, the Lord did not instruct him to write but to speak and tell the people: 'thus says the Lord' (e.g. Ezek. 2: 4; see 2: 7: 3: 1, 4).

Jeremiah four times refers to a scroll written by the prophet (Jer. 30: 2; 36: 2–32; 45: 1; 51: 60). Chapter 36 tells of Jeremiah dictating a scroll that contained 'all the words that the Lord had spoken to him',

---

[35] In the case of the Pentateuch and the historical books of the Old Testament, biblical scholars no longer attribute the texts to known, individual authors (e.g. Moses).

[36] See Schaper, 'The Literary History of the Bible', 112–16.

[37] On Isaiah, see U. Berges, 'Isaiah: Structures, Themes, and Contested Issues', in C. J. Sharp (ed.), *The Oxford Handbook of the Prophets* (Oxford: Oxford University Press, 2016), 153–70; and J. F. A. Sawyer, 'Isaiah', *Oxford Handbook of the Reception History of the Bible*, 52–63. On Jeremiah, see M. Leuchter, 'Jeremiah: Structures, Themes, and Contested Issues', *Oxford Handbook of the Prophets*, 171–90; on Ezekiel, see A. Mein, 'Ezekiel: Structures, Themes, and Contested Issues', ibid. 190–206; W. A. Tooman and P. Barter (eds), *Ezechiel: Current Debates and Future Directions* (Tübingen: Mohr Siebeck, 2017).

[38] See M. S. Odell, 'You Are What You Eat: Ezekiel and the Scroll', *Journal of Biblical Literature* 117 (1998), 229–48.

and, when this was burned, dictating an expanded version of the same scroll.[39] This chapter and Jeremiah 45: 1 ('the word that the prophet Jeremiah spoke to Baruch son of Neriah when he wrote these words in a scroll at the dictation of Jeremiah') at first glance might suggest that Jeremiah (under the influence of the Holy Spirit) dictated to Baruch what we know as Chapters 36–45. Evidence shows that the prophet did have a friend (who was a kind of secretary) called Baruch son of Neriah (Jer. 32: 12; 36: 4; 45: 1). But events narrated in Chapters 36–45 happened later. An account of their being 'dictated' seems to be a literary fiction, introduced to enhance their authority, rather than Jeremiah being given insight into later events.

In the case of Ezekiel, the structural and stylistic unity of the book that bears his name has led Andrew Mein to speak of it as 'this most homogeneous of prophetic books' and to agree that 'the book of Ezekiel' is 'largely the work of the prophet himself and of his exilic editors'.[40] Mein interprets Ezekiel's grotesque metaphors, violent rhetoric, and bizarre symbolic actions (in particular, his 'inability to mourn the death of his own wife (Ezek. 24: 15–27), who becomes merely a sign of Jerusalem's justified punishment') in the light of 'post-traumatic stress disorder, a syndrome common among modern refugees across a range of cultures'. The language and behaviour of the prophet express 'the devastating trauma' the exiles have suffered.[41] If Ezekiel himself, as much as or perhaps even more than his editors, directly fashioned the Book of Ezekiel, we must acknowledge the inspiring power of the Holy Spirit being at work in, with, and through a stressed and disordered person suffering a horrifying exile. The Spirit was also inspiring someone whose concepts and language deeply depended on a priestly tradition and whose priesthood exercised in exile was 'a genuine form of mediation'.[42]

Four Features of Prophecy

Before turning to Isaiah and what his book contributes to our project, let me recall four general features of prophecy reflected in the Old

---

[39] Schaper, 'The Literary History of the Bible', 119.

[40] Mein, 'Ezekiel', 192, 193, 195.   [41] Ibid. 195.

[42] Ibid. 195–6. For the ongoing influence of the prophet, see A. Mein, *Ezekiel through the Centuries* (Chichester: Wiley-Blackwell, 2017).

Testament testimony. First, in one way or another, prophets were all called to make known the divine mind and will. God was especially present to them, even to the point of identifying with what they said and did. Their personal judgement and human words became invested with divine authority. In the Old Testament, the expression 'the word of the Lord/God' occurs 241 times, and in 225 of these cases we deal with a prophetic utterance.[43] The prophets were understood to be mouthpieces of the divine Word. As much as anything, this language raises questions about the nature of the prophetic experience of God and the need to discern carefully what we may recover from the historical testimony. How can we validate human speech that is allegedly on behalf of God?[44]

Second, as well as proclaiming the divine Word, the prophets announced God's saving actions and intentions and, through dramatic, symbolic actions, denounced human failure. Thus Isaiah acted out a threatening future by going around for three years naked and barefoot like a prisoner of war (Isa. 20: 2–4). Jeremiah carried a yoke on his shoulders (Jer. 27: 1–2) as a sign of the yoke of Babylon imposed by God on Judah and her neighbours (Jer. 21: 1–10; 32: 3–5). Jeremiah also remained unmarried and childless to suggest the grim prospects that awaited Jewish parents and their children. As well as expressing some message, these symbolic gestures also mysteriously helped to bring about what they represented. The prophets shared in the dynamic role of God's revealing Word, which effected what it signified.

Third, the *intense immediacy* of their call is a further characteristic of the prophetic experience. In the case of Amos, for instance, his call came to him suddenly and directly, even though he lacked any relevant training and preparation. God abruptly swept Amos into a

---

[43] On biblical prophecy, see M. J. Boda and L. M. Wray Beal (eds), *Prophets, Prophecy and Ancient Israelite Historiography* (Winona Lake, IN: Eisenbrauns, 2013); R. E. Clements, *Old Testament Prophecy: From Oracles to Canon* (Louisville, KY: Westminster John Knox, 1996); H. B. Huffmon et al., 'Prophecy,' *ABD*, v, 477–502; W. Klein et al., 'Propheten/Prophetie', *TRE*, xxvii, 473–517; H. D. Preuss, *Old Testament Theology*, trans. L. G. Perdue, ii (Edinburgh: T. & T. Clark, 1996), 67–96; M. A. Sweeney, *The Prophetic Literature* (Nashville: Abingdon, 2005).

[44] On discerning the prophetic experience, see R. W. L. Moberly, *Prophecy and Discernment* (Cambridge: Cambridge University Press, 2006); O'Collins, *Revelation*, 48–53.

new existence. The shepherd turned prophet explained to the priest in Bethel: 'I am no prophet nor a prophet's son, but I am a herdsman and a dresser of sycamore trees, and the Lord took me from following the flock. The Lord said to me: "Go prophesy to my people Israel"' (Amos 7: 14–15; see 3: 8). Amos and other classical prophets, far from actively seeking a prophetic career, experienced a call coming to them from God, who unexpectedly overwhelmed them. As Jeremiah's complaints vividly illustrate, at times prophets followed their call with extreme reluctance (e.g. Jer. 20: 7–9).

Fourth, the prophetic experience comes across as a multi-levelled affair affecting the *entire existence of the subject* and a broad range of their spiritual and physical powers. While frenzy characterized the early bands of prophets (e.g. 1 Sam. 10: 5–7; 19: 20–4; 1 Kgs 22: 10, 12) and could be a medium for communicating divine revelation, it was not a fully human form for conveying God's saving message and became less prominent as time went by. To be sure, we meet an unusual psychological intensity, even abnormality, in Ezekiel's visions, ecstasy, shaking, dumbness, and possible temporal paralysis (e.g. Ezek. 3: 22–7; 4: 4–8; 24: 27; 33: 22). However, the classical prophets normally do not receive a divine message through ecstasy, dreams,[45] or similar states but rather by consciously using their various powers. They look, listen, answer, and deliver a message. Thus Isaiah's vision in the temple ends:

> I heard the voice of the Lord saying, 'Whom shall I send and who will go for me?' Then I said: 'Here am I! Send me.' And he said: 'Go and say to this people, "Hear and hear, but do not understand."'

(Isa. 6: 8–9)

Jeremiah provides another such case when the Lord questions him about the things he sees before communicating the divine intentions (Jer. 1: 11, 13; see also Amos 6: 1–2). Here and elsewhere, prophecy presents itself as a complex experience involving the whole person and various human powers.

---

[45] See, however, the visions in Daniel 7: 1–12: 13. Its dreams and visions distinguish Daniel from the other Old Testament prophetic books, which record some visions (e.g. Isa. 6 and Ezek. 1) but generally witness to words of God that prophets pass on to the people.

Isaiah

With the Book of Isaiah, we find prophets reaching the pinnacle of their powers and enjoying an inspiring impact on the origins of Christianity and its subsequent history.[46] Isaiah became the Old Testament book that, after the Psalms, was the most quoted and echoed in the New Testament. Isaiah proved to be a deep reservoir from which Christians drew fresh understanding of God. The acclamation 'holy, holy, holy' (Isa. 6: 3), which acknowledged the sacred otherness of the enthroned God,[47] was taken up by the Book of Revelation (4: 8)[48] and gave rise to the Jewish *Kedusha* and the Christian *Sanctus* (the *Trisagion* in the Eastern liturgy). Isaiah imagined an ideal, anointed ruler with a lyric language that later entered the New Testament, Christmas carols, and Handel's *Messiah*: 'a child has been born for us, a son given to us; authority rests upon his shoulders; and he is named Wonderful Counsellor, Mighty God, Everlasting Father, Prince of Peace' (Isa. 9: 6). Within a poem that pictured the coming, peaceful kingdom, three pairs of attributes expressed the charismatic endowments of the future king: 'The Spirit of the Lord shall rest on him, the spirit of wisdom and understanding, the spirit of counsel and might, the spirit of knowledge and the fear of the Lord' (Isa. 11: 2). By adding 'the spirit of piety', the Septuagint (Greek) translation completed this list to make up the seven gifts of the Holy Spirit that developed in Christian theology.

Jesus himself built on Isaiah's image of Israel as the vineyard of God (Isa. 5: 1–7; see also Ps. 80: 8–16), but gave it his own special twist. The prophet described a lovely vineyard prepared by God. The

[46] See Sawyer, 'Isaiah', 52: 'for 2,000 years there is hardly any aspect of western culture to which the language of imagery of Isaiah has not contributed something significant'.

[47] Sawyer shows how the 'Holy, holy, holy' echoes throughout the Book of Isaiah in the distinctive titles 'the Holy One of Israel' (24 times), 'the Holy One of Jacob', 'the Holy One', and related usage, including 'Holy Spirit' (Isa. 63: 10, 13, found elsewhere only in Ps. 51: 12) (ibid. 53).

[48] The Book of Revelation retrieved Ezekiel more frequently, citing or echoing that book twenty-four times. The author of Revelation brought into play the prophet's inspiring language and imagery to stir the imagination of Christians into seeing things differently and acting differently.

vineyard was set on 'a very fertile hill', with the stones cleared away and the slopes planted 'with choice vines'. The people of Israel themselves were identified with this well-appointed vineyard created by God. But the vineyard 'yielded wild grapes'. So God let it run down and become overgrown with briars and thorns. The vineyard that Jesus imagined remains, however, perfectly and obviously productive. The vines do not fail but produce abundantly. The problem is rather with the wicked tenants who become serial killers. They mistreat and murder the agents sent to them by the rich and powerful owner of the vineyard. Then they commit their supreme crime when they kill the owner's son. But the tenants have no chance of getting away with murdering the young man, claiming the vineyard for themselves, and making it their own property. They are out of their minds when they deal that way with the owner and those he sends to them. He will come quickly with an armed force, execute the murderers, and put his choice vineyard into the hands of other tenants (Mark 12: 1–12).

New Testament authors, perhaps Jesus himself,[49] and certainly his later followers treasured the fourth 'Servant Song' (Isa. 52: 13–53: 12) as an inspiring key for understanding the saving work of Jesus. The New Testament contains eleven quotations from and thirty-two allusions to this song or poem. By the end of the first century AD, Isaiah 53 had become *the* text for interpreting the redemptive impact of the crucifixion. When expounding the death of Jesus, Clement of Rome did not offer in explanation any words of his own, but simply quoted the whole of this passage (1 Clement 16). Nearly two thousand years later, Franco Zeffirelli did the same in his film *Jesus of Nazareth*. Looking at Jesus hanging dead on the cross, Nicodemus (played by Sir Laurence Olivier) recited with moving gravity Isaiah 52: 13–53:12. In the Roman rite, the fourth Servant Song remains the first reading appointed for the liturgy of the Word on Good Friday. Christianity has never left behind Isaiah and its inspiring power.

But what can we establish about the coming into being of this book, the development of which began about 700 BC and was substantially

---

[49] See G. O'Collins, *Christology: A Biblical, Historical, and Systematic Study of Jesus*, 2nd edn (Oxford: Oxford University Press, 2009), 78–9.

completed around 400 BC? How might it have reached its final form under the special influence of the Holy Spirit and through those gifted with the charism of biblical inspiration? Down to about 700 BC, Isaiah son of Amoz was active in Judah during the reign of four kings—a prophetic career reflected in Isaiah 1–39. Some of the material that constitutes the final text and the divinely inspired whole may come from Isaiah himself: for instance, the so-called 'Isaiah Memoir' (Isa. 6: 1–8, 18).[50] In general, Chapters 6–8 and 28–31 appear to be the original layer from which the full Isaiah scroll developed. There are later, editorial elaborations and additions, such as Isaiah 2: 6–22, and the oracles concerning Babylon (Chs 13, 14, 21). Collective authorship seems responsible for Chapters 24 to 27 (the 'Isaiah Apocalypse'), a loose collection of passages passing judgement on enemies and often picturing general doom. But there is also a brief indication of Isaiah's prophecies to King Ahaz being written down and entrusted to the prophet's disciples: 'bind up the testimony and the teaching among my disciples' (Isa. 8: 16).

Chapters 40–66 cannot be earlier than the sixth century, since they address situations that reflect the fall of Jerusalem in 586 BC (with the city in ruins in Isa. 44: 26–8), the deportation of much of Judah's population to Babylon (with the people in exile in Isa. 43: 5–6), and a return from exile.[51] Chapters 40–8 may well have been composed in or near Babylon, and Isaiah 49–55 in Jerusalem. Chapters 55 (or possibly 56) to 66 reflect what happened later, when some of the exiles had returned to Jerusalem. There may be a discrete reference to those responsible for assembling and editing the material in Chapters 40–66: 'this is the heritage of the servants [plural] of the Lord and their vindication from me, says the Lord' (Isa. 54: 17b). Significantly there is a transition from the servant (singular) of the servant poems to servants (in the plural).

Thus the picture emerges of the prophet Isaiah son of Amoz and then numerous authors and editors being responsible for the final

---

[50] Sawyer comments: 'most scholars would attribute some of the most powerful language and imagery, particularly in chapters 1–12, 28–31, and 36–9 to an original eighth-century prophet called Isaiah' ('Isaiah', 63).

[51] See, for example, the oracle (around 550 BC) about Cyrus II, the founder of the Persian empire (558–530 BC) (Isa. 44: 24–45: 8).

form of the Book of Isaiah. The later contributors, who obviously found the earlier material inspiring, brought about a striking unity. An initial vision of all nations streaming to Jerusalem when universal disarmament and peace come (Isa. 2: 1–4) is retrieved and expanded at the end (Isa. 56: 1–8; 60: 1–22; 66: 18–24). From being a place where judgement is passed, Jerusalem becomes a place of final salvation for the just ones from the nations, as well as for the righteous Israelites. The Temple will become 'a house of prayer for all people' (Isa. 56: 7). Both at the beginning and at the end, the Book of Isaiah highlights *God's universal kingship, the gathering of a worshipping community, and the centrality of Jerusalem,* themes that would reach their New Testament climax in the Book of Revelation. Isaiah, far from remaining a collection of fragments or a loosely connected anthology, develops and deepens in a unified fashion these central themes.

Thus those who acknowledge the divine inspiration that helped produce the Book of Isaiah need to reckon with the initial impulse given by the Holy Spirit from around 700 BC to Isaiah son of Amoz and his disciples. Later the Spirit guided many anonymous authors in making subsequent additions, and related groups in editing the text; by around 400 BC, they had substantially brought together in a coherent whole the Isaiah Scroll.

Along with other prophetic books in the Hebrew Bible, Isaiah was to inspire the Christian understanding of who Jesus was and what he had done. Marcion, Gnostics, and, later, the Manicheans put themselves outside mainstream Christianity by neglecting or denying any vital connection between the Hebrew prophets and the Gospel. But for the overwhelming majority of Christians, the inspired and inspiring prophetic witness was understood to illuminate the person and work of Jesus,[52] and to illuminate the appropriate way to live a faithful existence.

Sirach

To complete this sample of what we know about the human formation of Old Testament books and where/how the Holy Spirit was inspiringly

[52] See R. E. Heine, 'Early Christian Reception of the Prophets', *Oxford Handbook of the Prophets,* 407–22.

active, I have selected from wisdom writings Sirach, one of the longest books in the Bible, placed among the apocrypha by Protestants but considered inspired Scripture by Catholics and Orthodox Christians.[53] Written in Hebrew by a priestly schoolmaster, Jesus son of Sirach (Sir. 50: 27), before 180 BC, the work was translated into Greek after 132 BC by his grandson (Sir. prologue). From about AD 400, the original Hebrew text was lost, but from AD 1900 fragments of it have been discovered in Qumran, Masada, and an ancient Cairo synagogue. About two thirds of the original Hebrew have now been recovered.

Clearly set within the tradition of wisdom teaching, Sirach moves beyond earlier wisdom literature by being inspired by and retrieving biblical history in the 'Hymn in Honour of our Ancestors' (Chs 44–9), and by identifying Wisdom with the Torah or Law (Sir. 24: 23).[54] Ben Sira, a scholar of the Sacred Scriptures (Sir. 39: 3, 7–8), invites young students to his school (Sir. 51: 23) where they can learn something of his love for Lady Wisdom (Sir. 51: 13–30). Approaching the time of his death with grace and gratitude, Ben Sira seems radiant with the experience of what it has meant to be alive and in God's service.

This book differs from many biblical books through Ben Sira revealing his name as author and assuming responsibility for the book.[55] Along with the wisdom tradition, biblical history, and the Law, other sources (e.g. Ps. 119) show through. Many scholars have

[53] On Old Testament wisdom literature, see R. E. Murphy, *The Tree of Life: An Exploration of Biblical Wisdom Literature*, 3rd edn (New York: Doubleday, 2002); G. O'Collins, *Revelation*, 192–7. On Sirach, see P. W. Skehan and A. Di Lella, *The Wisdom of Ben Sira* (New York: Doubleday, 1987); and B. G. Wright, 'Sirach', in M. D. Coogan (ed.), *The Oxford Encyclopedia of the Books of the Bible*, ii (New York: Oxford University Press, 2011), 322–34.

[54] In the Hebrew Bible such rereading and reinterpretation by later authors of earlier texts is frequent: e.g. Micah 4: 1–4 (taken up by Isa. 2: 2–4) and Micah 4: 10 (taken by Isa. 13: 8; 26: 17; Jer. 4: 31). In *Gog of Magog*, Tooman has a fascinating study of how Chapters 38 and 39 of Ezekiel borrow from biblical texts of Genesis, the Holiness Code of Leviticus, Isaiah, and Jeremiah.

[55] W. M. Schniedewind points out: 'ancient Near Eastern literature is not so much the expression of an individual as it is the collective tradition of the group [...] The Hellenistic period saw the copying and transmission of the scrolls of scripture as "books", and traditions began to emerge about the authors of biblical books' ('Writing and Book Production in the Ancient Near East', *New Cambridge History of the Bible*, i, 46–62, at 55–6).

detected some influence from Stoic sources. Moreover, when Ben Sira reflects on friendship (Sir. 6: 5–17), he seems to draw on a Greek gnomic poet, Theognis (fl. sixth century BC).[56] The sage presents himself not only as having devoted himself to studying 'the law of the Most High' and prophetic literature (Sir. 38: 34; 39: 1) and as having pursued wisdom through prayer (Sir. 51: 3), but also as having learned much from travels to foreign lands (Sir. 34: 9–13; 39: 4; 51: 13). He has studied the collective wisdom of human beings, 'the wisdom of *all the ancients*' (Sir. 39: 1).

Study, prayer, travel, and steady reflection on his experience (on experience see e.g. Sir. 34: 9–13; 51: 13–22) have extended the learning of Ben Sira and deepened his understanding. Those four factors have enjoyed a deep impact on the sage, and fed into his writing. He is aware of his own authority as a teacher of wisdom. But he does not seem aware of being directed in his writing by the Holy Spirit. He writes 'inspiring' Scripture and will be cited or echoed thirty-four times in the New Testament. But Ben Sira does not claim that he communicates the 'inspired Word of God'.

[56] See B. J. Wright, 'Ben Sira and Hellenistic Literature in Greek', in H. Najman et al. (eds), *Tracing Sapiential Traditions in Ancient Judaism* (Leiden: Brill, 2016), 71–88, at 83–5.

3

The New Testament as Inspired
by the Old Testament

The books of the New Testament refer constantly to the Old Testament, especially in its Greek translation (LXX). They cite or echo most frequently the Psalms[1] and Isaiah,[2] with Deuteronomy, Exodus, and Genesis ranking next. We have already seen some spectacular examples of ways in which the Old Testament Scriptures 'inspired' and shaped New Testament interpretation: for example, Paul's understanding of Jesus as the New or Last Adam (against the background of Gen. 1–3); Paul's vision of 'all the families of the earth' being blessed through the call of Abraham and Sarah (Gen. 12); Hebrews taking up several psalms to represent the Trinity and their interrelationship; and the fourth Servant Song in Isaiah used to expound the saving work of Jesus.

Occasionally the Bible contains references to inspired authors reading the sacred texts they had inherited. Daniel (9:2, 24–7) prayerfully ponders some oracles of Jeremiah (25: 11–12; 29: 10–14). More often

[1] See S. P. Ahearne-Kroll, 'Psalms in the New Testament', in W. P. Brown (ed.), *The Oxford Handbook of the Psalms* (Oxford: Oxford University Press, 2014), 269–80; R. W. L. Moberly, 'The Old Testament in Christianity', in S. B. Chapman and M. A. Sweeney (eds), *The Cambridge Companion to the Hebrew Bible/Old Testament* (New York: Cambridge University Press, 2016), 388–406.

[2] See J. R. Wagner, 'The Prophets in the New Testament', in C. J. Sharp (ed.), *The Oxford Handbook of the Prophets* (Oxford: Oxford University Press, 2016), 373–87; S. Moyise and M. J. J. Menken (eds), *Isaiah in the New Testament* (London: T. & T. Clark, 2005); and, more widely, D. C. Allison, 'The Old Testament in the New Testament', in J. C. Paget and J. Schaper (eds), *The New Cambridge History of the Bible*, i (Cambridge: Cambridge University Press, 2012), 479–502; and S. E. Porter (ed.), *Hearing the Old Testament in the New Testament* (Grand Rapids, MI: Eerdmans, 2006).

such reading is presupposed, as, for example, when Matthew borrows words from Jeremiah (Matt. 2: 17–18) or Isaiah (Matt. 3: 3), and when Paul quotes by name Hosea (Rom. 9: 25) or David, the traditionally accepted author of the psalms (Rom. 11: 9–10). Texts can be cited through the rubric 'as it is written' (e.g. Rom. 3: 10; 8: 36); 'as it is written' obviously presupposes 'as we have read (or heard)'. The very heart of Christian faith, the death and resurrection of Christ, is attested as having happened 'according to the Scriptures' (1 Cor. 15: 4). Sometimes, as frequently in the Book of Revelation or in the prologue of John (evoking Gen. 1 and Prov. 8), the author quotes the inherited Scriptures without pausing to make any attribution, even a very general one. But the impact of the inspired Scriptures on the authors of the New Testament remains all-pervasive. They have repeatedly pondered the sacred texts.

Two late books in the New Testament, 2 Peter and 2 Timothy, reflect briefly on the production of the Old Testament Scriptures and their inspiring impact. 2 Peter 1: 20–1 draws a major conclusion from the Holy Spirit's work in influencing the prophetic utterances found in Scripture: 'no prophecy of [= found in] Scripture is a matter of one's own interpretation, because no prophecy ever came by unaided human will, but men and women moved by the Holy Spirit spoke from God' and, one must add, recorded in writing what had been said in prophecy.[3] Obviously the human will was also involved, albeit secondarily, when the Holy Spirit moved people to speak; the gift of prophetic inspiration did not rob the recipients of their freedom. We should also recall how 'prophecy' is open here to a broader sense, as in 'the law and the prophets' (e.g. Rom. 3: 21), where 'prophets' can include much of what is found in the Writings (e.g. Psalms and Proverbs). 'No prophecy of Scripture' is almost equivalent to 'no scriptural text or teaching'. The central thrust of the passage could be summed up positively: when receiving the Old Testament Scriptures, we should respect their God-inspired character and interpret them in the light of the Christ-event. This was precisely the approach of Matthew, Paul, and the author of the Book of Revelation, as we will see later in this

---

[3] On these two verses, see D. J. Harrington, *Jude and 2 Peter* (Collegeville, MI: Liturgical Press, 2003), 257–8, 259–60.

chapter. 2 Peter will talk about Paul's letters, understand them to take their place with 'the other [inspired] Scriptures', and note that he wrote 'according to the wisdom given him' (2 Pet. 3: 15–17).[4] 'The wisdom' given to Paul included being utterly imbued with the Old Testament Scriptures and constantly drawing on them to express his gospel. They were his interpretative matrix; his language was embedded in them. He loved the Scriptures and was inspired by them.

With an eye on the pastoral ministry, 2 Timothy 3: 16–17 also speaks positively of how the inspired Scriptures of the Old Testament may influence humankind, yet remains a little pedestrian in its vision: 'All Scripture [= every book and passage of Scripture] is inspired by God and [therefore] is useful for teaching, for reproof, for correction, and for training in righteousness, so that everyone who belongs to God may be proficient, equipped for every good work.'[5] However, the sixty-five quotations from the Old Testament in Romans show that these Scriptures were not merely 'useful' (that is to say, efficacious in a lesser sense) for Paul, but played a formative role in developing his thought. They 'trained' and 'equipped' him for his apostolic ministry. But as a reader and interpreter of the Scriptures, his imagination had been converted and transformed by the death and resurrection of Christ. As Richard Hays says, 'Paul could then engage Scripture with great imaginative freedom'.[6]

The inspiring influence of the Old Testament Scriptures on the New Testament authors needs to be expounded at length. But first we should note how, before those authors went to work, those Scriptures had already helped to 'inspire' Jesus' vision of his identity and mission. The previous chapter recalled his creative retrieval of Isaiah's image of the vineyard. Let me now introduce four other examples of Jesus' engagement with the Scriptures:[7] his use of 'the Son of man'; his

---

[4] Paul himself preferred to speak of 'the grace given to me' (e.g. Rom. 13: 3, 6; 15: 15; Gal. 2: 9).

[5] See J. D. Quinn and W. C. Wacker, *The First and Second Letters to Timothy* (Grand Rapids, MI: Eerdmans, 1995), 749–52, 759–65.

[6] R. B. Hays, *The Conversion of the Imagination: Paul as Interpreter of Israel's Scripture* (Grand Rapids, MI: Eerdmans, 2005), ix.

[7] T. Work, *Living and Active: Scripture in the Economy of Salvation* (Grand Rapids, MI: Eerdmans, 2002), 170–80.

praying and invoking the psalms; his biblically inspired vision of prophets as martyrs; and his reformulation of the love command.[8]

Jesus 'Inspired'

Sixty-nine times in the Synoptic Gospels Jesus calls himself '(the) Son of man', a Greek expression which in the Aramaic and Hebrew background has a number of meanings. It could be an oblique way for indicating the speaker's own self (e.g. Matt. 8: 20), or else could simply mean 'someone' or 'a human being' (e.g. Ps. 8: 4). It could also be a way of pointing to a prophet's insignificance when faced with God's glory and infinite power. Thus God addresses Ezekiel ninety-three times as 'son of man'. In Daniel 7: 13–14, the 'Son of man' seems to symbolize the angels (perhaps the archangel Michael) and/or the righteous and persecuted Jews who will be vindicated and given authority by God (Dan. 7: 18, 21–2, 27; 10: 13, 21; 13: 1), rather than referring to one individual, heavenly figure who represents the people.[9] The 'Son of man' did not appear in pre-Christian messianic expectations as a title for a deliverer to come in the last times. It was not a sharply defined concept with a specific content and reference.

According to the Synoptic Gospels, Jesus referred to himself as 'Son of man' in three contexts, each with its own fairly distinct meanings. He used this self-designation of (a) his earthly work and its (frequently) humble condition (e.g. Mark 2: 10, 28 parr.; Matt 11: 19 = Luke 7: 34; Matt. 8: 20 = Luke 9: 58); (b) his suffering, death, and resurrection (e.g. Mark 8: 31; 9: 31; 10: 33–4 parr.); and (c) his future coming in heavenly glory to act with sovereign power at the final judgement (e.g. Mark 8: 38; 13: 26–7 parr.; Matt. 25: 31–46).[10]

---

[8]   Ibid. 180.

[9]   On 'Son of man', see J. J. Collins, 'Daniel', in M. Lieb, E. Mason, and J. Roberts (eds), *The Oxford Handbook of the Reception History of the Bible* (Oxford: Oxford University Press, 2011), 77–88, at 84–5; D. R. A. Hare, *The Son of Man Tradition* (Minneapolis: Fortress Press, 1990); T. Slater, 'Son of Man', in S. E. Balentine (ed.), *The Oxford Encyclopedia of Bible and Theology*, ii (New York: Oxford University Press, 2015), 315–21.

[10]   On these passages see C. S. Keener, *A Commentary on the Gospel of Matthew* (Grand Rapids, MI: Eerdmans, 1999); U. Luz, *Matthew*, 3 vols, trans. J. E. Crouch (Minneapolis: Augsburg/Fortress, 1989–2005); J. Marcus, *Mark 1–8* (New York:

These classifications show how 'the Son of man' served to indicate Jesus' importance and even universal relevance. This was especially true of class (c) sayings. 'Son of man' was used to indicate what Jesus did rather than what he was. It never became a title in the normal sense.

But what of Jesus himself? Did any of the three classes of self-referential sayings derive from what he said in his ministry?[11] Waves of debate have flooded across the issue. A few scholars have even claimed that none of the 'Son of man' sayings come from Jesus himself. But there remain good and convergent reasons for maintaining that, while there was some editorial reworking, Jesus did speak of himself as 'Son of man', filled this biblical term with his own meanings, and was responsible for the three classes of 'Son of man' sayings listed above. Jesus took up an inherited expression and used it frequently but in his own way.

First, we do not find others addressing, describing, or confessing Jesus as the Son of man apart from four marginal cases (Acts 7: 56; Rev. 1: 13; 14: 14; Heb. 2: 6). In the last three cases we are dealing with quotations from the Old Testament; it is only in Acts 7: 56 that 'Son of man' functions as a kind of title. In the Gospels themselves other people address and speak about Jesus in a variety of ways, but never directly as 'Son of man'. According to John 12: 34, his audience remained bemused when Jesus referred to himself as 'Son of man'. Now, if the early Church had freely created the Son of man sayings, it would be strange that this designation for Jesus is not found on the lips of others. The puzzle disappears once we agree that we have here a genuine historical recollection: only Jesus used the term, and the evangelists and their sources faithfully recorded that fact.

Doubleday, 1999); J. Nolland, *The Gospel of Matthew* (Grand Rapids, MI: Eerdmans, 2005). On the Son of man in John's Gospel, see F. J. Moloney, *Johannine Studies, 1975–2017* (Tübingen: Mohr Siebeck, 2017), 185–260.

[11] D. R. Burkett, *The Son of Man Debate: A History and Evaluation* (Cambridge: Cambridge University Press, 1999). Provided recent findings from memory and oral tradition are also used, such criteria as multiple attestation are still valid in establishing what derives in some form from Jesus himself; see C. Keith (ed.), *Jesus, Criteria, and the Demise of Authenticity* (London: T. & T. Clark, 2012) on difficulties that have been raised.

Second, the Son of man sayings in which Jesus refers to his earthly activity are attested by both Mark (e.g. Mark 2: 10, 28) and the Q source[12] (e.g. Matt. 8: 20 = Luke 9: 58; Matt. 11: 10 = Luke 7: 34). The sayings dealing with the coming or apocalyptic Son of man likewise appear in Mark (e.g. Mark 8: 38; 13: 26; 14: 62) and Q (e.g. Matt. 24: 27 = Luke 17: 24). This double strand of tradition or multiple attestation encourages attributing to Jesus at least class (a) and class (c) of the Son of man sayings.

Third, as we have seen, there was some biblical background to Jesus' Son of man sayings, but there was scarcely any follow-up in the emerging Church. Later on, some fathers of the Church would use the expression as a way of referring to Christ's humanity as opposed to his divinity or to his being the Son of God. But in the first century 'Son of man' does not seem to have been useful in preaching the good news. It fails to appear in creedal or liturgical formulas. It was too flexible, or even vague: as we have shown, it ranges from the mysterious, heavenly being of Daniel 7 to simply serving as a circumlocution for 'I'. Linguistically it was an odd expression for Greek-speaking people. The fact that the designation was strange and unsuitable for the early Church's life and ministry suggests that the Son of man sayings did not derive from groups within the Church but from another source, which could only really be Jesus himself.

Fourth, the sayings about the coming Son of man sometimes imply a certain differentiation between this figure and Jesus. Thus Luke reports Jesus as declaring: 'every one who acknowledges me before others, the Son of man will acknowledge before the angels of God' (Luke 12: 8). Matthew modifies this Q saying to read: 'everyone who acknowledges me before others, I also will acknowledge before my Father who is in heaven' (Matt. 10: 32). Luke has preserved the original form of the saying, which indicates a certain unity of function between Jesus himself and the Son of man but at the same time introduces some differentiation between the two figures.

The differentiation makes sense once we recognize that it recalls a turn of phrase actually used by Jesus to distinguish his being acknowledged

---

[12] On Q, a hypothetical collection of Jesus' sayings, see B. Viviano, *What are they Saying about Q?* (Mahwah, NJ: Paulist Press, 2013).

in the present from his future judging. The distinction had its point in his ministry, but not later in the post-Easter situation where believers acknowledged the personal unity between the risen Jesus and the Son of man who would come in glory. Matthew's modification represents precisely that shift.

Fifth, there are some unusual features about the preservation of the Son of man sayings. The three classes are not blended together. Thus class (b), the passion predictions about the Son of man, do not press beyond the death and resurrection to include (c) statements about the future coming of the Son of man. Further, the (many) sayings about God's kingdom and, specifically, the parables never introduce the Son of man. As some wit put it, the kingdom has no Son of man and the Son of man has no kingdom. A partial exception comes in Matthew's story of the final judgement in which the Son of man (25: 31) is also called 'the king' (25: 34, 40). The absence of a clear connection between the Son of man and the divine kingdom is puzzling. After all, Daniel 7 was relevant for the functions of the Son of man, and the Danielic imagery included God's kingdom (Dan. 2: 44; 4: 3; 7: 27).

What can we make of the curious independence of the three classes of Son of man sayings, and of their separation from the kingdom sayings? These two features can be explained if we see the Gospels (and the traditions behind them) accurately preserving here distinctions that genuinely went back to Jesus' preaching and teaching. If early Christians had created the Son of man sayings, why did they not also feel free to blend the different classes of such sayings and to combine them with sayings about the kingdom of God? If they were the real authors of these sayings, why did they stop short in the way they used them?

I have developed something of the case that can be made for Jesus' speaking of the 'Son of man', an expression that he drew from the Scriptures (and other Jewish sources) and creatively adapted. Let me now introduce three further examples of the influence of the Sacred Scriptures on Jesus and his teaching, but without adding reasons for holding that these examples derive in some form from Jesus himself.[13]

[13] One could explore a fourth example, the parables and further material which are *both* 'the product of a religious imagination that is deeply grounded in the world of nature and the human struggle with it, *and* at the same time deeply

Richard Hays gathers examples in which Paul presents Jesus as the praying voice of some psalms.[14] Thus in Romans 15: 3 Christ speaks in the first person and addresses God in the words of Psalm 69: 9: 'the insults of those who insult you have fallen on me'. In Romans 15: 7–13, the suffering and vindicated Christ continues to use the words of psalms in prayer to God: for instance, 'I will confess you among the Gentiles, and sing praises to your name' (Ps. 18: 49). But did the historical Jesus himself identify with the psalmist and make his own the utterances of psalms? At the close of the Last Supper Jesus and his disciples went out to the Mount of Olives, 'after singing a hymn' (Mark 14: 26; par.). Presumably they sang the Hallel ('Praise'), which consisted of Psalms 113–18.[15] But the evangelist does not say anything specific about Jesus himself.

On the cross Jesus cried out (in Aramaic) the words of Psalm 22: 1: 'my God, my God, why have you forsaken me?' (Mark 15: 34).[16] More than any other example of Jesus' praying the psalms, the cry of dereliction encouraged Augustine and other fathers of the Church into expounding the psalms as *vox Christi ad Deum* ('the voice of Christ addressing God [the Father]'). A good case can be made for this cry coming from the last moments of the crucified Jesus.

The question of the Messiah as David's son prompted Jesus to recall Psalm 110: 1: 'David himself said in the Holy Spirit, "The Lord said to my lord, sit at my right hand until I put your enemies under your feet"'

---

rooted in the traditions of Israel which speak of God as creator of heaven and earth and all that is in them' (S. Freyne, *Jesus, a Jewish Galilean: A New Reading of the Jesus Story* (London: T. & T. Clark, 2004), 59; emphasis added).

[14] Hays, 'Christ Prays the Psalms: Israel's Psalter as Matrix of Early Christology', *The Conversion of the Imagination*, 101–18.

[15] Joel Marcus, *Mark 9 –16* (New Haven, CT: Yale University Press, 2009), 968. Commenting on Matthew's reference to the hymn, Ulrich Luz wonders whether it 'means the second part of the Hallel' or 'a different, new thanksgiving hymn' (*Matthew 21–28*, trans. J.E. Crouch (Minneapolis, MN: Augsburg Fortress, 2005), 887).

[16] On the historicity and meaning of this cry of abandonment, see G. O'Collins, *Jesus Our Redeemer: A Christian Approach to Salvation* (Oxford: Oxford University Press, 2007), 140–8; R. E. Brown, *The Death of the Messiah: A Commentary on the Passion Narratives in the Four Gospels*, ii (New York: Doubleday, 1994), 1043–58, 1085–8; J. Marcus, *Mark 9–16*, 1054–5, 1061–4.

(Mark 12: 36; parr.). These words led Jesus to claim, at least implicitly, to be Israel's rightful king and, seemingly, to have an even more exalted status. The appeal that Jesus made to this verse appears to have encouraged its being frequently cited in the New Testament (seventeen further times) and to have sponsored, in particular, the image of his *priestly* 'interceding for us' at the right hand of God (e.g. Rom. 8: 34; Heb. 8: 1).

Reflecting on what he learned from Jeremiah and other prophetic texts 'inspired' Jesus' lament: 'Jerusalem, Jerusalem, you kill the prophets and stone those who are sent to you' (Luke 13: 34 = Matt. 23: 37). The Scriptures (and, obviously, the fate of John the Baptist) underpinned Jesus' conviction about prophets being persecuted and martyred (see e.g. Luke 11: 47–51 par.).

Finally, Jesus creatively reformulated the love command.[17] When questioned about 'the first commandment', he responded from within the scriptural tradition by first quoting the *Shema* ('Hear, O Israel') on the love of God (Deut. 6: 4–5) and then adding another biblical text on the love of neighbour (Lev. 19: 18): 'Hear, O Israel, the Lord our God, the Lord is one; you shall love the Lord your God with all your heart, and with all your soul, and with all your mind, and with all your strength. The second is this, you shall love your neighbour as yourself' (Mark 12: 28–34).

Jesus took up the Scriptures but innovated in two ways: first, by combining the two classic Old Testament texts about love of God and love of neighbour, respectively. Jesus distinguished but would not separate the vertical relationship to God and the horizontal relationship to neighbour. Together they form a twofold commandment of love that transcends all the other commandments in importance, summarizes the key values of the Jewish Torah, and furnishes a basic framework for understanding and applying the law of God.

The second innovation introduced by Jesus involved going beyond defining 'neighbour' narrowly as one's kin and one's people. In Leviticus 19: 18 'neighbour' meant one's fellow Israelite; a few verses later 'neighbour' was slightly extended to include 'resident aliens'

---

[17] See J. P. Meier, 'Widening the Focus: The Love Commandments of Jesus', in *A Marginal Jew: Rethinking the Historical Jesus*, iv (New Haven, CT: Yale University Press, 2009), 478–646.

(Lev. 19: 33–4). Jesus, however, defined 'neighbour' in a way that went beyond family, ethnic relationships, and contacts with resident aliens. He spoke out on the need to love even one's enemies, whoever they were (Luke 6: 27–35).

When Luke records Jesus' teaching on love for God and neighbour, he at once has Jesus tell the story of the Good Samaritan in answer to the question, 'and who is my neighbour?' (Luke 10: 29). Even if this parable may not have belonged originally in that setting, it goes back to Jesus and lets us glimpse his universal application of neighbourly love. In this story the hero is neither the Jewish priest nor the Levite but a despised and even hated outsider, a Samaritan. Jesus holds up this compassionate person as an example for everyone, a model for human conduct when faced with someone who is deeply distressed and to whom one should show 'pity and kindness, even beyond the bounds of one's own ethnic and religious group'.[18]

By the ways the Scriptures influenced him in what he said and did, Jesus exercised a prophetic ministry. He exemplified par excellence the presence and power of *prophetic* inspiration. But recording the Jesus story in written texts under the impact of *biblical* inspiration was left to others—primarily the four evangelists.

Matthew Inspired and Inspiring

On any showing, the Sermon on the Mount (Chs 5–7) embodies much of Matthew's programme; it presents Jesus as claiming that he has come to 'fulfil' the Law and the prophets (Matt. 5: 17). What that fulfilment involves emerges from the biblical patterns which have influenced Matthew in shaping his presentation of Jesus right from the start.

Through the lineage of Jesus (Matt. 1: 1–17), the evangelist draws together the story of Israel. Three sets of fourteen generations each[19] take the reader from Abraham to King David, from David to the exile in Babylon, and from the exile to the birth of Jesus. In summary form, the origins of Jesus illustrate the collective impact of the Scriptures on

---

[18] J. A. Fitzmyer, *The Gospel According to Luke X–XXIV* (New York: Doubleday, 1985), 884.

[19] In Hebrew, 'David' has the numerical value of fourteen.

Matthew. They also encourage the evangelist to indicate the full scope of what has happened.

An 'angel of the Lord' assures Joseph that the child whom Mary carries is 'from the Holy Spirit'. The evangelist added: 'all this took place to fulfil what had been spoken by the Lord through the prophet: "Look, the virgin shall conceive and bear a son and they shall call his name Emmanuel", which means "God is with us"' (Matt. 1: 18–25). This is the first of ten 'fulfilment' formulas that Matthew introduced into his Gospel from Chapter 1 to Chapter 27. The evangelist had in mind Isaiah 7: 14, which in the original Hebrew announces the conception of a child to be born of a 'young woman (*almah*)'. This sign is best understood as a son who will be born to the wife of the king (Ahaz) and who will thus ensure the continuation of the Davidic dynasty through the faithful providence of YHWH, once again shown to be 'God with us'. David's line will not disappear and God will be faithful to Israel (see 2 Sam. 7: 8–16). The Greek translation (the Septuagint) renders *almah* as *parthenos* or 'virgin', as in the version quoted by Matthew 1: 23.[20] He most likely knew the Hebrew original but decided to use the Greek translation. Three comments are called for here.

First, we do not have any evidence that in pre-New Testament times the Greek version of Isaiah 7: 14 was 'understood to predict a virginal conception, since it need mean no more than that the girl who is now a virgin will ultimately conceive (in a natural way)'.[21] Second, the first of Matthew's ten fulfilment formulas should presumably be interpreted in the light of the other nine. In those subsequent cases, Matthew looks for an appropriate biblical text to illuminate some event he reports.[22] In other words, he moves from event to text, rather than creating some 'event' out of a biblical text. One can reasonably hold that, after receiving from an oral or written tradition

[20] J. F. A. Sawyer writes: this is 'by far the most often-quoted verse from Isaiah in Christian art and architecture as well as [in] literature, liturgy, and theological discourse' ('Isaiah', *Oxford Handbook of the Reception History of the Bible*, 52–63, at 58).

[21] R. E. Brown, *The Virginal Conception and Bodily Resurrection of Jesus* (London: Geoffrey Chapman, 1974), 64; see also R. E. Brown, *The Birth of the Messiah*, new edn (New York: Doubleday, 1993), 143–50.

[22] On the fulfillment formulas, see Brown, *Birth of the Messiah*, 96–104.

an account of the virginal conception, Matthew looks for a suitable text to illuminate the story and finds such a text in the Greek version of Isaiah 7: 14.[23] Third, Isaiah 7: 14 anticipates the promise of a just and peaceful king, called 'Mighty God' and 'Prince of Peace', whose reign will have no end (Isa. 9: 1–7). As Emmanuel or 'God with us', the risen Christ will assure his disciples: 'All authority in heaven and on earth has been given me [. . .] I am with you always, to the end of the age' (Matt. 28: 18, 20).

Matthew continues to cite prophets who bear witness to the unfolding of the child Jesus' life—in his birth at Bethlehem, the flight into Egypt, Herod's massacre of young boys, and Joseph's decision to live in Nazareth (Matt. 2: 6, 15, 17–18, 23). Although various interpreters have 'found the evangelist's appeal' to Hosea, Jeremiah, Micah, and 'the prophets' 'arbitrary and contrived', Ross Wagner 'uncovers a deeper logic at work', a set of 'fundamental correspondences between the story of Jesus and the story of his people Israel, correspondences founded in God's providential ordering of both'.[24] Even when this claim about a deeper logic is not judged to be firmly vindicated, at the very least the appeal to the Old Testament reveals something of what was at work on Matthew in the process of his writing. Inspiring Jewish Scriptures influenced an inspired author, whose Gospel will lead off the canon of the Christian Scriptures, as a bridge between the Old and New Testaments.

The life of Jesus in Matthew's Gospel continues to follow providentially the episodes of Israel's history: at his baptism he passes through the waters like his people on their exodus from Egypt (Matt. 3: 13–17). Then, unlike the Israel of old, when led into the wilderness he does not test the Lord and worship false gods (Matt. 4: 1–11). Fulfilling the words of Isaiah 8: 23–9: 1, Jesus inaugurates his ministry in Capernaum in Galilee (Matt. 4: 12–17). Like a new Moses, Jesus ascends a mountain and, with sovereign authority, teaches the law of God's kingdom (Matt. 5: 1–7: 29). Love in practice sums up 'the Law and the prophets' (Matt. 7: 12; see 22: 40). Once again we see how the

---

[23] On the virginal conception in Matthew and Luke, see G. O'Collins, *Christology: Origins, Developments, Debates* (Waco, TX; Baylor University Press, 2015), 286–96.

[24] Wagner, 'The Prophets in the New Testament', *Oxford Handbook of the Prophets*, 373–87, at 378.

inspired Scriptures, whether specifically quoted (as in the account of the temptation in the wilderness) or gathered under the rubric of 'the Law and the prophets', guide Matthew's composition and prove 'useful' (2 Tim. 3: 16) as he himself produces an inspired text.

Accounts of Jesus' healing the sick introduce (Matt. 4: 23–5) and follow the Sermon on the Mount (Matt. 8: 1–17). Matthew understands the healing of the sick and deliverance of the demon-oppressed to fulfil Isaiah 53: 4: 'he himself took our infirmities and he carried our diseases' (Matt. 8: 17). Phrases from Isaiah also feature when Jesus responds to John's question: 'Are you the one who is to come, or do we wait for another?' (Matt. 11: 2–5). The evangelist then quotes Isaiah 42: 1–4 to summarize the ministry of compassion and justice exercised by Jesus (Matt. 12: 17–21). The prophetic Scriptures continue to have their inspiring influence on the evangelist.

This influence manifests itself once more when Matthew reports the parables of Jesus. He understands the parabolic teaching to fulfil the words of Psalm 78: 2: 'I will open my mouth to speak in parables; I will proclaim what has been hidden from the foundation of the world' (Matt. 13: 35). He finds words that Isaiah used in rebuking unrepentant Israel (Isa. 6: 9–10) suitable for interpreting the purpose of Jesus' parables (Matt. 13: 14–15).

When Matthew tells the story of Jesus' entrance into Jerusalem and what ensues in his actions and teachings, the evangelist follows Mark by introducing, for instance, Isaiah (Matt. 21: 33), the Psalms (Matt. 21: 42), and Daniel (Matt. 24: 30). But he also introduces further quotations and echoes: for example, Isaiah 62: 11 and Zechariah 21: 5 (Matt. 21: 5), and Psalm 8: 3 (Matt. 21: 16), to understand events and words in the Jesus story. New quotations and echoes from the Old Testament appear when Matthew tells the story of Jesus' betrayal, arrest, trial, and crucifixion: 25: 35–6 (Isa. 58: 7), 26: 63 (Isa. 53: 7), 26: 67 (Isa. 50: 6), 27: 9–10 (Jer. 32: 6–9; Zech. 11: 12–13), 27: 30 (Isa. 50: 6), and 27: 43 (Ps. 22: 8). Inherited Scriptures constantly colour the evangelist's narrative; he continues to be inspired by the sacred texts. Traditions about the message, miracles, and martyrdom of Old Testament prophets supply language for telling the story of Jesus.

Some commentators have suggested that many details in the passion narratives of Matthew and the other evangelists (such as the offer of vinegar to the dying Jesus, the distribution of his clothing, the mockery which he suffered, and his repeated loud cry at death) were not historically factual but entered the narrative through reflection on Psalms 69 and 22 and on further Old Testament texts. In other words, the evangelists (and/or the traditions from which they drew) moved from their inherited scriptural texts to create events which never happened. Yet one can more plausibly argue that through the earliest traditions these details go back to the historical event of the crucifixion. To be sure, they were expressed and reshaped by the evangelists in the inspiring language of the Psalms and other biblical books, but the basic details came from the history underlying the passion narratives.[25] In telling the story of the last hours of Jesus, Psalm 22 provided a key source of language for Matthew and the other evangelists. What was originally a psalm of lament and thanksgiving became *the* passion psalm or—more accurately—*the* crucifixion psalm.

Far from using a superficial prediction–fulfilment scheme that might suggest a proof-texting apologist, Matthew appeals to Old Testament texts that provide an authoritative commentary on the story of Jesus. What the inspired Scriptures had indicated (or at least foreshadowed) in 'the Law and the prophets' and the language these texts provided forged the presentation and interpretation that Matthew offered for the life of Jesus. This inspired author articulated his message through Old Testament Scriptures that were themselves inspired and inspiring.

The Apostle Paul

Paul began his masterpiece by confessing that 'the gospel of God' had already been 'promised beforehand through his [God's] prophets in the holy Scriptures' (Rom. 1: 2). In an earlier letter, the apostle had insisted on the unique character of 'the gospel of Christ' which he (Paul) proclaimed (Gal. 1: 8–9). Yet, significantly, he proposed Abraham as the model for Christian faith (Gal. 3: 6–14),[26] and presented the promised inheritance of Abraham as coming through Christ and not through the Law (Gal. 3: 15–18). Paul's reflections on 'the gospel of

---

[25] See Brown, *Death of the Messiah*, i, 14–17.

[26] See also Rom. 4: 1–25 on the righteousness and faith of Abraham.

God/Christ', already promised through the Old Testament 'prophets', understood prophets in a wider sense and appealed to texts from Genesis, Exodus, Leviticus, and Deuteronomy. But he also drew on Isaiah 54: 1, when he developed an allegory about Hagar and Sarah, in which the latter represents the descendants of Abraham who, through Jesus Christ, will be the true heirs to the divine promise (Gal. 4: 21–5: 1).

Richard Hays has illustrated how 'the interpretation of Israel's Scripture was central to the apostle Paul's thought'. Hence he argues that 'we can learn from Paul's example how to read Scripture faithfully'.[27] Reading devotedly and interpreting the Sacred Scriptures amounts to being inspired by them. In a particular way, Paul seems to have been inspired by Isaiah. The seven letters that scholars normally acknowledge as authentic (Romans, 1 Corinthians, 2 Corinthians, Galatians, Philippians, 1 Thessalonians, and Philemon) contain eighty-nine Old Testament quotations and, of these, thirty-one come from Isaiah. These letters also contain around fifty allusions to the text of Isaiah.[28] Paul found in Isaiah, Hays maintains, 'not only a *warrant* for his apostolic ministry to Gentiles but also a direct prophetic *prediction* of it',[29] or, in roughly equivalent terms, an inspired and inspiring encouragement for that ministry. As Paul claimed in a more global way, 'the Law and the prophets' together bear inspired witness to the divine righteousness now revealed through the Gospel (Rom. 3: 21).

When Paul struggles in Romans 9–11 with the question of God's mysterious faithfulness to Israel, the apostle looks for inspired insights from the Sacred Scriptures to conclude that, through Jesus Christ, God shows mercy both to Israel and the nations. In developing his case, Paul appeals to Genesis 18: 10, 14; 21: 12; 25: 23 (Rom. 9: 7, 9, 12), Exodus 9: 16 (Rom. 9: 17), Leviticus 18: 5 (Rom. 10: 5), Deuteronomy 29: 4; 32: 4, 21 (Rom. 9: 14; 10: 6–8, 19; 11: 8), 1 Samuel 12: 22 (Rom. 11: 1–2), 1 Kings 19: 10, 14, 18 (Rom. 11: 3, 4), Job 41: 11 (Rom. 11: 35), Psalms 19: 4; 69: 22–3, and 35: 8 (Rom. 10: 18; 11:

[27] Hays, *The Conversion of the Imagination*, viii.

[28] See J. R. Wagner, *Heralds of the Good News: Isaiah and Paul 'In Concert' in the Letter to the Romans* (Leiden: Brill, 2002); F. Wilk, *Die Bedeutung des Jesajabuches für Paulus* (Göttingen: Vandenhoeck & Ruprecht, 1998).

[29] Hays, *The Conversion of the Imagination*, 26.

9–10), Jeremiah 18: 6 (Rom. 9: 21), Hosea 1: 10; 2: 23 (Rom. 9: 25–7), Joel 2: 32 (Rom. 10: 13), and Malachi 1: 2–3 (Rom. 9: 13). But it is, above all, Isaiah that Paul cites (Rom. 9: 20, 27–9, 33; 10: 11, 15, 16, 20, 21; 11: 8, 26–7, 34). Isaiah even appears as a colleague of Paul in preaching the Gospel: 'Lord, who has believed our message?' (Rom. 10: 16, quoting Isa. 53: 1). The apostle construes Isaiah, in particular Chapters 40–55, as witnessing to the Gospel.

Perhaps the greatest homage Paul pays to the sacred nature of the inherited Scriptures comes when he cites prophetic writings as the very voice of God or what God 'says': 'those who were not my people I will call "my people", and her who was not beloved I will call "beloved"' (Rom. 9: 25). God's response guarantees the salvation of a remnant (Rom. 11: 4). God's voice confirms the apostle's confidence about the final salvation of 'all Israel': 'This will be my covenant with them, when I take away their sins' (Rom. 11: 27). Scripture can be 'useful' not only 'for teaching' (2 Tim. 3: 16) but also for finding words to put into the mouth of God.

When citing the activity of the Holy Spirit, Paul writes lyrically of the Spirit praying 'in us' (Rom. 8: 26–7). When reflecting on issues concerned with marriage and marriage relations, the apostle believes he also is being guided by the 'Spirit of God' (1 Cor. 7: 40). In the same letter he expounds and interprets other experiences of the Holy Spirit (e.g. 1 Cor. 14: 13–19). But he nowhere claims, or at least nowhere explicitly claims, that what he writes is inspired by the Spirit or comes from the Spirit active with and through him. The author of the Book of Revelation, however, maintains that the messages to seven Christian communities of Asia Minor are, in fact, what 'the Spirit says to the churches' (Rev. 2: 1–3: 22).

The Book of Revelation

Replete with visions, from the inaugural vision of the exalted Christ (Rev. 1: 9–20) to the final vision of the new Jerusalem (Rev. 21: 1–22: 5), the Book of Revelation or 'the Apocalypse of Jesus Christ' (Rev. 1: 1) draws much of its vivid language and inspiration from the Scriptures, transforming earlier images through the visionary's imagination. Of its 404 verses, well over half (275 verses) contain one or more quotations from or allusions to the Hebrew Bible or to its Greek translation (the

Septuagint)—above all, Isaiah, Ezekiel, and Daniel. In the New Testament no book has been more 'inspired' by the inherited Scriptures,[30] and no other book contains such a wealth of visions to be communicated to the author's audience. It is the only visionary text among the twenty-seven books of the New Testament.

The author (of a work that has features of an apocalypse, a prophecy, and a circular letter) identifies himself as 'John' (Rev. 1: 1, 4, 9; 22: 8).[31] But the traditional identification of this 'John' with the apostle John, son of Zebedee, is made doubtful because he refers to apostles as figures from the past (Rev. 21: 14) and does not claim to be one of them. Nevertheless, the author has received the divine mandate to write down what he 'has seen and what will come after this' (Rev. 1: 19). They will be 'blessed' who read and hear the divine revelation that comes through Jesus Christ and 'an angel', as the end time is near (Rev. 1: 1–3). Using an inclusion, the book introduces at the end the same, initial motivation for obeying this authoritative message: 'these words are trustworthy and true, for the Lord, the God of the spirits of the prophets, has sent his angel to show his servants what must soon take place' (Rev. 22: 6); 'It is I, Jesus, who sent my angel to you with this testimony for the churches' (Rev. 22: 16). This is nothing less than a work of divine 'prophecy' (Rev. 1: 3; 22: 10, 19; another inclusion). The author is

---

[30] See E. V. Allen, I. Paul, and P. Woodman (eds) *The Book of Revelation: Currents in British Research on the Apocalypse* (Tübingen: Mohr Siebeck, 2015); J. Fekkes, *Isaiah and Prophetic Traditions in the Book of Revelation: Visionary Antecedents and their Development* (Sheffield: JSOT Press, 1992); S. Moyise, *The Old Testament in the Book of Revelation* (Sheffield: Sheffield Academic Press, 1995).

[31] On the question of the work's genre, see C. R. Koester, *Revelation: New Translation with Introduction and Commentary* (New Haven, CT: Yale University Press, 2014), 104–12; see further R. Bauckham, *The Climax of Prophecy: Studies in the Book of Revelation* (Edinburgh: T. & T. Clark, 1993); C. Rowland, 'Revelation', *Oxford Handbook of the Reception History of the Bible*, 161–72. In *Prophets of Old and the Days of the End* (Leiden: E. J. Brill, 1996), Eibert Tigchelaar has demonstrated how apocalyptic works, in particular sections of the Book of Zechariah, deliberately reactualize the meaning of texts by reading them afresh in the light of public events. The Book of Revelation does this by rereading biblical texts in the context of events happening in the wider Roman Empire, not least in the province of Asia (1: 1–3: 22), and in the context of practices in the Roman Empire (Rev. 13–19). For a brilliantly suggestive study of Revelation's reworking of sacred texts, see Michelle Fletcher, *Reading Revelation as Pastiche: Imitating the Past* (London: T. & T. Clark, 2017).

conscious of being inspired and of his God-given, prophetic authority (Rev. 10: 11; 22: 9). Revelation ends with a solemn warning
against altering the text (Rev. 22: 18–19). Divine authority stands
squarely behind the whole message.[32]

With its pictures and language (themselves repeatedly inspired by
the inherited Scriptures), the Book of Revelation has itself enjoyed an
inspiring impact on the subsequent religious, literary, artistic, and
musical imagination of Christians.[33] Sculpture, illuminated books,
stained glass, mosaics, engravings, and paintings spread images from
the apocalyptic world of the last book of the Bible. The altarpiece in
Ghent completed in 1432 by Jan van Eyck, for instance, drew on
Revelation 7: 9–17 to depict a multitude of people worshipping the
Lamb. The triumphal arch mosaics of the church of Cosmas and
Damian in Rome exemplified a straightforward adoption of the
symbol of the slain Lamb. A sequence of fifteen woodcuts by Albrecht
Dürer (1471–1528) have popularized for a lasting audience some of
Revelation's central images.[34] *The Light of the World* by Holman Hunt
(1827–1910) brought alive for millions of viewers the words of Jesus,
'I am standing at the door, knocking; if you hear my voice and open
the door, I will come in to you and eat with you, and you with me'
(Rev. 3: 20). Radiant elements in the extraordinarily popular image of
the Virgin Mary in the Basilica of Our Lady of Guadalupe, Mexico
(coming from a 1531 vision reported by Juan Diego), recall the
woman clothed with the sun of Revelation 12: 1–4.

Calling Jesus Christ 'the Alpha and the Omega, the first and the
last, the beginning and the end' (Rev. 22: 13; see also 1: 8; 21: 6) fed
into a hymn (*Corde natus*) of Aurelius Prudentius Clemens (d. around
410), still sung in the popular version by J. M. Neale (d. 1866): 'Of the
Father's love begotten, / Ere the worlds began to be, / He is Alpha
and Omega, / He the source, the ending be, / Of all things that are
and have been / And that future years shall see: / Evermore and

---

[32] See Rowland, 'Revelation', 166.

[33] See I. Boxall and R. Tresley (eds), *The Book of Revelation and its Interpreters: Short
Studies and an Annotated Bibliography* (Lanham, MD: Rowman & Littlefield, 2016);
J. Kovacs and C. Rowland, *Revelation through the Centuries* (Oxford: Blackwell, 2004).

[34] On the work and biblical interpretation of Dürer, see D. H. Price, 'Dürer,
Albrecht', *OEBA*, i, 280–5.

evermore.' From ancient times, religious art has also symbolized Christ by the letters alpha and omega. A hymn by Charles Wesley (d. 1788), 'Love Divine, All Loves Excelling', culminates in praise as worshippers cast their crowns before the throne of God—a gesture that recalls what the four elders do in Revelation 4: 10.[35]

The Divine Comedy of Dante was deeply influenced by Revelation. As Ronald B. Herzman has written, 'no work of medieval literature draws so directly and comprehensively from the Book of the Apocalypse as do the last cantos of the *Purgatorio*, wherein the pageant of Church history presented there for the pilgrim and the reader would be unintelligible without some knowledge of the Apocalypse'. Herzman adds: 'even apart from [such] concentrated references, the poem is studded with quotations from the Apocalypse'. The pilgrimage to the New Jerusalem of the 'scribe and visionary' who, as 'both exile and even a kind of martyr', wrote Revelation proved a model for Dante, who is 'both poet and pilgrim'.[36]

Nevertheless, attention to the impact of the Book of Revelation on Dante's *Comedy* should not lead us to ignore the way he has absorbed and re-elaborated the Bible. He creatively 'bends' the biblical text 'to his own needs and aims'.[37] We can see this, for instance, in his version of the Lord's Prayer (*Purgatorio*, canto XI), which Dante takes from Matthew 6: 9–13, expands with such themes as angels, love, and peace, and puts into the mouths of those who have sinned through pride.

This very brief sampling of the inspiring impact of the Book of Revelation can bring us to some (also necessarily brief) reflections on the influence of the Scriptures in the history of Christianity. Often described as the 'reception history of the Bible', this scriptural impact may also be better characterized as the 'inspiring history of the Bible'.

---

[35] Over the centuries, the interpretation of Revelation has also involved serious conflicts over such matters as the thousand-year reign of the saints on earth (Rev. 20: 1–6). But, beyond such conflicting views, the work has also exercised a widely positive and inspiring impact on Christians (and others); see Koester, *Revelation*, 29–65; and R. K. Emmerson and B. McGinn (eds), *The Apocalypse in the Middle Ages* (Ithaca, NY: Cornell University Press, 1992).

[36] R. B. Herzman, 'Dante and the Apocalypse', *The Apocalypse in the Middle Ages*, 398–413, at 398, 413.

[37] P. Boitani, 'Dante and the Bible: A Sketch', *Oxford Handbook of the Reception History of the Bible*, 281–93, at 282.

4

The Reception and Inspiring History of the Scriptures

Famously Søren Kierkegaard appeared to trivialize the importance of Jesus' historical existence by maintaining:

> If the contemporary generation [of Jesus] had left nothing behind them but these words: 'We have believed that in such and such a year God appeared among us in the humble figure of a servant, that he lived and taught in our community, and finally died', it would be more than enough.[1]

This paradoxical speculation deftly put aside the inspired writings that the early Christians left us: the four Gospels in which they revisited their experience of Jesus through the prism of memory and the other twenty-three books of the New Testament in which they interpreted the whole story of Jesus (including his crucifixion and resurrection) and showed how they lived out their faith in him. They also understood their faith in Christ within the matrix of the inherited Old Testament Scriptures. Kierkegaard's hypothetical reduction of what Christians need for their life of faith dispensed with the New Testament and, in fact, with the whole Bible. But this hypothesis aimed, not to set aside the full heritage from the first Christian disciples, but to jolt the reader into thinking about the heart of the matter.[2]

---

[1] *Philosophical Fragments* (Princeton, NJ: Princeton University Press, 1963), 130.

[2] For Kierkegaard himself, 'the Bible provided innumerable literary images and tropes; it provided him with ethical imperatives and ammunition for cultural critique; and perhaps most important of all, it provided him with spiritual nourishment and direction in his relationship with God' (P. Martens, 'Kierkegaard and the Bible', in J. Lippitt and G. Pattison (eds), *The Oxford Handbook of Kierkegaard*

In fact, the impact of the inspired Scriptures in the story of Christianity has been universal and essential.[3] That story could be described as the reception and practice of the Scriptures, along with scandalous failures to receive and practise them. The history of the Christian Church is simply unimaginable without the Bible. All Christians inhabit the 'history of effects (*Wirkungsgeschichte*)' caused by biblical inspiration.

Let me turn to add further evidence that illustrates the inspiring influence of the Scriptures, both Old and New Testament, in the life of the worldwide Church. I begin with the liturgy, recognizing how the Bible is at the heart of liturgical celebration.[4]

Inspiring Christian Worship

Christians have been initiated into the Church community with a baptismal formula that follows the mandate from the risen Christ at the end of Matthew's Gospel: 'Make disciples of all nations, baptizing them in the name of the Father and of the Son and of the Holy Spirit' (Matt. 28: 19). The tripartite structure of this New Testament formula for baptism provided the outline for two early creeds (both almost entirely biblical in their language), the Apostles' Creed and the Nicene-Constantinopolitan Creed, which have played central roles in Christian worship.

Those who are baptized know themselves to follow the example of Christ, who, at the start of his public ministry, received baptism at the hands of St John the Baptist. The inspired Scriptures encourage and illuminate their experience. They know themselves to be assumed once and for all into the dying and rising of Christ, who had himself

(Oxford: Oxford University Press, 2013), 150–65, at 150); see L. C. Barrett and J. Stewart (eds), *Kierkegaard and the Bible*, 2 vols (Aldershot: Ashgate, 2010).

[3] In the words of Gerhard Ebeling, the history of Church is 'the history of the interpretation of Holy Scripture' (*The Word of God and Tradition: Historical Studies Interpreting the History of Christianity*, trans. S. H. Hooke (London: Collins, 1968), 26).

[4] See G. Rouwhorst, 'The Bible in Liturgy', in J. C. Paget and J. Schaper (eds), *The New Cambridge History of the Bible*, i (Cambridge: Cambridge University Press, 2012), 822–42.

referred to his coming death as a 'baptism' (Mark 10: 38; Luke 12: 50). Having become God's adopted sons and daughters, they are initiated into the Church, 'a people claimed by God' (1 Pet. 2: 9–10). Their 'old self is crucified with him [Christ], so that their sinful self might be destroyed' and 'they might no longer be enslaved to sin' (Rom. 6: 6). Baptism, therefore, calls on them to 'make no provision for the flesh' nor 'gratify its desires' (Rom 13: 14), a scriptural passage which dissipated the darkness of doubt for St Augustine of Hippo, flooded his heart with peace, and opened the way for his being baptized. The Gospels and some New Testament letters provide abundant, inspiring light towards accepting and understanding the basic sacrament that turns people into Christians.

In a single, interconnected process of Christian initiation, baptism and confirmation (the sacrament in which the Holy Spirit descends more fully upon those who have been baptized), reach their goal in the Eucharist (Greek for 'thanksgiving'), the greatest of the sacraments and the central act of worship in the life of the Church. Repeatedly, deeply, and eloquently the Scriptures prove their inspiring power in the celebration of the Eucharist, which comes directly from what Jesus said and did on the night before he died.

Convergent New Testament traditions about the Last Supper support that conclusion, even while they differ slightly over details. For instance, on the one hand, Paul (1 Cor. 11: 23–6) and Luke (22: 14–20) witness to the instruction to 'do this in memory of me', and, on the other hand, Mark (14: 22–5) and Matthew (26: 26–9) report 'this is my body' (without the 'for you' found in the tradition from Paul and Luke) and 'my blood of the covenant' (without qualifying it as the 'new' covenant, as do Paul and Luke). But these and further differences are secondary. The Gospels laid the ground for the development of the Eucharist.

Evidence from Justin Martyr in the second century witnesses to the early emergence of the Liturgy of the Word and the Liturgy of the Eucharist.[5] The former constitutes the first part of the Mass, with

---

[5] See B. D. Spinks, *Do This in Remembrance of Me: The Eucharist from the Early Church to the Present Day* (London: SCM Press, 2013), 30–4; B. D. Spinks, 'The Bible in Liturgy and Worship', in E. Cameron (ed.), *The New Cambridge History of the Bible*, iii (Cambridge: Cambridge University Press, 2012), 563–77.

opening prayers of praise and thanksgiving, readings from the Bible, followed ideally by a homily, intercessions for the Church and the world (see 1 Tim. 2: 1–6), and (on Sundays and some other days) the Creed or confession of faith. Then follows the Liturgy of the Eucharist, with the preparation of the gifts, thanksgiving to the Father for the gifts of creation and redemption, the invocation of the Holy Spirit or *epiclesis*,[6] the words of institution and remembrance (or *anamnesis*), 'do this in memory of me' (1 Cor. 11: 24; Luke 22: 19), the Lord's Prayer (Matt. 6: 9–13), a sign of reconciliation and peace (sometimes coming earlier, at the end of the Liturgy of the Word), sharing in communion, and a final blessing. Thus the assembly moves from word and worship to the Eucharistic meal.

The inspired Scriptures supply the essential 'ingredients' for the entire Mass. The opening words ('in the name of the Father and of the Son, and of the Holy Spirit') come straight from Matthew 28: 19, and the opening greeting ('the grace of our Lord Jesus Christ and the love of God and the fellowship of the Holy Spirit be with you all') comes directly from 2 Corinthians 13: 13. The *Gloria* opens with words from Luke 2: 14 ('glory to God in the highest and on earth peace to those whom he favours') and integrates biblical language (e.g. 'Lord', 'heavenly', 'Father', 'praise', 'glory', and 'mercy'). In the *Gloria* the 'Lamb of God' who 'takes away the sin of the world' echoes John 1: 29, while 'sitting at the right hand of the Father' evokes various New Testament texts (e.g. Mark 12: 36; Heb. 1: 3). The Apostles' Creed remains throughout a web of biblical terms, as does the Nicene-Constantinopolitan Creed, with the exception of 'of one being with the Father'. Even then it can be argued that the original Greek, *homoousios*, echoes the LXX version of God's self-presentation to Moses as 'I Am Who I Am', with *eimi* (from *einai*, to be) corresponding to *ousia* (being). Many of the ancient collects chosen for the 1970 *Missale Romanum* (sometimes called the Paul VI Missal) have firm links to the language of the New Testament.[7]

---

[6] In the Eucharistic Prayer, the *epiclesis* is the prayer asking the Spirit to descend upon the gifts of bread and wine to change them into the body and blood of Christ for the spiritual profit of those who receive them.

[7] See G. Moore, *Vatican II and the Collects for Ordinary Time* (Bethesda, MD: International Scholars Publications, 1998).

Scripture readings form the heart of the Liturgy of the Word: a first reading (from Old or New Testament), a responsorial psalm (from the Old Testament), and a passage from one of the four Gospels. On Sundays and other more important days, two readings, one from the Old Testament and one from the New Testament, accompanied by a psalm, precede the Gospel. The Liturgy of the Word would be simply unthinkable if we eliminated the inspired and inspiring Scriptures.

In the Liturgy of the Eucharist, phrases and longer passages from the Scriptures punctuate the text: from the 'Holy, holy, holy' (Isa. 6: 3), through the words of Eucharistic institution, the Lord's Prayer, the prayer for peace (citing John 14: 27, 'peace I leave with you, my peace I give you'), 'the Lamb of God who takes away the sins of the world' (before communion, citing John 1:29, 36), and on to the humble confession, 'Lord, I am not worthy to receive you, but only say the word and I shall be healed' (echoing Matt. 8: 5–13). Scriptural phrases recur throughout the Liturgy of the Eucharist. Along the way, the prayers repeatedly deploy biblical language and phrases, as in the preparation of the gifts ('the bread of life' from John 6: 22–71, 'the fruit of the vine' from Mark 14: 25, and 'spiritual drink' from 1 Cor. 10: 3). The frequent use of the biblical title 'Lord' could also catch our attention. The First Eucharistic Prayer (the ancient Roman Canon) follows the New Testament by naming Jesus as 'Lord' five times, as well as addressing God the Father as 'Lord' four times. The Prayers for Mass (and the divine office) repeatedly conclude 'through Christ our Lord', as well as often being addressed to 'Lord God', 'Lord our God', or simply 'Lord'. When we join these and many other dots, we see how much the Liturgy of the Eucharist cites or at least alludes to the inspired Scriptures.

The examples of baptism and the Eucharist show how the Bible and liturgical texts blend together seamlessly to exert their inspiring power. Matthew Levering has called the liturgy 'the primary context for the proclamation, interpretation, and *enactment of God's revelation*'.[8]

---

[8] M. Levering, *Engaging the Doctrine of Revelation* (Grand Rapids, MI: Baker Academic, 2014), 3; emphasis added. See also P. Caldwell, *Liturgy as Revelation* (Minneapolis: Fortress, 2014). In 'The Bible in Medieval Liturgy, c. 600–1300', J. Dyer recalls the antiphons and other sung parts of the Eucharist and writes: 'for all practical purposes the medieval liturgy was the singing of the Bible' (R. Marsden and

Hearing and participating in the revelatory communication richly offered by liturgical celebrations, to which Levering draws attention, is largely (but not wholly) equivalent to letting the inspiring Scriptures come home to us. We will return later to the connection between 'revealing' and 'inspiring' (as well as that between 'revealed' and 'inspired').

The divine office or liturgy of the hours has been closely aligned with the celebration of the Eucharist. The recital and very often the singing of the psalms make up the substance of the liturgy of the hours. The divine office surrounds the psalms with detail: antiphons (regularly drawn from the psalms), Scripture readings, hymns, and prayers. But without the inspired and inspiring psalms, the liturgy of the hours could not exist.

In the first complete commentary ever composed on the psalms, Augustine of Hippo interpreted them as Christ 'praying for us as our priest', 'praying in us as our head', and 'being prayed to by us as our God'. On our side, 'we pray to him, through him, and in him; we speak with him and he speaks with us' (*Expositions of the Psalms 73–98*, 85. 1).[9] Augustine's very Christ-centred understanding of the psalms recaptures the inspiring quality that belongs essentially to them.

Hymns, Preaching, and Drama

Let us fill out other ways in which the Scriptures can have an inspiring impact on those who hear or read them. Hymns, preaching, and drama accompany and sometimes match the impact produced by worship and the divine office.

(1) *Christian hymns* enjoy rich links with the Bible.[10] Verbal images and Christological titles[11] drawn from the inspired Scriptures give life

---

E. A. Matter (eds), *The New Cambridge History of the Bible*, ii (Cambridge: Cambridge University Press, 2012), 659–79, at 679.

[9] Trans. M. Boulding (Hyde Park, NY: New City Press, 2002), 220, 221.

[10] See J. R. Watson, 'The Bible and Hymnody', in J. Riches (ed.), *The New Cambridge History of the Bible*, iv (Cambridge: Cambridge University Press, 2012), 725–49.

[11] Christological titles are distinctive names that denote attributes of Jesus and illuminate his being and saving work. Of the 130 titles found in the New Testament,

and substance to hymns and liturgical chants. We might recall here the poignant words sung three times at the veneration of the cross on Good Friday: 'Behold the wood of the cross on which hung the Saviour of the world.' The verbal image 'Saviour of the world' (taken from John 4: 42 and 1 John 4: 14) comes through powerfully. This English rendering works more effectively than the Latin original, which ends with a verb and not a title (*'ecce lignum crucis in quo salus mundi pependit'*).

One can think of biblical images in such a well-loved, traditional hymn as 'O come, O come Emmanuel', and its subsequent line, 'O come now, Wisdom from on high, who orders all things mightily'. The images of Emmanuel and Wisdom succeed remarkably well in this Advent carol. One could mention also the way in which verbal images and titles taken from the Scriptures operate in other classic hymns: 'Love divine, all loves excelling', 'Soul of my Saviour', 'Christ the Lord is risen today', and 'At the name of Jesus'. Based on Philippians 2: 6–11, this last hymn naturally uses 'Lord' but adds other such biblically based titles as 'King of glory' and 'the mighty Word'. Frederick William Faber (1814–63) took over Thomas's Easter confession from John 20: 28, introduced Jesus' name, and added 'my all' to begin brilliantly: 'Jesus, my Lord, my God, my all'.

In the context of biblical titles and names, two further classical hymn-writers should be recalled: Isaac Watts (1674–1748)[12] and John Newton (1725–1807). The eleven stanzas in 'Join all the glorious names' by Watts exploit the titles and images of Jesus to name him, for instance, as 'Great Prophet of my God', 'my Shepherd', 'Jesus my great High Priest', and 'my dear almighty Lord'. The penultimate verse of Newton's 'How sweet the name of Jesus sounds' names Jesus

---

only eighteen occur more than ten times, and only seven more than twenty times. These seven are 'Christ' (540 times); 'Lord' (used of Jesus 485 times); 'Son of Man' (85 times); 'Son' (83 times); 'Son of God' (43 times, as well as 'Son of God the Most High' twice); 'King' (38 times); and 'Lamb' (30 times, as well as 'Lamb of God' used twice in John's Gospel).

[12] See B. Grom, 'Watts, Isaac', *OEBA*, ii , 453–7; see also J. R. Watson, 'Wesley, Charles', ibid. 457–65.

in ten, scriptural ways: 'Jesus, my shepherd, brother, friend, / my prophet, priest, and king, / my lord, my life, my way, my end, / accept the praise I bring'.

These more recent examples of inspiring hymns that bring scriptural language alive should not lead us to gloss over the rich musical life, equally based on the Bible, that flourished in Eastern and Western Christianity from the ancient times. Liturgical hymns, going back to the fifth and sixth centuries, continue to inspire those who attend the liturgies of Eastern Christianity, whether Orthodox or Catholic. One of the glories of Western civilization, the medieval repertoire of plainsong (also known as Gregorian chant) has not lost its evocative religious power. Whether in the original Latin or in translated texts, it continues to be widely used in the Roman Mass and liturgy of the hours.

One of the oldest and most beautiful songs of praise to the Mother of God in the Byzantine East, the *Akathistos* consists of twenty-four strophes and is usually sung standing (hence its name, 'A-kathistos') during the Saturday vigil service of the fifth week in the Greek Lent. The first part of the text is based on the infancy narrative of Luke's Gospel, interspersed with some apocryphal elements and the repeated 'Hail Mary!' (literally 'Rejoice, Mary!', itself derived from the Annunciation scene). The second part contemplates the birth of Jesus in its salvific impact on the whole cosmos. The fact that the *Akathistos* has been attributed to two patriarchs of Constantinople, Sergius (patriarch 610–38) and St Germanus (patriarch 715–30), and to St Romanos the Melodian (d. about 560) reflects its importance.

Among the oldest Marian antiphons in Gregorian chant and an antiphon imbued with biblical language, the *Salve Regina* dates back at least to the eleventh century. Its tenderly devotional language and exquisite setting have made it enduringly popular in the Catholic world and beyond. The *Stabat Mater* ('the Mother was standing [by the cross]'), a dramatic medieval hymn inspired by John 19: 25–7, describes the suffering of the Virgin Mary during her Son's crucifixion and became widely used at Mass and during the Stations of the Cross. Along with the *Ave Maria* (inspired by Luke 1: 28, 42–3) and the *Magnificat* (Luke 1: 46–55), the *Stabat Mater* was set to music by Bach, Brahms, Dvořák, Gounod, Haydn, Palestrina, Schubert, Verdi, Vivaldi, and other famous composers. Not all of them created settings for each one of these three texts, but some of them composed many scores for one or other of the texts. Palestrina, for instance, left more than forty versions of the *Magnificat*. The most celebrated composition of all is arguably Bach's setting for the *Magnificat*. That prayer of Mary continues to inspire fresh compositions: for instance, 'Tell out, my soul, the greatness of the Lord', words by Timothy Dudley-Smith (b. 1926) and music by Walter Greatorex (1877–1949).

The Bible has proved a rich source of imagery, language, and inspiration for the Masses composed by Bach, Beethoven, Brahms, Byrd, Haydn, Mozart, Palestrina, and further classical composers.[13] These Masses let the worshippers hear and be inspired by the consistent voice of the Scriptures. The oratorios or sacred operas of George Frederick Handel include not only the *Messiah* but also his interpretation of other biblical stories, for instance in *Saul* (1739) and *Judas Maccabeus* (1747).[14] With other composers, he encouraged biblical opera, which flourished from the nineteenth century into the twentieth (e.g. Richard Strauss's 1905 version of the martyrdom of John the Baptist, *Salome*).[15]

Inspired biblical texts continue to be disseminated and brought alive by numerous modern musicians. They include not only such religious composers as John Bell (b. 1949), Sydney Carter (1915–2004), Richard Connolly (b. 1927), Lucien Deiss (1921–2007), Eleanor Farjeon (1881–1965), Joseph Gelineau (1920–2008), Marty Haugen (b. 1950), Sir James MacMillan (b. 1959),[16] Graham Maule (b. 1958), John Rutter (b. 1945), Jan Struther (1901–53), Sir John Tavener (1944–2013),[17] Ralph Vaughan Williams (1872–1958), Christopher Willcock (b. 1947), and Brian Wren (b. 1936), but also popular artists and songwriters such as Bob Dylan (b. 1941). Over many years Dylan has creatively engaged

[13] See D. R. Melamed, 'Bach, Johann Sebastian', *OEBA*, i , 61–9; B. Lodes, 'Beethoven, Ludwig van', ibid. 78–831; P. Berry, 'Brahms, Johannes', ibid. 115–19; P. Polzonetti, 'Haydn, (Franz) Josef', ibid. 401–5.

[14] See D. W. Rooke, 'Handel, George Frideric', ibid. 391–6.

[15] See E. M. Good, 'Music and the Bible', in B. M. Metzger and M. D. Coogan (eds), *The Oxford Illustrated Companion to the Bible* (New York: Oxford University Press, 2003), 535–8.

[16] See N. A. Brown, 'MacMillan, James', *OEBA*, ii , 1–5.

[17] See 'Tavener, John', ibid. 395–8.

with biblical texts, images, and ideas.[18] His work, that of David Hewson (b. 1960), known by his stage name 'Bono', and the best-selling songs of the Canadian Leonard Cohen (b. 1934) demonstrate how all manner of music, and not merely religious music composed for worship, can let the Scriptures come alive and prove inspiring.[19] *Jesus Christ Superstar* (lyrics by Tim Rice and music by Andrew Lloyd Weber) became the longest-running musical in London's East End.[20]

(2) *Preaching or proclaiming the Word of God* involves or should constantly involve the powerful presence of the Scriptures. Preceded by John the Baptist (Mark 1: 1–8), Jesus proclaimed the good news of God (Mark 1: 14–15) and sent the Twelve to preach (Mark 6: 7–13). Peter (Gal. 2: 7–8), Paul, and other Christian missionaries proclaimed Jesus crucified and risen from the dead as Christ, Lord, and Son of God (Rom 1: 1–6, 15–16; 10: 14–18; Gal. 1: 15–16).

Great Christian preachers have included St Ephrem (d. 373), St John Chrysostom (d. 407), St Augustine of Hippo (d. 430), St Leo the Great (pope 440–61), St Antony of Padua (d. 1231), Martin Luther (d. 1546), George Fox (d. 1691), Jacques Bénigne Bossuet (d. 1704), Louis Bourdaloue (d. 1704), John Wesley (d. 1791), and Blessed John Henry Newman (d. 1890).[21] Their preaching was deeply shaped by the Scriptures. Sometimes, in fact, their sermons took the form of commentary on books of the Bible: for instance, John Chrysostom on the Gospel of Matthew, and Augustine on the Psalms.

The preaching of some modern theologians also succeeds at taking their hearers inside the message of the Scriptures. In 'The Incarnation in Selected Christmas Sermons', Marguerite Shuster illustrates how such theologically sophisticated preachers as Karl Barth, Gustavo Gutiérrez, and Karl Rahner often reach the human heart in moving

---

[18] See M. J. Gilmour, 'Bob Dylan's Bible', in M. Lieb, E. Mason, and J. Roberts (eds), *The Oxford Handbook of the Reception History of the Bible* (Oxford: Oxford University Press, 2011), 355–68; A. L. Glazer, *Tangle of Matter and Ghost: Leonard Cohen's Post-Secular Songbook of Mysticism(s) Jewish and Beyond* (Brighton: Mal Academic Studies, 2017); V. Nicolet-Anderson, 'Cohen, Leonard', *OEBA*, i , 221–4; M. A. Powell, 'Christian Music, Contemporary', ibid. 202–10.

[19] See T. Erhardt, 'The Bible in Music', *New Cambridge History of the Bible*, iv, 681–92.

[20] See B. Murdoch, 'Musicals', *OEBA*, ii, 136–40.

[21] A. Knight, 'Sermons', *OEBA*, ii, 347–57.

and compelling ways.[22] In 'Sermons on Romans 8: 18–25', she recalls classical preachers like John Chrysostom and John Wesley. Chrysostom emphasized the resurrected glory awaiting his hearers, a glory that 'must not be bartered for the attractions of this life'. Wesley gave 'prominence to the non-human creation'.[23] Hope in a glorious future for human beings entails a hope for the whole created world (and a conscientious care for it). When preachers neglect the resurrection of the body, they often ignore the future of the material world. Paul's inspired text, however, invites preachers to proclaim the way in which, here and hereafter, the natural world and humanity are essentially interconnected. Biblical preaching can and should have such an inspiring impact.

(3) *Drama* has also played its part in communicating the vitality of the Scriptures.[24] Medieval 'mystery plays' characteristically developed inspiring, biblical themes. They highlighted, for example, the connection between Adam and Christ as New/Second Adam by having the same actor portray both Adam and Christ.[25] The gifts coming from the Second Adam were contrasted with the damage done by the First Adam.

The performance of plays that present the narrative of Christ's passion continues in Austria, England, Italy, the Philippines, Spain, and other parts of the world. The Wintershall Players have been staging the passion of Jesus for large audiences in Trafalgar Square (London) every Good Friday since 2010. The Oberammergau Passion (Bavaria), performed for the first time in 1634, has continued ever since. Sunday-school nativity plays characteristically prove adept in sustaining an inspiring knowledge of the infancy narratives of Matthew and Luke.

[22] In S. T. Davis, D. Kendall, and G. O'Collins (eds), *The Incarnation: An Interdisciplinary Symposium on the Incarnation of the Son of God* (Oxford: Oxford University Press, 2002), 373–96.

[23] In S. T. Davis, D. Kendall, and G. O'Collins (eds), *The Redemption: An Interdisciplinary Symposium on Christ as Redeemer* (Oxford: Oxford University Press, 2004), 321–42, at 325.

[24] See L. R. Muir, 'Staging the Bible', *New Cambridge History of the Bible*, ii, 860–73.

[25] See R. Woolf, *The English Mystery Plays* (Berkeley, CA: University of California Press, 1980); and B. Murdoch, *Adam's Grace: Fall and Redemption in Medieval Literature* (Cambridge: D. S. Brewer, 2000).

For the liturgy on Palm Sunday and Good Friday, the use of several readers (for Christ, the crowd, and individuals like Judas and Pilate) brings the passion story into sharper focus. So too does the practice of joining with others in following the Stations of the Cross, whether inside a church or out in the open. For many years on Good Friday evening, Pope John Paul II led the faithful in Rome along the Stations of the Cross erected at the Colosseum. Pope Francis continues to do the same.

(4) *Films*, both (a) those that directly take up the biblical narratives, like Darren Aronofsky's *Noah*, Luca Bernabei's series from Adam to Paul, Franco Zeffirelli's *Jesus of Nazareth*, and Mel Gibson's *The Passion of Christ*, and (b) those that engage more subtly with the Scriptures, like Denys Arcand's *Jésus de Montreal* and Martin Scorsese's *Silence*, have constantly had their impact in bringing the inspired texts to bear on the popular imagination. Lloyd Baugh has magisterially examined 'Jesus films', both those which graphically display the Gospel stories and those which produce their effect by presupposing and hinting at the life and work of Christ.[26]

Prayer

Church history offers a vantage point from which to observe key patterns in the inspiring power of the Scriptures. We examine here some patterns of prayer.

Prayer is not about getting something done but being, through the power of Christ and his Spirit, the selves we can be in God's presence. The personal prayer of Christians cannot be sustained without input from the inspired and inspiring Scriptures. In particular, for two thousand years the followers of Jesus have found the Lord's Prayer (Matt. 6: 9–13) endlessly rich in its meaning and inspiring power. They have cherished, translated, interpreted it: from Tertullian, Origen, and St Cyprian of Carthage in the third century, St Cyril of Jerusalem, St John Chrysostom, and St Augustine in the fourth and

---

[26] L. Baugh, *Imaging the Divine: Jesus and Christ-Figures in Film* (Kansas City, MO: Sheed & Ward, 1997). See G. Ortiz and W. R. Telford, 'The Bible in Film', *New Cambridge History of the Bible*, iv, 668–80; R. G. Walsh, 'Jesus Movies', *OEBA*, i, 497–505.

fifth centuries, through St Thomas Aquinas in the thirteenth, Martin Luther, John Calvin, and St Teresa of Avila in the sixteenth, into the seventeenth century with Lancelot Andrewes, and down to Charles Péguy and others in the twentieth.[27]

The river Marne, which flows north-west across central France, was the scene of an epic battle at the start of World War I, when the German forces were halted and repelled as they advanced rapidly on Paris. Among the thousands of soldiers who died in the early days of the Battle of the Marne was Péguy, a prophetic thinker and great poet. An atheist from the age of twenty, he returned to his Catholic faith six or seven years before he was killed. St Joan of Arc was his lifelong heroine, as he struggled with the sufferings which human beings endure and took solace in the hope which they can find through divine love. In 'A Vision of Prayer', one of the plays found in Péguy's *Basic Verities*, it is God who comments at length on the words of the Lord's Prayer.[28] God introduces the opening words of the parable of the prodigal son (Luke 15: 11–32), and closes by declaring: 'It always ends with embraces, and the father crying even more than anyone else.' Progressive, chant-like repetition turns God's words into an astonishing tribute to the tender love at the heart of the 'Our Father'.

Another twentieth-century poet, Edwin Muir (1887–1959), also witnessed to the enduring, inspiring impact of the 'Our Father'. In March 1939, his wife, with whom he had translated several works of Franz Kafka, was seriously ill, and for the second time in his life the world was threatened with a terrible war. He found himself returning to a prayer he had learned as a boy, and it came alive with fresh power. Muir later described his experience:

> Going to bed alone, I suddenly found myself (I was taking off my waistcoat) reciting the Lord's Prayer, in a loud, emphatic voice—a thing I had not done for many years—with deep urgency and profound and disturbed emotion. When I went on I became more composed; as if

[27] See K. Stevenson, *The Lord's Prayer: A Text in Tradition* (Minneapolis: Fortress Press, 2004).

[28] See 'I Am Their Father', in R. Atwan, G. Dardess, and P. Rosenthal (eds), *Divine Inspiration: The Life of Jesus in World Poetry* (New York: Oxford University Press, 1998), 300–3, where it is God who ponders the words 'Our Father who art in heaven'.

it had been empty and craving and were being replenished, my soul grew still; every word had a strange fullness of meaning which astonished and delighted me. It was late; I had sat up reading; I was sleepy; but as I stood in the middle of the floor half undressed saying the prayer over and over, meaning after meaning sprang from it, overcoming me again with joyful surprise; and I realized that [this] simple petition was always universal and always inexhaustible, and day by day sanctified human life.[29]

In his turmoil Muir was surprised by joy as he was flooded with new and life-giving insights from the traditional words of the 'Our Father'.

The *Didache*, a manual for Christian conduct and worship to be dated around AD 100, followed, in a slightly edited form, Matthew's text of the Lord's Prayer and added: 'for yours is the power and glory for ever and ever'. Then the *Didache* immediately directs Christians to recite it three times a day (8. 3), a direction which will turn up again in the fourth-century *Apostolic Constitutions* (7. 24). Apparently the *Didache* is referring to the three hours of prayer which Jews had practised (e.g. Ps. 55: 17; Dan. 6: 10) and which Christians continued to practise (Acts 2: 15; 3: 1; 10: 3, 9). Clearly by the start of the second century the Lord's Prayer was understood to be central to Christian life—a centrality also suggested by the way the *Didache* places the prayer between its teaching on baptism and the Eucharist and so implies that it is an essential part of the believers' worship and witness.[30]

The immense amount of literature on the Lord's Prayer shows how it has been experienced and treasured by Christians of all ages. A building which stands to the east of Jerusalem on the Mount of Olives vividly attests the universal, inspiring influence of the Lord's Prayer. The Emperor Constantine, soon after he gave religious freedom to Christians in 313, began a building programme in Palestine centred on three caves: the cave of Jesus' birth in Bethlehem, the tomb cut of rock near to Golgotha, and a cave on the Mount of Olives which tradition linked with Jesus' teaching and ascension. Over this latter cave a church was built under the direction of Constantine's

---

[29] E. Muir, *An Autobiography* (London: Methuen, 1964), 246.

[30] See P. J. Tomson, 'The Lord's Prayer (*Didache* 8) at the Faultline of Judaism and Christianity', in J. A. Draper and C. N. Jefford (eds), *The Didache: A Missing Piece in the Puzzle in Early Christianity* (Atlanta: SBL Press, 2015), 165–87.

mother, St Helena; a raised sanctuary covered the cave. Persians destroyed the church in 614; five centuries later the Crusaders erected an oratory in the ruins. By that time, the cave and the site had become exclusively associated with the teaching of Jesus and, especially, with his teaching the 'Our Father'. After the foundations of Helena's church were uncovered in the early twentieth century, the present church of the Pater Noster was built on the same site. Tiled panels in the church and the adjacent cloister were decorated with the Lord's Prayer in sixty-two languages. Up to the year 2000, other versions of the Lord's Prayer were added, and one can now read the prayer in over one hundred versions.[31] Like the story of his birth, death, and resurrection, the prayer Jesus shared with his disciples has gone out to influence all nations and cultures. Whoever we are, we can do no less than treasure this inspiring prayer with deep thanks and say or sing it with quiet devotion.

The text of the *Spiritual Exercises* of St Ignatius Loyola (d. 1556) repeatedly introduces the Lord's Prayer, and depends throughout on the inspiration provided by the Gospels.[32] As popular as ever, and not merely with Catholics but also with Anglicans and other Christians, 'doing' the Spiritual Exercises, which takes more or less an entire month, aims at finding the will of God for one's life and receiving insight and encouragement in following one's personal call. After proposing a prologue (the 'First Principle and Foundation' for Christian and, indeed, human living), Ignatius divides the Exercises into four parts or 'weeks'. These weeks can vary in length and do not necessarily consist of seven days. During the 'first week' those making the Exercises meditate on sin and its consequences, with the aim of experiencing a deep repentance or total turning to God as revealed in the person of the crucified Jesus. During the 'second week' the

[31] On the church of the Pater Noster, see J. Murphy-O'Connor, *The Holy Land: An Oxford Archaeological Guide from Earliest Times to 1700*, 5th edn (Oxford: Oxford University Press, 2008), 143–4.

[32] See D. L. Fleming, *Draw Me into Your Friendship: A Literal Translation and Contemporary Reading of the Spiritual Exercises* (St Louis, MO: Institute of Jesuit Sources, 1996); J. A. Munitiz and P. Endean, *Saint Ignatius of Loyola: Personal Writings* (London: Penguin, 1996). For commentaries, see A. de Mello, *Seek God Everywhere: Reflections on the Spiritual Exercises of St. Ignatius* (New York: Doubleday, 2010); M. Ivens, *Understanding the Spiritual Exercises* (Leominster, UK: Gracewing, 1998).

contemplations and meditations focus on the life of Jesus. The 'third week' turns to meditate on his passion and death, and in the 'fourth week' those making the Exercises contemplate Christ's resurrection and risen life.

Over more than 450 years since the Exercises came into existence, innumerable men and women have taken a month out to make them. Very many members of religious institutes do so fully at least once and sometimes twice, at their entrance into religious life and at the end of their spiritual training. As my summary above and, more fully, the guide book of the *Exercises* show, they coherently channel the inspiring power of the Gospels to bring believers closer to God and to their fellow human beings.

Theological Developments

Since the third century, the Scriptures have played a decisive role in forming Christian teaching and settling doctrinal controversies at synods and councils.[33] They generated the creed at the First Council of Nicaea (325) and its fuller form at the First Council of Constantinople (381). At the Councils of Ephesus (431) and Chalcedon (451), the Book of the Gospels was enthroned to symbolize the presence of the risen Christ and the paramount importance of the Scriptures—a practice that was followed at the Second Vatican Council (1962–5).[34]

Over the centuries the letters of Paul have played an inspiring role when fresh developments spring up in theological thinking. Let me take three examples of those whom the apostle has steered away from unacceptable, if widespread, notions and practices and towards positions that belong more to the good news of Jesus Christ.

(a) In a late-fourth-century and early-fifth-century debate with Pelagius and his followers, Augustine insisted that human beings cannot achieve salvation through their own sustained efforts. He denied that original sin amounted to no more than Adam's bad

[33] T. Graumann, 'The Bible in Doctrinal Developments and Christian Councils', in J. C. Paget and J. Schaper (eds), *The New Cambridge History of the Bible*, i (Cambridge: Cambridge University Press, 2012), 798–821.

[34] See R. de Maio, *The Book of the Gospels at the Ecumenical Councils* (Vatican City: Biblioteca Apostolica Vaticana, 1963).

example, which did not harm interiorly his descendants and left intact their natural use of reason and will. He refused to join Pelagius in reducing the free gift of grace to the good example provided by Christ. To be sure, the Pelagian controversy provoked from the ageing Augustine some extreme assertions about God electing only some people for eternal salvation. But Augustine left the Christian Church permanently in his debt by insisting that the divine initiative always enjoys the priority and that human faith itself is a gift from God. When God crowns the merits of the saved, he does nothing else than crown the divine gifts.

This anti-Pelagian controversy frequently took its shape from opposing views of what Paul meant in Romans 1–11. Augustine's interpretation of Romans guided his resistance to the exegesis of Pelagius and his followers.[35]

(b) Martin Luther (d. 1546) ranks with Augustine as one of the outstanding interpreters of Paul's letters. In Luther's case, however, it is his commentary on the Letter to the Galatians that takes centre stage; it circles around 'the agonizing struggles of the individual believer and the glorious assurance that faith in Christ remedies them'.[36] Luther read Galatians as 'proclaiming the good news of the Christ who is God's self-giving to the godless and the undeserving'.[37]

Luther incorporated much of what he had gleaned from Galatians in his *Freedom of the Christian*, 'a popular tract of enormous importance. Here the revolutionary force of Paul's letter' was 'harnessed by Luther as never before or since'. But, as John Riches adds,

> even though Galatians undoubtedly provided Luther with support and encouragement, it was also the letter which provided one of the key texts for the Roman Catholic counter-challenge to the Reformation at the Council of Trent. The phrase 'faith working through love' (Gal. 5: 6) became a slogan for those who argued that faith alone could

---

[35] See T. de Bruyn, *Pelagius' Commentary on Romans* (Oxford: Oxford University Press, 1993); M. Edwards, 'Augustine and Pelagius on the Epistle to the Romans', *Oxford Handbook of the Reception History of the Bible*, 609–20; B. R. Rees, *Pelagius: Life and Letters* (Woodbridge: Boydell Press, 1998).

[36] P. Matheson, 'Luther on Galatians', *Oxford Handbook of the Reception History of the Bible*, 621–34, at 632.

[37] Ibid. 633.

not bring justification; it needed to be informed by love infused into the soul.[38]

After both sides in this crucial debate had maintained for centuries that they held fast to the Scriptures, ecumenical dialogue in the twentieth century uncovered significant points of convergence. The Lutheran World Federation and the Holy See jointly endorsed an official Common Statement Concerning the Lutheran–Catholic Joint Declaration on Justification (31 October 1999).[39]

(c) In Chapter 1, we examined the teaching of Karl Barth on biblical *inspiration*. But this concern should not lead us to ignore what he expounded on God's *self-revelation* in Christ. More than any other theologian he brought about after the First World War a renewed concern to elucidate the nature of divine revelation. The importance of Barth's commentary on Romans, especially in its game-changing, second edition of 1922,[40] lay essentially in his rediscovery of the biblical revelation of God as *the* decisive category for theological thought. Barth demanded a return to the authentic sources of faith and theology, the revealed Word of God to which the Bible witnesses.[41] The inspiring words of Paul's Letter to the Romans aroused Barth's interest and led him to break with the humanist distortions of liberal theology and insist on granting revelation, in which God speaks and makes himself known, the serious consideration it warrants.

Recalling and highlighting biblical texts and themes which suffered from neglect have triggered fresh developments in theology.[42] One could, for instance, dwell on the centrality of the exodus for the

[38] J. Riches, 'Galatians', ibid. 149–60, at 151.

[39] The complete text was published by the Pontifical Council for Promoting Christian Unity, N. 98 (1998 III), 81–93.

[40] Trans. E. C. Hoskyns (Oxford: Oxford University Press, 1933).

[41] See T. Gorringe, 'Karl Barth on Romans', *Oxford Handbook of the Reception History of the Bible*, 590–608; G. O'Collins, *Foundations of Theology* (Chicago: Loyola University Press, 1971), 31–6, 191–4.

[42] In *Reading Sacred Scripture: Voices from the History of Biblical Interpretation* (Grand Rapids, MI: Eerdmans, 2016), Stephen Westerholm and Martin Westerholm take up Augustine, Barth, Luther, and many other influential interpreters (from Irenaeus to the present) and show how they read and reacted to the Scriptures as the Word of God.

liberation theology of Latin America.[43] The exodus has become a living, inspiring symbol of God's liberating power for Bible-reading groups and other poor communities. For feminist theology, long neglected scriptural passages have been retrieved and have shown their vitalizing impact. In its treatment of 'God', the second volume of the four-volume *Interpreter's Dictionary of the Bible* neglected the female images of God found in the Old Testament prophets and elsewhere.[44] In a supplementary volume that appeared fourteen years later, Phyllis Trible summarized these female images and their impact.[45]

Official Teaching Retrieves Forgotten Texts

Official teaching coming from church councils repeatedly illustrates the same phenomenon: neglected biblical texts can finally come into their own and drive what a particular council has to say. The scriptural index of the two-volume *Decrees of Ecumenical Councils* reveals where such developments have occurred.[46] Let me take one striking example.

For its teaching on the Jewish people, the Dogmatic Constitution on the Church, *Lumen Gentium* (Light of the Nations), of the Second Vatican Council (1962–5) first selected some of the privileges listed by Romans 9: 4–5 to speak of 'the people to whom the covenants and promises were given and from whom Christ was born according to the flesh'. Then the Constitution aligned itself with Paul in stating that 'according to the [divine] election, they [the Jews] are a people most dear on account of the fathers; for the gifts and calling of God are without regret (Rom. 11: 28–9)' (*Lumen Gentium*, 16). Before Vatican II, no ecumenical council had either cited those two passages from Romans or spoken well of the Jews. Now prompted by Pope John XXIII and other friends of the Jewish people and aiming

[43] See S. M. Langston, *Exodus through the Centuries* (Oxford: Blackwell, 2006); P. Noguera, 'Exodus in Latin America', *Oxford Handbook of the Reception History of the Bible*, 447–59. The exodus as a story of hope that provides visions of a promised land has also been misused by various communities, as Langston's book reminds us.

[44] (Nashville: Abingdon Press, 1962), 407–36.

[45] *Interpreter's Dictionary of the Bible: Supplementary Volume*, 'God, Nature of, in the OT' (Nashville: Abingdon Press, 1976), 308–9.

[46] N. P. Tanner (ed.) (London/Washington, DC: Sheed & Ward/Georgetown University Press, 1990).

to proscribe effectively any anti-Semitism, the Council found a scriptural warrant in the classical texts of Paul about God's irrevocable election of Israel.[47]

In a longer treatment of the Jewish people that appeared a year later in Vatican II's Declaration on the Relation of the Church to Non-Christian Religions, *Nostra Aetate* (In Our Age), the Council once again quoted Romans 9: 4–5 (*Nostra Aetate*, 4) and, in a reference to Romans 11: 28–9, recalled the use of that passage in *Lumen Gentium*, 16 (*Nostra Aetate*, 4, fn. 11). Undoubtedly what was said about Judaism in *Nostra Aetate* was longer and more significant—especially in view of the emerging Catholic–Jewish dialogue.[48] Nevertheless, driven by what Paul had written in Romans, the decisive step towards *rapprochement* had already been taken in *Lumen Gentium*. Once again Romans proved itself crucial in notable developments, this time in official teaching.

Literature

Before completing this chapter, we need to pay homage to the extraordinary impact of the Bible on literature.[49] The Scriptures, either directly, or through the beauty and power of various translations (e.g. the Vulgate, the Luther Bible, the Douay Bible, and the Authorized Version) and their use by classical writers, have profoundly affected medieval Latin, English, German, Italian, and other languages and literature.[50] For writers of different nations and cultures, the Bible has

[47] On these verses from Romans, see B. Byrne, *Romans* (Collegeville, MN: Liturgical Press, 1996), 285–7, 351–2; J. A. Fitzmyer, *Romans* (New York: Doubleday, 1993), 545–7, 626; D. Moo, *The Epistle to the Romans* (Grand Rapids, MI: Eerdmans), 559–68, 729–32.

[48] On results of the post-conciliar, interfaith dialogues, see J. L. Heft (ed.), *Catholicism and Interfaith Dialogue* (New York: Oxford University Press, 2012).

[49] See E. A. Matter, 'The Bible in the Spiritual Literature of the Medieval West', *New Cambridge History of the Bible*, ii, 693–703.

[50] Besides the works of Robert Alter, see R. Atwan and L. Wieder (eds), *Chapters into Verse: Poetry in English Inspired by the Bible*, 2 vols (New York: Oxford University Press, 1993); N. Frye, *The Great Code: The Bible and Literature* (London: Routledge & Kegan Paul, 1982); D. L. Jeffrey, 'The Hebrew Bible in Art and Literature', in S. B. Chapman and M. A. Sweeney (eds), *The Cambridge Companion to the Hebrew Bible/Old Testament* (New York: Cambridge University Press, 2016), 426–46; D. Norton, *A History of the English Bible as Literature* (New York: Cambridge University Press, 2000); S. E. Porter,

proved a rich source of language, imagery, and inspiration, and not least through the figure of the redeeming Christ himself inspiringly displayed in the four Gospels.[51]

With imagination and vitality, poets of all ages have taken up the Scriptures. In the early period we find Ephrem the Syrian (d. 373), an influential theologian whose medium was poetry;[52] Ambrose of Milan (d. 397), the father of liturgical song in the West;[53] Venantius Fortunatus (d. around 610), the author of some of the greatest poems/hymns in Western Christianity;[54] the anonymous *Exultet* or Easter Proclamation sung on the vigil of Easter Sunday; and the *Veni, Creator Spiritus* (Come, Creator Spirit) attributed to Rabaunus Maurus (d. 856). In the Middle Ages came Wipo of Burgundy (d. after 1046), who composed the Easter sequence *Victimae paschali laudes* (Praises to the Easter Victim); Hildegard of Bingen (d. 1179), who created the music to which her Latin poems on Christ the Redeemer and the Virgin Mary were sung;[55] and Thomas Aquinas (d. 1274), who wrote such exquisite Latin lyrics as *Adoro te devote* (I Adore You Devotedly).

M. A. Hayes, and D. Tombs (eds), *Images of Christ Ancient and Modern* (Sheffield: Sheffield Academic Press, 1997), 206–398; L. Ryken, J. C. Wilhoit, and T. Longman III (eds), *Dictionary of Biblical Imagery* (Downers Grove, IL: InterVarsity Press, 1998). For the interpretation of the Bible in literature, the visual arts, music, and dance, see A. Swindell et al., 'Interpretation, History of', *Encyclopedia of the Bible and its Reception*, xiii (Berlin: De Gruyter, 2016), 131–47.

[51] See e.g. R. Kiely, ' "Graven with an Iron Pen": The Persistence of Redemption as a Theme in Literature', *The Redemption*, 277–94.

[52] Ephrem, like Augustine of Hippo, Martin Luther, John Donne, George Herbert, and many other Christian writers, revelled in the paradox of divinity and humanity being joined in the one person of Christ. In a 'Hymn on Nativity', Ephrem wrote: 'He was happy but he sucked Mary's milk, and from his blessings all creation sucks' (Atwan et al. (eds), *Divine Inspiration*, 21).

[53] J. Fontaine et al., *Hymnes/Ambroise de Milan* (Paris: Cerf, 1992).

[54] His *Crux fidelis* (Faithful Cross) links the tree from which Adam and Eve took the forbidden fruit with the tree on which Christ was crucified. Two of his poems/hymns became an integral part of the Holy Week liturgies in the Western Church: *Vexilla Regis prodeunt* (The Banners of the King Go Forward) and *Pange, lingua, gloriosi proelium certaminis* (Sing, [My] Tongue, of the Battle of the Glorious Struggle).

[55] Saint Hildegard of Bingen, *Symphonia: A Critical Edition of the Symphonie armonie celestium revelationum*, trans. B. J. Newman (Ithaca and London: Cornell University Press, 1988); A. L. Clark, 'Hildegard of Bingen', *OEBA*, i, 430–4.

These were followed by John of the Cross (d. 1591), Jean de La Ceppède (d. 1623), and Henry Vaughan (d. 1695); and, nearer our own time, Gerard Manley Hopkins (d. 1889), Miguel de Unamuno (d. 1936; he composed a series of eighty-nine poems on the bleeding Christ painted by Velázquez), T. S. Eliot (d. 1965), and Kevin Hart (b. 1954). The scope of biblically inspired poetry varies. Vaughan's 'The Dwelling Place' takes up John 1: 38 ('Lord, where are you dwelling?') to exploit the deeper meanings that the evangelist allows for. Partly to vindicate in 'theorems' his orthodox faith, de La Ceppède wrote 520 sonnets visualizing the events recorded in the last chapters of the four Gospels.[56] From the fourth century down to our own day, Christian poetry bears persistent witness to the inspiring quality of the Scriptures.

The Visual Arts

The influence of the Bible on painting (including icons), sculpture, architecture, mosaics, tapestry, and other forms of the visual arts in the West and beyond (in Africa, Asia, Latin America, and Oceania) has been exceptional.[57] The exhibition 'Seeing Salvation' held at the National Gallery, London (February–May 2000), and its accompanying catalogue, *The Image of Christ*,[58] displayed that profound influence eloquently. The roll call of those who rendered the Scriptures in painting and sculpture is immense: from the anonymous artists who decorated catacombs, through Giotto and Beato Angelico, and then through Leonardo da Vinci, Raphael, Michelangelo, Caravaggio, Rembrandt, El Greco, and Blake,[59] to Chagall and other modern

[56] See K. Bosley (ed. and trans.), *From the Theorems of Master Jean de La Ceppède* (Manchester: Carcanet Press, 1993).

[57] See J. Mitchell, 'The Bible in Public Art, 600–1050', *New Cambridge History of the Bible*, ii, 755–84; C. M. Kauffmann, 'The Bible in Public Art, 1050–1450', ibid. 785–820; D. H. Price, 'The Bible and the Visual Arts in Early Modern Europe', ibid. iii, 718–61; M. Wheeler, 'The Bible in Art', ibid. iv, 693–706; S. E. Porter, M. A. Hayes, and D. Tombs (eds), *Images of Christ Ancient and Modern* (Sheffield: Sheffield Academic Press, 1997).

[58] G. Finaldi (ed.) (London: National Gallery, 2000).

[59] See E. Mason, 'Elihu's Spiritual Sensation: William Blake's Illustrations of the Book of Job', *Oxford Handbook of the Reception History of the Bible*, 460–75.

artists. In several publications, David Brown has opened up ways in which artists have meaningfully visualized events of Jesus' life and death.[60] Inspired by the Gospels, these artists have in their turn left works that remain inspiring for generation after generation.

John Mitchell summarizes the early place of the Bible in the visual arts: 'The half millennium following the effective disintegration of the Roman world system in the decades around 600 witnessed an engagement with the Bible in the public visual area that was dynamic, inventive and extremely varied.'[61] Mitchell reminds us not to neglect the splendid decorations of Gospel books (like the Book of Kells) and other biblical manuscripts. Robin Cormack corrects any unqualified description of stained-glass windows as 'the Bible of the poor': 'Art was not just the Bible of the illiterate but something much more complicated. As Photios argued in the ninth century, seeing the sacred events as icons reinforced faith in their historical reality.' Cormack adds: 'While the words of the Bible taught Christian morality and values, icons offered models of saints who had lived according to their values and turned the abstract into Christian truth.'[62]

In 'The Bible as Iconography', A. C. Labriola summarizes something of the history of personages, events, and objects in the Bible being rendered as visual images.[63] Over and over again, Christian artists linked Old Testament personages, events, and objects with their counterparts in the New Testament. By depicting such scenes in sequence, these artists conveyed a sense of God's action moving human history forward. (We saw an example of this in Chapter 2, with Masaccio linking Adam and Eve with Christ, the New Adam.) The Bible tells a story to be recognized, valued, and celebrated. The visual arts have led the way in appreciating this inspiring story, as Labriola showed brilliantly in his teaching career.

[60] See e.g. D. Brown, 'Images of Redemption in Art and Music', *The Redemption*, 295–320.

[61] 'The Bible in Public Art, 600–1050', 783.

[62] R. Cormack, 'Icons of the Eastern Church', *New Cambridge History of the Bible*, ii, 821–34, at 833–4.

[63] *Oxford Handbook of the Reception History of the Bible* , 175–99.

Inspiring Scriptures Misused

This chapter has brought together something of the *positively* inspiring effects of the Scriptures. But it does not intend to deny the misuse of the Bible that has persisted since the beginning of Christianity. As William Shakespeare warned in *The Merchant of Venice*, 'the devil can cite Scripture for his purpose' (Act 1, scene 3).

Some books of the Bible have proved particularly open to such misuse: for instance Judges, which records an endemic exercise of violence.[64] Reading the Book of Jonah as if it were an historical work (and not as an extended parable that saves its religious punch for the last few lines) has landed many in absurd puzzles: how could the prophet have survived inside the great fish? Was Nineveh such a huge city that it took three days to cross (Jonah 3: 3)? Some readers, ignoring the way in which the Pentateuch records zoological views of ancient times, have been startled to find hares listed among animals that chew the cud (Lev. 11: 6; Deut. 14: 7). For many centuries some texts (e.g. Matt. 27: 25; John 8: 44; 1 Thess. 2: 15–16) have been deployed in the cause of anti-Semitism.[65] The Old Testament injunction to execute female sorcerers (Exod. 22: 18) was taken to 'justify' the burning of witches.

In 1633 the Roman Inquisition condemned Galileo Galilei (1564–1642) for endorsing the system first proposed by Nicolaus Copernicus (1473–1543), a Polish (priest) astronomer who had argued that the earth moves around the sun and not vice versa. The condemnation of Galileo still symbolizes the enduring image of an official church refusing to accept new discoveries and trying to curb scientific freedom. The negative stand of many Christians towards the theory of evolution advanced by Charles Darwin (1809–82) further reinforced the image of an anti-scientific church and even the triumph of science over religion.[66] Some Christians have misunderstood the purpose of

---

[64] See D. M. Gunn, 'Judges', ibid. 89–103.

[65] See T. Nicklas, 'The Bible and Anti-Semitism', ibid. 267–80.

[66] See J. H. Brooke, 'Samuel Wilberforce, Thomas Huxley, and Genesis', ibid. 397–412; N. A. Rupke, 'The Bible and Science', *New Cambridge History of the Bible*, iv, 707–24; G. O'Collins and M. Farrugia, *Catholicism: The Story of Catholic Christianity*, 2nd edn (Oxford: Oxford University Press, 2015), 188–90.

the creation narratives of Genesis (to present the relationship between God the Creator and alienated human beings) and searched for help in understanding the mechanics of creation. The early chapters of the Bible are not in the business of providing factual accuracy in scientific (and historical) matters. Too many Christians have ignored the wise comment of St Augustine of Hippo about the inspiration of the Holy Spirit having a religious purpose and not aiming to promote scientific truth: 'We do not read in the Gospel that the Lord said, "I am sending you the Paraclete to teach you about the course of the sun and the moon." After all he wanted to make Christians, not astronomers' (*Contra Felicem Manichaeum*, 1. 10).[67]

For many people, the priest-palaeontologist Pierre Teilhard de Chardin (1881–1955) represents the end of old antagonisms between science and religion. Far from finding the evolution of the species in conflict with inspired truth, Teilhard acknowledged the wisdom and power of God who, through laws implanted in creation, arranged for a marvellous development from within.

Preachers, church officials, artists, political leaders, and other Christians have repeatedly misappropriated and misinterpreted the Scriptures in all manner of bad causes. But *abusus non tollit usum* (abuse does not take away use), or, as we might put it, diseased and destructive abuse does not rule out a healthy and life-giving use of the Bible.

---

[67] *Answer to Felix, a Manichean*, in *The Manichean Debate*, trans. R. Teske (Hyde Park, NY: New City Press, 2006), 286. Notoriously many have read the divine injunction to rule over the earth (Gen. 1: 26–30) and to care for the garden of Eden (Gen. 2: 15–25) as a licence to exploit and even ravage our planet. It was meant to be our beautiful, spiritual home (Ps. 104), with which we should reconnect before it is too late.

5

Revelation, Tradition, and Inspiration

The first four chapters of this book gathered information from two Christian thinkers who have grappled with the nature of biblical inspiration (Karl Barth and Raymond Collins), from four books of the Old Testament (Genesis, Psalms, Isaiah, and Sirach), from Jesus (the praying voice of the psalms), from three New Testament writers (Matthew, Paul, and the 'John' of the Book of Revelation), and from the post-New Testament inspiring history of the Bible (in worship, hymns, preaching, drama, films, personal prayer, theological developments, official teaching, literature, and art). That account of the Bible's reception history was more or less confined to Christians. A lengthier treatment would include the inspiring impact of the Scriptures in Islam, Hinduism, and so forth.[1]

We noted what both Barth and Collins contribute to a theology of biblical inspiration: for instance, by questioning any attempts to identify God's self-revelation simply with inspiration. The inspired Bible bears witness to revelation but is to be distinguished from revelation. Beyond question, the Holy Spirit who inspired and sanctified the scriptural texts made them a permanent means for revealing God (and the human condition) and for bringing about God's saving purposes.

---

[1] See e.g. J. Holton, 'Gandhi's Interpretation of the Sermon on the Mount', in M. Lieb, E. Mason, and J. Roberts (eds), *The Oxford Handbook of the Reception History of the Bible* (Oxford: Oxford University Press, 2011), 542–56; W. A. Saleh, 'The Hebrew Bible in Islam', in S. B. Chapman and M. A. Sweeney (eds), *The Cambridge Companion to the Hebrew Bible/Old Testament* (New York: Cambridge University Press, 2016), 407–25.

The sanctifying work of the Spirit includes (but is not restricted to) these texts, and makes them suitable and even powerful instruments for communicating the good news. Nevertheless, as Donald Bloesch has written, 'the Bible is not in and of itself the revelation of God'. It is a 'divinely appointed means and channel of this revelation'.[2]

In *Holy Scripture: A Dogmatic Sketch*, John Webster may seem to identify inspiration *tout court* with the divine self-revelation when he writes: 'Scripture is revelation'.[3] But he presses on to explain the inspired Scriptures as a/the major means for communicating the divine self-presence: 'through the Holy Scripture God addresses the church with the gospel of salvation'.[4]

Our Chapter 1 closed with Collins stating firmly that adequate treatments of biblical inspiration should begin with the reality of the Scriptures themselves. To this advice, I would add that any such treatments remain inadequate unless they *also* treat the inspiring impact of the Bible in the life of post-New Testament Christianity. Hence, after reflecting on the reality of several inspired books of the Old and New Testament (Chapters 2 and 3), I included something on the subsequent, inspiring history of the Scriptures (Chapter 4). The inspired Scriptures have as such continued to be inspiring.

This fifth chapter has a mapping function in that it will spell out the interrelationship between revelation, tradition, and the divine–human inspiration of Scriptures before directly examining inspiration. I am more convinced than ever that the Second Vatican Council exemplified the best approach in *Dei Verbum* ('the Word of God', a constitution promulgated on 18 November 1965). This document dedicated Chapter 1 to revelation and Chapter 2 to tradition, in order to provide a clear context for presenting the inspired Scriptures in Chapters 3–6. Hence let us sketch an account, in turn, of revelation, tradition, and biblical inspiration, and then take a position on their interrelationship.

---

[2] D. G. Bloesch, *Holy Scripture: Revelation, Inspiration & Interpretation* (Carlisle: Paternoster Press, 1994), 57.

[3] John Webster, *Holy Scripture: A Dogmatic Sketch* (Cambridge: Cambridge University Press, 2003), 31.

[4] Ibid. 32.

The Self-Revelation of God

'Revelation' (a term of Latin origin, *re-velare*) literally means 'taking away the veil', and points to the self-disclosure of God who was previously and mysteriously unknown. Classic episodes of such self-disclosure would include the story of God revealed to Moses at the burning bush (Exod. 2: 23–4: 17), Isaiah's vision of the heavenly throne room (Isa. 6: 1–13), and the risen Christ encountering Paul (1 Cor. 9: 1; 15: 8; Gal. 1: 12, 15–16). Primarily, revelation refers to this personal self-manifestation of God, the divine Truth (upper case and in the singular), who invites and enables the human response of faith. No mere cognitive affair, revelation is primarily the self-communicative presence of God, who becomes present and is known to be present as Saviour.

Secondarily, revelation also encompasses the communication of hitherto unknown truths (lower case and in the plural) about God, human beings and the created universe.[5] Revelation is first received, and then expressed verbally in propositions. Theology should distinguish between *personal* revelation or encountering God in faith and *propositional* revelation. While recognizing both forms, theology should allow for the priority of personal revelation. Bloesch put matters this way: 'I do not wish to downplay or deny the propositional element in revelation, but this element is in the service of the personal.'[6]

The Old Testament witnesses to ways in which the personal self-revelation of God is communicated through (a) *words* and (b) *events*, both events of public history and those of personal history. Let us consider each in turn, beginning with divine self-revelation through words. Distinguishing between himself as a true prophet of God's Word and his false colleagues, Jeremiah asked: 'Who has stood in the council of the Lord so as to see and to hear his words? Who has given heed to this word so as to proclaim it?' The Lord adds apropos of the false colleagues: 'I did not speak to them, yet they prophesied. If they had stood in my council, then they would have proclaimed my

---

[5] On revelation see G. O'Collins, *Revelation: Towards a Christian Interpretation of God's Self-Revelation in Jesus Christ* (Oxford: Oxford University Press, 2016), and the select bibliography, ibid. 215–16.

[6] Bloesch, *Revelation, Inspiration & Interpretation*, 284.

words to my people' (Jer. 23: 18, 21–2). Through proclaiming 'the good news of God', Jesus manifested the divine kingdom that was breaking into the world (Mark 1: 14–15). He communicated the divine revelation through his words and not least through the psalms he quoted—right through to the cry of dereliction on the cross taken from Psalm 22: 1. The risen Christ revealed the good news directly to Paul, who then announced it to the Gentiles (Gal. 1: 6–16). The same emphasis on word as the avenue of divine self-disclosure comes through the summary of revelation history that majestically opens the Letter to the Hebrews: 'Long ago God *spoke* to our ancestors in many and various ways through the prophets, but in these last days he *has spoken* to us through the Son' (Heb. 1: 1–2).

The Bible also records innumerable *events* that conveyed some self-disclosure of God: from the stories shrouded in mystery of Abraham, Sarah, and their descendants (Gen. 12–50), the poetic account of the deliverance from Egypt (Exod. 15: 1–21), the deportation to Babylon and the return from exile (Isa. 40–66), through to the self-manifestation in the incarnation (Matt. 1: 18–25; John 1: 1–18), episodes in the life and ministry of Jesus (e.g. his miracles and transfiguration), the crucifixion, the resurrection, the post-resurrection appearances, and the descent of the Holy Spirit at Pentecost.

Along with such events of sublime, 'public' importance, the Scriptures also witness to 'ordinary', everyday sights, states of anxiety and joy, and quiet learning from life's experiences that serve to reveal God and the divine purposes. God has spoken and continues to speak 'in many and diverse ways' (Heb. 1: 1). Jeremiah sees an almond branch (Jer. 1: 11–12), a pot on the boil (Jer. 1: 13–14), and a potter at work (Jer. 18: 1–12), and these sights all bring him God's revelation. Psalms of individual lamentation and thanksgiving repeatedly attend to such all-pervasive human troubles as sickness, loneliness, false accusation, and straight-out persecution. Picturing these situations and their experience of divine activity on their behalf (e.g. Pss 3, 6–7, 12, and 22), sufferers transcribe an inner dialogue in which the 'word of God (*locutio Dei*)' responds to the 'word of a human being (*locutio hominis*)'. The psalms also testify to vivid and varied ways in which Israelites experienced the divine presence and power through activities in which they regularly engaged—like pilgrimages to Jerusalem, worship in the temple, and sharing in sacred music led by an ancient orchestra

(Ps. 150). Chapter 2, above, recalled how Ben Sira learned wisdom and the knowledge of God through his travels and study of the Law and biblical history. The parables of Jesus constantly point to common experiences (such as farmers sowing their crops, women preparing dough for the oven, and rich people hosting banquets), which manifest the power and purpose of God's kingdom.

It is in a Christo-centric fashion that the whole history of revelation is summarized by the closing verse of John's Prologue: 'No one has ever seen God. It is God the only Son, who is close to the Father's heart, who has made him known' (John 1: 18). With the Holy Spirit, Christ is simultaneously the revealer (or agent) of divine self-revelation, the revelation (or active process of disclosure), and the content of revelation. This Christo-centric reading of history leads the New Testament to assign to the Logos, now incarnate, the role of mediating creation, through which the divine revelation also reaches human beings (e.g. John 1: 3; 1 Cor. 8: 6; Col. 1: 15–16; Heb. 1: 2–3).

All human beings are offered the revelation of God mediated through (a) the orderly and beautiful works of creation and (b) their own, inner spiritual reality. The author of the Book of Wisdom highlighted (a), and criticized nature worship that took 'the luminaries of heaven' to be 'the gods that rule the world'. Delighting 'in the beauty of these things, people assumed them to be gods'.[7] They should have known 'how much better than these is their Lord, for the author of beauty created them'. 'If the people were amazed at their power and working', Wisdom goes on to say, 'let them perceive from them how much more powerful is the One who formed them'. The argument reaches its climax with the statement: 'from the greatness and beauty of created things comes a corresponding perception of their Creator' (Wis. 13: 1–9).

Centuries before the Book of Wisdom was written, the order and beauty of the cosmos which God created and continues to sustain in existence inspired the vivid hymn that is Psalm 104. Other psalms also praise creation's beauty and harmony: 'the heavens are telling the

---

[7] Developing this argument, Paul interpreted idolatry as an utterly foolish attempt to deny the real God and so evade accountability for immoral actions. When human beings culpably refuse to know God from the world in which they live, they suffer severe consequences (Rom. 1: 18–32).

glory of God, and the firmament proclaims his handiwork' (Ps. 19: 1). They poetically celebrate the Creator's power and intelligence that can be experienced and recognized in the created world (e.g. Ps. 8; see also Job 38–9). Jesus himself was to invoke the self-witness that God offers when dispensing sunlight and rain for all human beings, good and bad alike (Matt. 5: 44), and when providing for the birds of the air and the lilies of the field (Matt. 6: 25–31).

Cosmic revelation 'out there' should not, however, lead us to neglect the deepest, inner hungers of human beings, classically expressed by St Augustine of Hippo at the start of his *Confessions*: 'You have made us for yourself, O Lord, and our heart is restless until it rests in you' (1.1). Every human being reveals something of God in his or her dynamic self-questioning and openness to the infinite. 'In here', each mind and heart constantly put God on display, if implicitly, through a ceaseless drive towards life, meaning, and love.[8]

Before leaving the theme of revelation, we need to attend to its triple 'time-key': (a) back then, (b) here and now, and (c) to come definitively in the future. In terms of (a), the prologue to Hebrews witnesses to the *past* revelation that has been completed by Jesus Christ: 'Long ago God spoke to our ancestors in many and various ways to the prophets, but in these last days he has spoken to us by the Son' (Heb. 1: 1). Hebrews recognizes the fullness of the divine self-disclosure communicated through Jesus, and attributes that fullness to his identity as the Son of God. But God's revelation is also (b), a memory that is 'living'; it also happens here and now. The Book of Revelation represents the divine self-disclosure as occurring in the *present*: for instance, in the messages that the risen and exalted Christ addresses through the Holy Spirit to seven churches in Asia. Believers should hear in faith 'what the Spirit is saying' to them right now (Rev. 2: 1–3: 22). The divine revelation comes across as a living event in the present. Likewise, Paul understands that here and now the divine 'righteousness is revealed' to elicit the faith of human beings and bring them into a right relationship with God (Rom. 10: 14–17). In the Book of Acts, right from the day of Pentecost, apostolic preaching can call forth repentance and faith (Acts 2: 37–42). Finally, (c) a *future*

[8] See O'Collins, *Revelation*, 64–6.

and final revelation will bring the definitive climax of the divine self-communication. Chapter 3 cited the language of Jesus about the coming Son of man, the final manifestation of the glorified Christ at the end of human history. The New Testament underlines this future, divine self-disclosure that will be the second coming of Christ (e.g. 1 Cor. 1: 7–8; Heb. 9: 28; 1 John 3: 2). To sum up: the New Testament presents the divine self-revelation as something that has happened (past or 'foundational'), that is happening (present and experiential), and that will happen (future and in hope).[9]

Tradition

Responding with faith to God's revelation and shaped by their experiences of the divine self-communication, believers from the start of biblical history followed up their encounters with God by handing on to the next generation an account of what they had experienced. For centuries memories were rehearsed and transmitted orally before being regulated by writing. Thus Abraham, Sarah, and other half-glimpsed figures, prompted by their experiences of the divine self-disclosure, set going the traditional narrative of the believing community with its ethical values, worshipping practices, and forms of leadership.[10] Eventually tradition would create the Scriptures.

The prophets typically heard the Word of God (revelation in the primary sense) and passed on the messages they received (revelation in the secondary sense). Sometimes consoling and supportive but sometimes dramatically unsettling, the prophetic messages shaped and reshaped the biblical tradition. In Chapter 2 we saw how the powerful language and imagery of an eighth-century prophet, Isaiah, had such an impact. In less dramatic ways, Ben Sira and other authors of wisdom literature educated people in what they had learned from God and about God.

The story of Moses, with its movement from revelation in the primary sense to revelation in its secondary sense, suggests paradigmatically the constant reframing of tradition. In Midian the God of his ancestors

[9] For more on this triple time-key of revelation, see ibid. 101–20.

[10] For a further account of tradition and a bibliography on tradition, see ibid. 121–43.

appears to Moses at the burning bush and commissions him to accept a leadership role in delivering the people (Exod. 2: 43–4: 17). Moses is to take a message to 'the elders of Israel' and say to them: 'The Lord, the God of your ancestors, the God of Abraham, Isaac, and Jacob, has appeared to me, saying, "I will bring you up out of the misery of Egypt"' (Exod. 3: 16–17). Moses delivers the message to the people and assumes his leadership role. The divine appearance, or theophany, at Horeb prefigures a second theophany (at Sinai) when God establishes a covenant with Israel (Exod. 19–31)—a life-changing set of experiences that reframes forever the people's tradition.

The unsurpassable highpoint of biblical history, and what we can call the climax of 'foundational' revelation, came with Jesus and his Holy Spirit, the apostles, and other first-century disciples. What they received through their new experiences of God reinterpreted and refashioned what they were to hand on. The apostolic generation's experience of Christ and his Holy Spirit led them, not to abandon monotheistic faith, but to recast it as belief in the Father, Son, and Holy Spirit. In this and other new ways, by building into the religious tradition their experiences of God's new messages to them and actions on their behalf, first-century Christians formed and fashioned the normative tradition of Christianity that they launched.

Some members of the apostolic community, inspired by the Holy Spirit, set down in writing the story of the making of the foundational tradition and how they had understood, expressed, and acted upon (or sinfully failed to act upon) their encounter with God through Christ and his Spirit. These inspired Scriptures (like the Old Testament Scriptures) emerged *from* tradition, and were interpreted and actualized within the living tradition of the community. More will be said below about the relationship between tradition and the Sacred Scriptures, as well as about biblical inspiration (both related to and distinct from revelation). Here I wish to point out only how the inspired Scriptures originated from and within the tradition that had been triggered by experiences (in faith) of the divine self-revelation. Thus tradition preceded the composition of the Sacred Scriptures, included those Scriptures, and extended beyond them. Tradition transmits, interprets, and applies the inspired texts, but it also hands on much more besides—in the vital and varied ways of worshipping, living, and believing of the whole community.

In *Revelation: From Analogy to Metaphor*, Richard Swinburne rightly recognizes how revelation preceded the writing of the inspired Scriptures, but omits the process of tradition when he writes: Scripture 'is a true record of revelation which existed before it'.[11] The sequence is rather: revelation, tradition, and then the writing of inspired Scriptures. Swinburne has little or nothing to say about the key, mediating role of tradition. His limited view of tradition concerns itself only with the particular issue of 'unwritten traditions'.[12] Moreover, Scripture includes much more than 'a true record of revelation'; we will come to this later. Biblical inspiration (which Swinburne does not discuss), as we shall see, is a special, God-given impulse to set down in writing various things, which include, but go well beyond, words and events of revelation.

Revelation, Tradition, and Scripture

Before moving to examine biblical inspiration in depth, let me pull matters together and outline in seven ways the complex relationship between revelation, tradition, and the Scriptures. A visualization of these interrelationships is provided at the end of the chapter (see Figure).

First, the apostles and those associated with them experienced the fullness of foundational revelation and salvation (through Christ and the Holy Spirit) and faithfully responded by expressing, interpreting, and applying this once-and-for-all experience in their preaching. In and through preaching the good news (Rom. 10: 14–15), the conferral of baptism (Rom. 6: 3–11), and the celebration of the Eucharist (1 Cor. 11: 23–6) they fully founded the Church. The apostolic age brought not only the founding of the Church but also the composition of the twenty-seven inspired books of the New Testament. Under a special guidance of the Holy Spirit these books (which drew on experiences and memories as well as on oral and written traditions) fixed for all time the preaching of Peter, Paul, and the rest as the normative response to the full, albeit not yet definitive, revelation of God in Christ and through the Holy Spirit. The sacred authors were

[11] R. Swinburne, *Revelation: From Analogy to Metaphor*, 2nd edn (Oxford: Oxford University Press, 2007), 137.

[12] Ibid. 188–9, 212, 310, 313, 315.

not necessarily aware of doing this. The results of their activities may not be measured by their conscious intentions, as we shall see later. They never lived to witness what they had achieved.

Second, the books of the New Testament, together with the inspired writings of the Old Testament, do not as such coincide with revelation. The difference between revelation and Scripture is the difference between a lived (and living) reality and a written (and inspired) record. We cannot simply identify revelation with the Bible. The Scriptures witness to the human experience of the foundational revelation of God, as well as to the vivid and varied ways in which men and women responded to (or failed to respond to), remembered, and interpreted that experience. The scriptural witness remains distinct from the experience of revelation itself, just as a written record differs from any reality we live through.

Where foundational revelation came *before* the Scriptures (or, at least, before the writing of all the Scriptures), what we can call 'dependent' revelation has continued *after* the writing of all these Scriptures ended. Hearing, reading, and praying over the Scriptures can bring about now the experience of (dependent) divine revelation. As they speak to people, biblical texts help initiate what believers experience today of God's self-communication. Even so, in this period of dependent revelation, the Scriptures differ from revelation in the way in which an inspired and inspiring written record differs from the living reality of an encounter with God.

Third, and analogously, *tradition* never literally coincides with revelation. Tradition can hand on revealed truths (or what can be called propositional revelation), but cannot literally pass on the personal experience of God's self-revelation. It may prove revealing in the sense of recalling moments of revelation, interpreting those moments, and offering means to experience revelation (always in dependence upon God's grace). Yet revelation remains distinct from tradition as a lived experience is to be distinguished from the community's expression of that experience which is transmitted through history. We cannot identify *tout court* either tradition or Scripture as such with the event and experience of God's revealing and saving presence.

Fourth, how should the post-apostolic tradition of the Church be understood and how does it relate to Scripture? All active members of the Church are, in fact, engaged in the *process* of transmitting tradition and bringing about (under the power of the Holy Spirit) the experience of the divine self-communication. They do so by pondering the Scriptures, celebrating the Eucharist, administering and receiving the other sacraments, preaching and evangelizing, serving the poor and the suffering, composing sacred music, writing icons, sharing in pilgrimages, and through all the other authentic beliefs and healthy practices that make up the total reality of the Church and give Christians their continuity, identity, and unity. Seen as an active process (*actus tradendi*), the tradition of the post-apostolic Church embraces the Scriptures but obviously extends well beyond them. Handing on, interpreting, and applying the Scriptures is only one, albeit major, part of tradition's activity.

In transmitting all this living heritage, the Holy Spirit remains the principal, if invisible, agent of tradition. During his final discourse in John's Gospel, Jesus promises that the Paraclete will come and remind the disciples of all that he had said to them (John 14: 26; 16: 4). At stake are the elucidation and understanding of what Jesus has revealed, and not a mere recalling of words said by him (John 2: 22; 12: 16).[13] The Spirit works to make the Church a genuine 'remembering community' that can maintain its identity through continuity with the apostolic generation, and can do so by constantly discerning authentic tradition within the diverse particular traditions.

What traditions truly express the foundational revelation and so help the good news of Christ to remain living and effective in the life of the Church? Four questions can assist in the work of discernment. (a) Does some specific tradition help the faithful to be led more clearly by the Holy Spirit and the risen Christ? (b) Does it enhance their common worship? (c) Is any decision about this or that tradition illuminated and supported by prayerful reflection on the Scriptures? (d) Does such a decision inspire believers to serve the needy more generously? I am not alleging that these questions can be answered easily and at once. But if we do not even ask these questions, it seems

---

[13] On these verses, see A. T. Lincoln, *The Gospel According to John* (London: Continuum, 2005), 141, 344–5.

difficult, if not impossible, to discern faithfully the customs that embody the true tradition and what Christ is calling us to reform and change in what we have received from the past. Revision and reform can be true but they can also be false, as Yves Congar classically recalled in *True and False Reform in the Church*.[14]

Fifth, in the active process of tradition there exists a *mutual priority*. On the one hand, authentic tradition seeks to remain faithful to the normative account of Christian origins and identity to which the inspired Scriptures witness. On the other hand, fresh challenges and a changing context require tradition to do what the Scriptures cannot do by themselves. It must interpret and apply them, so that they can become the revealing Word of God to new readers and hearers today. In this way tradition (and the Christian life to which it gives shape and force) not only forms an extended commentary on the Scriptures but also allows them to come into their own and let Christ speak to people.

Sixth, in this whole process the members of the *magisterium* (i.e. the bishops) have a special but not exclusive role as 'carriers' of tradition and mediators (always subordinate to Christ the Mediator) prompting the living event of divine self-revelation. Tradition as an action is thus exercised in a particular way by the bishops, inasmuch as they transmit officially matters of faith and practice. By formulating (normally with others) statements of faith—this was classically done in the Nicene-Constantinopolitan Creed of 381—they introduce new elements into the tradition and its narrative that will be transmitted to the next generation of believers.

Recently the exercise of the magisterium at the Second Vatican Council (1962–5) modified what would be handed on. As an engine for far-reaching change in the Catholic Church and beyond, Pope Francis is currently influencing the traditions of church governance and life that will be transmitted to the next generation. A living tradition necessarily means a tradition that develops and changes, with the changes maintaining the apostolic identity of the Church and coming not only from popes and bishops but also, and often even

---

[14] Trans. P. Philibert (Collegeville, MI: Liturgical Press, 2011).

more, from others who are charismatically endowed, like St Francis of Assisi (d. 1226) and St Teresa of Avila (d. 1582).[15]

Seventh and lastly, the whole people of God will not transmit all that they received exactly as they received it. Language shifts occur; the flux of experience calls forth fresh interpretations and activities; emerging signs of the times offer their special message to believers; new devotions emerge; and technological advances offer remarkable challenges and possibilities (e.g. for preaching the good news). Francis of Assisi introduced the Christmas crib, which has continued to be widely displayed in Christian churches and homes. As bishop of Truro, Bishop Edward Benson (1829–96) started the Advent service of carols and lessons, which has spread around the world and well beyond Anglican churches. Social media now include such resources for prayer and reflection as 'Pray as You Go' and 'Sacred Space'.

Certainly an essential continuity is maintained. The dependent revelation which is experienced now remains essentially continuous with the original, foundational revelation that the apostolic generation received in faith. At the same time, the whole Church, no less than

Old Testament history	New Testament history	Post-New Testament Church
Foundational revelation	Foundational revelation completed	Dependent revelation
Tradition (encompassing oral witness to revelation, inspired Scriptures, and much else)		
Writing of inspired Scripture Impact of earlier on later books of the OT	Inspired Scripture completed Impact of OT books	Inspiring role of all the Scriptures

Figure: interconnection between revelation, tradition, and inspiration

[15] See S. H. Hughes, 'Teresa of Avila', *OEBA*, ii, 398–402.

members of the magisterium, modifies to some degree the aggregate of beliefs, customs, and practices (tradition as 'object', the *traditum*) which one generation of believers transmits to the next.

To draw all of this together, understood either as the active process (*actus tradendi*) or as the object handed on (the *traditum*), tradition includes Scripture rather than simply standing alongside it. In both senses tradition is much more extensive than Scripture.

6

The Inspired Scriptures

Formation, Content, and Five Characteristics

The last chapter engaged itself with the complex relationship between God's self-revelation, tradition, and the inspired Scriptures. A document from the Second Vatican Council (1962–5) on divine revelation summed up three essential moments in this relationship: tradition and Scripture 'flow from the same well-spring' (past or foundational revelation), 'in some fashion form together one thing' (present or dependent revelation), and 'move towards the same goal' (the final fullness of revelation and salvation) (*Dei Verbum*, 9). Revelation as foundational made the Jewish-Christian tradition and Scripture possible. If there had been no well-spring of revelation or, to put it personally, no self-manifestation of the triune God, that tradition and Scripture would not have come into existence. During the phase of dependent revelation, while tradition interprets and actualizes Scripture, in its turn Scripture challenges and purifies tradition. At the end, the face-to-face revelation of God (1 John 3: 2) will bring tradition and Scripture to their goal, and replace them.

Kevin Vanhoozer fills out the laconic language about tradition and Scripture now 'form[ing] together one thing'. He writes: 'Scripture and tradition are paired [...] norms for doing theology, for seeking knowledge of God and knowledge of self.'[1] Elsewhere he asks: 'What is tradition if not a form of life to know and glorify God? And what is Scripture if not a certain use of language to name God?'[2]

---

[1] K. J. Vanhoozer, 'Scripture and Tradition', in K. J. Vanhoozer (ed.), *The Cambridge Companion to Postmodern Theology* (Cambridge: Cambridge University Press, 2003), 149–69, at 166.

[2] Ibid. 149.

Let me examine further the relationship between revelation and biblical inspiration, and lay the ground for setting forth three characteristics of biblical inspiration: its authority, a major consequence that is biblical truth, and the function of the canon. First, how might we describe further the distinction between the inspired Scriptures and the foundational revelation recorded in the Old Testament and New Testament? Let us begin by considering the formation of the Bible, which illustrates some differences between the divine self-disclosure and the inspired Scriptures. We will then be in a position to reflect on the *content* of the Bible in relation to revelation.[3]

The Formation of the Bible

The divine self-revelation takes place as a living, interpersonal event. God initiates, at particular times and in particular places and for particular persons, some form of self-disclosure. This divine initiative reaches its goal and revelation happens when human beings respond in faith to God's self-disclosure.

As such, the Scriptures are not a living, interpersonal event in the way just described. They are written records, which by a special impulse of the Holy Spirit came into existence through the collaboration of some believers (and others, like Persian kings, as we will see below) at certain stages in the foundational history of God's people. The Scriptures differ then from revelation in the way that written texts differ from something that happens between persons—in this case between human persons and the three divine Persons. Hence, while it makes perfectly good sense to say 'I left my Bible on the bus', it does not make sense to say 'I left revelation on the bus'. One could say, of course, 'when travelling on the bus into the city, God's revealing word came alive for me'. That could be a treasured, even dramatic,

---

[3] Whenever the divine revelation is simply identified with the Jewish-Christian Bible, this makes it difficult, if not impossible, to recognize how the revelation of God is, in various ways, also offered to those who follow 'other' religious faiths or none at all, and who do not accept the Bible or may not even know about its existence. Such a simple identification would involve holding '*extra Scripturam nulla revelatio* (outside Scripture no revelation)'.

moment in my life, but the event of revelation was not an object, such as a book, which I could leave behind.

In the long history of the Bible's composition, the gift of divine revelation and the special impulse to write inspired Scriptures were not only distinguishable but also separable. Either directly or through such mediators as the prophets, the apostles, and, above all, Jesus himself, the foundational revelation has been offered, in principle, to all people; God's self-communication was and is there for everyone. The special impulse to write some Scriptures was, however, a particular charism given only to those who, under the guidance of the Holy Spirit, composed or helped to compose the sacred texts that came to be known as the books of the Old and New Testament. To be sure, the potential readership of the Scriptures includes everyone. But the charism to write such Scriptures was given only to a limited number of persons.

Even in the case of the biblical authors themselves, the self-revelation of God and the charism of inspiration did not coincide. Receiving in faith the divine self-manifestation was one thing; being led by the Holy Spirit to set certain matters down in writing was another. God's revelation impinged on their entire lives. In cases that we know, the charism of inspiration functioned only for limited periods in their history. The divine revelation was operative in St Paul's life before and after his call/conversion (around AD 36). Around AD 50 he wrote his first (inspired) letter that has been preserved for us (1 Thessalonians), and he went on to compose other letters during the 50s and into the early 60s. The divine self-communication affected Paul's entire history, the charism of divine inspiration only the last decade or so of his apostolic activity.

The Content of the Bible

Reflection on the content of the Bible yields another angle on the difference I wish to express. The Scriptures witness to and interpret various persons, words, and events that mediated the divine self-revelation. The Letter to the Hebrews acknowledges the Son of God as the climax in a series of mediators of revelation (Heb. 1: 1–2). A wide variety of events manifested God and the divine will: from the exodus, an exile in Babylon and the return from that exile, births of various children (reaching a highpoint with John the Baptist and Jesus himself), through to a crucifixion, resurrection, and descent of the Holy Spirit. Prophetic utterances, creeds (e.g. Deut. 26: 5–9; Rom. 1: 3–4), hymns (e.g. Phil. 2: 6–11; Col. 1: 15–20), summaries of proclamation (e.g. 1 Cor. 15: 3–5), and—supremely—the parables, beatitudes, and other words from Jesus himself disclosed the truth of God (and of human beings).

At the same time, the Bible *also* records matters that do not seem to be connected, or at least not closely connected, with divine revelation. The language of courtship and human love fashions the Song of Songs, an inspired book that, paradoxically, has no explicitly religious content. Alongside lofty prescriptions to guide the worship and life of Israel as a holy people, Leviticus includes many regulations about wine and food, about the sick and diseased (in particular, about lepers), about sexual relations, and about other matters that hardly seem to be derived from divine revelation. This book (that probably took its final shape in the sixth or fifth century BC) contains pages of rituals and laws which usually look as if they came from ancient human customs rather than from some divine disclosure. From the period after the Babylonian exile, the Book of Ezra quotes some letters concerned with the rebuilding of Jerusalem and its Temple and written by and to King Artaxerxes and King Darius (4: 11–22; 5: 6–17; 6: 1–12; 7: 11–26). Political leaders and administrators of an empire produced this correspondence, rather than some divine oracles.

From the same post-exilic period, the Book of Proverbs puts together the moral and religious instruction that professional teachers offered the Jewish youth. This wisdom of the ages is based on lessons drawn from common human experience, and is in part (Prov. 22: 17–24: 34) modelled upon the *Amen-em-ope*, an Egyptian book of wisdom.[4] Where religious faith supports Proverbs' view of an upright human life, Ecclesiastes seems to use reason alone to explore the meaning of existence and the (limited) value of life which ends in the oblivion of death.

[4] See J. Schaper, 'The Literary History of the Hebrew Bible', in J. C. Paget and J. Schaper (eds), *The New Cambridge History of the Bible*, i (Cambridge: Cambridge University Press, 2012), 105–44, at 123–4.

Admittedly, one might argue that in human love, ancient religious traditions, the administration of empires, the experience of the ages, and the use of reason, God is also at work to disclose truth about our nature and destiny, and about the Creator from whom we come and to whom we go. Any theology that proposes dramatic, special events as the *only* appropriate means for mediating God's Word would be a diminished version of revelation. God can certainly use 'ordinary' channels for communicating with human beings and shedding light on the divine and human mystery.

Nevertheless, whole sections of the Bible (e.g. much of wisdom literature) speak more of our human condition and less vividly of divine revelation. That the inspiration of the Holy Spirit also operated in the formation of these books is no immediate gauge of the 'amount' of divine self-revelation to which they witness. They may proclaim matters of revelation less intensely and closely than other parts of the Bible. Simply from divine inspiration being active in the composition of a book, one cannot draw any necessary conclusions about the degree to which God's self-revelation shows through that book.

Add too the way many chapters of the Bible focus on the human story of individuals and groups: for instance, many passages in the historical books of the Old Testament. Some of this material seems a long way from God's saving self-communication. Take, for example, the story of a concubine being murdered and the subsequent revenge on the Benjamites (Judg. 19: 1–20: 48), Saul's visit to the witch of Endor (1 Sam. 28: 1–25), and, for that matter, the death of Ananias and Sapphira (Acts 5: 1–11). One might argue that such stories illustrate how people failed to respond to the overtures of divine revelation. Human failures, sins, and even atrocities were also recorded under the influence of divine inspiration. But that fact does not as such guarantee anything specific about their positive value for revelation. In short, an inspired record is one thing, revelatory 'content' is another.

The latest document to come from the Pontifical Biblical Commission, *The Inspiration and Truth of the Sacred Scripture*, describes the Scriptures as God addressing us in human words or, as its subtitle puts it: *The Word that Comes from God and Speaks of God for the Salvation of the World*. Serving the faithful transmission of the record of revelation, the Bible is 'the authoritative source for knowledge about God'.[5] Recognizing different ways in which the inspired Scriptures originated from God, the document highlights the divine revelation becoming 'a written text', and focuses on the books of the Bible functioning as 'a privileged vehicle of God's revelation'.[6]

Unquestionably, through much of the Spirit-inspired Scriptures, God addresses individuals and the community at large. Yet the Biblical Commission had to work hard to press into this scheme human matters that are less closely connected with the divine self-revelation, such as the human love between a young woman and a shepherd that is vividly and even erotically celebrated in the Song of Songs. The document speaks of this book being open to a more 'theological dimension' and 'additional meanings', which, in fact, the history and practice of Christian mysticism added later.[7] In its origins, however, the Song of Songs was an imaginative drama of human love, rather than some self-disclosure of God that became 'a written text'.[8]

But when it reaches some classical challenges for biblical interpretation, the Commission introduces the question: which passages should be 'considered perennially valid' and which 'relative', or 'linked to a culture, a civilization, or even the mentality of a specific period of time'? The document adds: 'the status of women in the Pauline epistles raises this type of question'.[9] The Commission then dedicates pages to what these epistles say about the submission of women to their husbands, the silence of women in ecclesial gatherings, and the

---

[5] Biblical Commission, *The Inspiration and Truth of Sacred Scripture*, trans. T. Esposito and S. Gregg (Collegeville, MI: Liturgical Press, 2014), xxi, 4.

[6] Ibid. 47, 60.

[7] Ibid. 86–8. Vatican II's Constitution on Divine Revelation, *Dei Verbum* (the Word of God), prompts a similar comment when it declares: 'Sacred Scripture is the speech of God (*locutio Dei*) as it is attested in writing under the inspiration of the divine Spirit' (DV 9). Beyond question, we can often call the Scriptures 'the speech of God'. Yet much of the Bible originated as the speech of human beings (*locutio hominis*). That *locutio hominis* can readily *become* the speech of God for those who, with attentive openness, read it during the present history of its inspiring impact.

[8] See D. Garrett, *Song of Songs*, Word Biblical Commentary 23B (Nashville: Thomas Nelson, 2004).

[9] Biblical Commission, *The Inspiration and Truth of Sacred Scripture*, 150.

role of women in the assembly of the faithful.[10] Rather than being 'a word that comes from God' or a revelation that turns into 'a written text', such examples should be understood as items recorded under the impulse of divine inspiration, but with the content coming more from human beings and particular cultures of the world.

An acceptance of other (human) sources for the inspired texts of the Bible appears also in the general conclusions to *The Inspiration and Truth of the Sacred Scripture*. There the Commission 'fully' recognizes that 'the literature of the Old Testament is greatly indebted to Mesopotamian and Egyptian writings, just as the New Testament books draw extensively on the cultural heritage of the Hellenistic world'.[11] Once again, while saying that the Scriptures were all written under the divine inspiration, we should, nevertheless, acknowledge how not infrequently they record what comes from human beings in their cultural and religious diversity.

Biblical Inspiration

If it is an error to identify revelation *tout court* with the Bible, what precisely are we to make of the divine activity of inspiration that (in and through human authors) produced the Scriptures, the unique record of the foundational Jewish-Christian experiences of God and the human responses those experiences evoked (or failed to evoke)? By witnessing to collective and individual experiences and the new self-identity those experiences initiated, the Bible offers subsequent generations the possibility of sharing (to a degree) in those experiences[12] and accepting that new identity. Thus the Scriptures are both an effect and a cause of the divine self-revelation. The record of what was experienced *then* helps to instigate and interpret the experience of God's self-communication *now*. Later we will return to this 'inspiring' impact of the Scriptures. Here we need to disentangle various meanings of 'inspiration'.

[10] Ibid. 153–4.   [11] Ibid. 166.

[12] Believers today experience the risen Christ (in the liturgy and beyond), but not exactly in the same way as those who witnessed his appearances after his death and burial; see D. Kendall and G. O'Collins, 'The Uniqueness of the Easter Appearances', *Catholic Biblical Quarterly* 54 (1992), 287–307.

'In-spiration', understood broadly, describes a double agency, a 'spiritual' influence from God that empowers human beings to think, speak, or act in ways which go beyond their normal capacity. 'Breathing into' them—inspiration—in some fashion takes them beyond the level and the way in which they would usually perform. *Biblical* inspiration can be called a special impulse from the Holy Spirit, given during the long history of the chosen people and the much shorter apostolic age, to set down in writing both experiences of the divine self-revelation and other things which are not necessarily closely tied to revelation. This distinguishes biblical inspiration from *prophetic* inspiration, a God-given impulse to speak (and act symbolically) in certain ways. Such prophetic inspiration to *speak* may be associated with the biblical inspiration to *write*. But, characteristically, the Old Testament prophets were speakers (and actors) rather than writers. It was generally left to others to collect, expand, arrange, and publish their prophetic utterances. These (frequently anonymous) writers, as the immediate authors of the prophetic books of the Bible, received the charism of biblical inspiration. Nevertheless, their charism obviously presupposed that Isaiah, Jeremiah, Ezekiel, and others had received the prophetic charism to speak (and act).

It was natural for the Second Letter of Peter to describe the written texts of the prophetical books as if they were the *spoken words* of the prophets: 'no prophecy of Scripture is a matter of one's own inspiration, because no prophecy ever came from the impulse of a human being, but human beings moved by the Holy Spirit spoke from God' (2 Pet. 1: 20–1). Both the spoken word and the written word enjoyed a divine origin and authority.[13] Distinctions between them were not firmly drawn. The author of the Book of Revelation likewise blurred distinctions between the spoken (prophetic) word and the written word when he called his book 'words of prophecy' to be listened to (Rev. 22: 18).[14] This blurring of distinctions between the spoken and the written was encouraged by the fact that many believers, rather

---

[13] See R. Bauckham, *Jude, 2 Peter* (Waco, TX: Word Books, 1983), 228–35; G. L. Green, *Jude & 2 Peter* (Grand Rapids, MI: Baker Academic, 2008), 229–34.

[14] See R. Bauckham, *The Climax of Prophecy: Studies on the Book of Revelation* (Edinburgh: T. & T. Clark, 2003); H. B. Huffmon et al., 'Prophecy', *ABD*, v, 447–502, at 494–5, 500.

than reading the texts, heard them proclaimed in their liturgical assemblies.

Hence, almost inevitably, the early Church understood the sacred writers to have the role of prophets, and later theologians like Thomas Aquinas interpreted biblical inspiration as prophetic.[15] However, precisely as such, biblical inspiration was a God-given impulse to write rather than (merely) to say something. Therefore, from this point on, unless otherwise noted, 'inspiration' will be taken in the sense of biblical inspiration.

Since the books of the Bible were written under a special impulse and guidance of the Holy Spirit, we may call the Bible itself 'the Word of God'. Thus the effect of inspiration was to invest human words with the authority of being also the Word of God, which allows us to qualify the Scriptures as 'sacred'. We may also name God as the 'author' of Scripture, provided we intend 'author' in the wider sense of 'instigator', 'cause', or 'source' and not precisely in the sense of literary author.[16] Classical Latin bequeathed to later Latin various meanings for *auctor* which include 'writer' but go well beyond that limited meaning.[17] It was in a broader sense that, right from early times, the Church insisted on the divine authorship of the Bible and, in particular, on the role and authority of one and the same God who stood behind the history of the Jewish people and their Scriptures. Thus the First Council of Toledo (AD 400) anathematized those who claimed that there was 'one God of the old Law and another God of the Gospels' (DzH 198).

[15] See his treatise on prophecy in *Summa Theologiae* IIa IIae, 171–4.

[16] The classic formula, 'one and the same God is the author of both the New and Old Testaments, that is, of the Law and the Prophets and the Apostles', is found in the fifth-century *Statuta Ecclesiae Antiqua* ('the Ancient Statutes of the Church'), and aimed at safeguarding the divine origin and authority of all the scriptural books against attempts (e.g. from Marcion and Manicheans) to exclude many of them (e.g. the whole of the Old Testament) (DzH 325). For details and bibliography, see '*Statuta Ecclesiae Antiqua*', in F. L. Cross and E. Livingstone (eds), *The Oxford Dictionary of the Christian Church*, 3rd edn (Oxford: Oxford University Press 2005), 1549–50.

[17] See P. G. W. Glare (ed.), *Oxford Latin Dictionary* (Oxford: Oxford University Press, 1982), 204–6; besides 'writer', Glare lists twelve other clusters of meaning for 'auctor'.

Here and now we need to face in detail the question: what form did the 'special impulse' of inspiration take or not take? Our answers will also affect what is meant by calling God the 'author' of the Scriptures. At least five points should enter a preliminary account.

Characteristics of Inspiration

First, the Nicene-Constantinopolitan Creed of 381 professed faith in the Holy Spirit 'who spoke through [Greek *dia*; Latin *per*] the prophets' (DzH 150; ND 12). Other early creeds expressed this activity of the Spirit at greater length: '[the Holy Spirit] spoke in/through [*en*] the law and proclaimed in/through the prophets [. . .] and spoke in/through the apostles' (DzH 44); '[the Spirit] spoke in/through [*en*] the law and in/through the prophets and in/through the Gospels' (DzH 46); '[the Spirit] spoke through [*dia*] the law and the prophets and the evangelists' (DzH 48). The language about the Spirit speaking through the prophets could claim a background, albeit a limited one, in the relatively few cases where the prophetic books refer to empowerment by 'the spirit' (Isa. 61: 1; Ezek. 2: 1–2; Mic. 3: 8; Zech. 7: 12). This language, together with the teaching about God as the *auctor* of the two testaments, opened up the way for appropriating to the Holy Spirit the divine dictation/inspiration involved in writing not only the prophetic books but also the other books of the Old and New Testament.

In its 1442 Decree for the Copts, the Council of Florence taught: '[The Holy Roman Church] professes that one and the same God is author of the Old and New Testaments, i.e. of the Law, the Prophets, and the Gospel, because by the dictation/inspiration [*dictante*] of one and the same Holy Spirit, the saints of both covenants have spoken. She accepts and venerates these books' (DzH 1334; ND 208). A century later, in 1546 at its fourth session, the Council of Trent spoke of the books of the New Testament coming 'from the apostles through the dictation/inspiration [*dictante*] of the Holy Spirit' (DzH 1501; ND 210).[18]

---

[18] The translation of Trent's decree on the sacred books and apostolic traditions offered in N. P. Tanner (ed.), *Decrees of the Ecumenical Councils*, ii (London/ Washington, DC: Sheed & Ward/Georgetown University Press, 1990) could

In Chapter 2, we noted a literary fiction found in the Book of Jeremiah and representing the prophet as 'dictating' to Baruch a scroll that contained 'all the words that the Lord had spoken' to him (Jer. 36: 2–32). The passage, where the Vulgate (Latin) translation uses *loqui ex ore* and not *dictare*, suggests a double dictation: from the Lord to Jeremiah and from Jeremiah to Baruch. In classical and then ecclesiastical Latin, *dictare* enjoyed not only the strict sense of 'dictate words to be written down', but also the wider sense of 'prescribe', 'prompt', or 'order'.[19] It was the narrower sense, however, that prevailed in what came to be called the *verbal dictation* account of how inspiration functioned. This view was encouraged by the picture of Moses receiving stone tablets on which 'the finger of God' had written the Law (Exod. 24: 12; 31: 18; Deut. 9: 10).

In this view, the inspired writers heard a heavenly voice dictating words which they were to reproduce. They obediently set down the texts that were given to them. In Chapter 1, we recalled how some Christian art reflects this reduction of the inspired authors to the status of mere stenographers. Such a view interprets inspiration in a mechanical way that dramatically reduces the human role in composing the Scriptures. The sacred writers cease to be real authors, and become at best mere secretaries who faithfully transcribe the divine dictation. A set of recording machines could have served God's purposes just as well. In the verbal dictation theory, the divine causality counts for everything, the human causality for nothing or next to nothing.

Some of the fathers of the Church used images that similarly minimized the role of the biblical writers. In the second century, Athenagoras described the Old Testament prophets as flutes played by a divine musician (*Legatio pro Christianis*, 9. 1).[20] Gregory the Great

---

create a little confusion here by rendering (in the same paragraph) 'Spiritu sancto dictante' as 'at the inspiration of the holy Spirit', and then 'traditiones [...] a Spiritu sancto dictatas' as 'dictated by the holy Spirit' (p. 663).

[19] See Glare, *Oxford Latin Dictionary*, 538. The Councils of Florence and Trent seem to have used *dictare* in the broader sense.

[20] B. Pouderon (ed. and trans.), Sources Chrétiennes 379 (Paris: Cerf, 1992), 99.

(d. 604) believed that the human authors enjoyed no more significance in producing the Bible than a pen in the hand of a stenographer.[21]

Those who endorsed verbal dictation theories mistakenly believed that affirming the Sacred Scriptures to be the inspired Word of God entailed denying that they are *also* a genuinely human word. They wrongly imagined that God and the human authors competed rather than collaborated. Apart from this basic theological flaw, the verbal dictation approach could not satisfactorily explain the many differences of form and style exhibited by the inspired authors. Did the Holy Spirit's style change from the period when Paul's letters were composed to the later period when the Gospels were composed? If the human writers played no effective part in the literary process, such differences could come only from a mysterious, even arbitrary, divine decision to vary the style and alter the form.

The naive model of verbal dictation may linger on in the fantasy of fundamentalism. But it is an error to be dispelled. Most Christians have made their peace with the genuinely human activity involved in the social and literary processes that produced the inspired Scriptures. They would agree with the Second Vatican Council's teaching about the biblical writers being 'true authors' who 'made use of their own powers and abilities' (*Dei Verbum*, 11).

The second characteristic worth noting is that the inspired authors wrote in various genres but not in all possible forms of literature. They wrote proverbs, psalms, letters, gospels, apocalypses, and so forth. But the Bible contains no epic poetry (like Homer), no works for the theatre (like ancient Greek drama), no novels (in the modern sense), and no 'critical' history (in the modern sense).

The last point may be the most important. Christians have been prone to read biblical history through modern spectacles. Undoubtedly, the historical books of the Old and New Testaments convey much trustworthy information. The honesty of Hebrew historiography put it in a class by itself in the Middle Eastern world. It recorded King David's shameful sins of adultery and murder (2 Sam. 11: 1–27), along with many other embarrassing failures on the part of leaders and people. It showed itself superior to the stereotyped, empty, and often falsified glorification of monarchs found in the annals of other nations.

Nevertheless, the religious significance of events from the story of salvation mattered much more to the Hebrew historians than a material exactitude. They felt no overwhelming curiosity that would have pushed them into clarifying the record when different sources provided conflicting details. Who killed Goliath—David or Elhanan (1 Sam. 17; 2 Sam. 21: 19)? Did the site of the Temple in Jerusalem cost David 50 shekels of silver or 500 shekels of gold (2 Sam. 24: 24; 1 Chron. 21: 25)? In the New Testament, Matthew (1: 1–17) and Luke (3: 23–38) give us irreconcilable genealogies of Jesus. Repeatedly details in the stories of Jesus' ministry, death, and resurrection cannot be reconciled into a single, coherent account. It has rightly been argued that the Gospels provide a substantially reliable account of what Jesus said, did, and suffered in the last years of his life.[22] But this well-founded conclusion should not be pushed to the point of treating the Gospels as if they were *modern* biographies, just as we should not gloss over the fact that the historical books of the Old Testament should be classified as popular history. In short, just as the Bible did not exemplify all the forms of literature extant in ancient times, so it did not miraculously anticipate future genres, like modern, 'critical' history.

Third, some biblical authors demonstrated unusual talent as writers and produced works of considerable literary power and beauty. They played their part in making the Bible a rich source of imagery, language, and 'inspiration', not least in the world of music, literature, and the visual arts, as we saw in Chapter 4. Nevertheless, the gift of divine inspiration did not mean that the *literary* level shown by the

---

[22] See R. A. Burridge, *What are the Gospels? A Comparison with Graeco-Roman Biography* (Grand Rapids, MI: Eerdmans, 2004); J. D. G. Dunn, *Christianity in the Making*, i: *Jesus Remembered* (Grand Rapids, MI: Eerdmans, 2003); P. R. Eddy and G. A. Boyd, *The Jesus Legend: A Case for the Historical Reliability of the Synoptic Jesus Tradition* (Grand Rapids, MI: Baker Academic, 2007); M. Hengel and A. M. Schwemmer, *Geschichte der frühen Christentums*, i: *Jesus und das Judentum* (Tübingen: Mohr Siebeck, 2007); C. S. Keener, *The Historical Jesus of the Gospels* (Grand Rapids, MI: Eerdmans, 2009); G. O'Collins, *Jesus: A Portrait* (London: Darton, Longman & Todd, 2008).

sacred authors was necessarily higher than that of other writers. The special impulse from the Holy Spirit did not miraculously raise (but rather respected) the writing talents of those who received it. The first nine chapters of 1 Chronicles belong to the canon of inspired Scripture, but these dreary genealogies will not excite too many readers in the modern world. Divine inspiration could be at work in such a dull form of human writing, as well as in the political correspondence of King Artaxerxes and King Darius incorporated in Ezra (see above). In itself the gift of inspiration did not automatically guarantee anything about the literary standard of the results.

Fourth, we should likewise be cautious about claiming that inspiration necessarily entails a uniformly *high religious power and impact,* which lifts all the Scriptures above non-inspired writings. Although all Scripture is inspired, Bloesch succinctly notes that 'this does not imply that all the Scripture has equal value'.[23] Of course, the Gospels, the Psalms, Isaiah, the letters of St Paul, and many other books of the Bible continue to fire readers with their special spiritual quality. But experience shows how Augustine's *Confessions,* *The Imitation of Christ* of Thomas à Kempis, and the works of St Teresa of Avila consistently exert a greater religious influence than the Letter of Jude, 2 Maccabees, and the purity regulations from Leviticus. A striking and enduring spiritual impact is not necessarily the result of some text having been written under the influence of biblical inspiration, nor is limited spiritual impact an index that a text could not have been inspired by the Holy Spirit.

The constraints that we detect in the literary and religious power of inspired writings stem from the themes being treated (e.g. genealogies and purity regulations) and the limited human talents behind them, albeit talents exercised under special divine impulse. Inasmuch as they are human books, they inevitably reflect the limitations of a community's culture and of the writers' own individual capacities.

Fifth, like the charisms of prophecy and apostleship, the gift of inspiration was *not strictly uniform.* Just as there were major and minor prophets, and just as Peter and Paul clearly acted as more significant

---

[23] D. G. Bloesch, *Holy Scripture: Revelation, Inspiration & Interpretation* (Carlisle: Paternoster Press, 1994), 121.

apostles than some others listed among the Twelve, it seems reasonable to hold that the evangelists, for example, enjoyed a 'higher' degree of inspiration than was the case for the authors of Nahum (a brief prophetic book that takes a very different view of Nineveh from what we find in the Book of Jonah), 2 Maccabees, and the Letter of Jude. All the inspired authors received a special divine impulse to put together and express something in writing. Yet there could be different degrees in the Holy Spirit's presence and activity on their behalf.

Allowing for considerable variety in the gift of inspiration becomes even more important when we recall such cases as the insertion of letters from and to Persian kings into the text of Ezra (see above), the impact of an Egyptian book of wisdom on Proverbs (see above), the author(s) of a Canaanite hymn of praise which was probably the source of Psalm 29 (see Chapter 2 above), and the Greek poet Theognis, who seems to have contributed to the text of Ben Sira (Sir. 6: 5–17; see Chapter 2 above). Unlike other biblical works such as Isaiah, where anonymous Jewish writers completed the work of an eighth-century prophet, the earlier texts taken up into the inspired books of Ezra, Proverbs, the Psalms, and Sirach unquestionably derive from 'outsiders', non-Israelites. Through the foreknowledge and activity of God, what they wrote was already earmarked for its place in the Sacred Scriptures of Israel. It seems necessary to recognize some divine inspiration at work in advance when the kings (and their scribes), those who addressed letters to them, an Egyptian wisdom writer, one or more Canaanites, and Theognis composed their texts, which provided source material for three canonical books of the Old Testament. The same conclusion should also be reached when reflecting on (a) those who fashioned, transmitted, and modified ancient Middle Eastern myths that supplied some of the source material for the first eleven chapters of Genesis, and (b) those who provided the oral folklore that did the same for Genesis 12–50.

2 Maccabees, written between 124 BC and 63 BC, offers a spectacular example of texts (in this case letters) originally written in other contexts achieving inspired status by being incorporated in biblical texts. Even before we reach the introduction of 2 Maccabees, we read two letters. The first was sent by the Jews in Jerusalem to exhort the Jews in Egypt to observe the new feast of Hanukkah, which had been inaugurated in Judaea just over forty years earlier (2 Macc. 1: 1–9).

The second was addressed by Jerusalem Jews and some others not only to the Jews in Egypt but also, specifically, to Aristobulus, who belonged to 'the family of the anointed priests and teacher of King Ptolemy' (2 Macc. 1: 10–18).[24] This second letter argued that the new eight-day festival was legitimate, even though it had not been prescribed by the Mosaic law. Both letters belong to religious communications between communities of Jews. Through divine providence and inspiration, they were invested with the value that eventually allowed them to be prefixed to 2 Maccabees.

2 Maccabees goes on to quote diplomatic correspondence sent from King Antiochus V (of the Seleucid dynasty with Antioch as its capital),[25] his brother Lysias, and two Roman envoys, Quintus Memmius and Titus Manius. In early December 164 BC, Lysias addressed a friendly letter to the Jews, promising to promote their 'welfare' (2 Macc. 11: 16–21). Two similarly friendly letters by Antiochus are quoted: one he sent to Lysias (2 Macc. 11: 22–6) and the other to the Jewish 'senate' or council of elders (2 Macc. 11: 27–33). The Roman envoys asked the Jewish council to despatch someone to them 'promptly', so that 'we may make proposals appropriate for you' (2 Macc. 11: 34–8). These four letters came from non-Jews and yet, once again through the advance knowledge and provident activity of God, the texts of 'outsiders' were destined to achieve the authoritative status of inspired Scripture.

James Barr correctly held that inspiration 'must extend over the entire process of production' that led to the final texts. But he might have added that the 'large number of anonymous persons' involved in that process could in some cases be 'outsiders' and not necessarily members of the Jewish community.[26] In the gift of inspiration one must allow for various possibilities, including that of its being also granted to non-Israelite 'outsiders'.

[24] 'The anointed priests had descended from Zadok (2 Chr. 31: 10); from them the high priests were chosen. One branch of this priesthood moved to be in Egypt with Ptolemy I.'

[25] Founded by Sileucus I Nicator, one of Alexander the Great's generals, the Seleucid empire extended over Syria and much of Western Asia from 311 to 65 BC.

[26] J. Barr, *Holy Scripture: Canon, Authority, Criticism* (Philadelphia: Westminster, 1983), 27.

Some diversity in the intensity of the divine inspiration at work could also stem from the nature of the themes being treated. In the case of the four Gospels, recording and interpreting the life, death, and resurrection of Jesus surely 'raised' the degree of inspiration affecting the four evangelists. Since the revealing and saving self-communication of the tripersonal God reached its acme with Jesus Christ, a 'higher' and 'stronger' impulse of divine inspiration would have accompanied the written witness to that highpoint.

Another reason for proposing a non-uniform, diverse gift of divine inspiration comes from a conclusion to be drawn from examining outstanding writers who have peopled post-New Testament Christian history. Frequently divine gifts seem to be proportionate to other divinely gifted qualities. In particular, the thirty-five doctors of the Church—for instance, Ambrose of Milan, Athanasius of Alexandria, Gregory the Great, Hildegard of Bingen, and Teresa of Avila— embodied extraordinary human and Christian characteristics; they were gifted by God in what they did as writers and as spiritual leaders. In a similar but not identical way, one would expect a 'higher' charism of inspiration to match the total dedication and effective leadership of Paul of Tarsus. To be sure, this argument applies only to the inspired writers whom we can identify and know to some extent, and these are unquestionably in the minority among authors responsible for composing the final texts of the Bible. But we do know a few, such as Paul, and his specific charism as an inspired writer matched the graced quality of his life in general.

When discussing 'some characteristic qualities of inspiration', the Biblical Commission agrees that the charism of inspiration was not uniform for 'all the authors of the biblical books'. It was only 'analogously the same'.[27] This remark remains quite isolated in the Commission's text, which nowhere treats in any detail 'the analogy of inspiration'. Yet this lonely remark reminds me that I could also have presented this fifth point in terms of the analogy of inspiration. Instead of inspiration being always monolithically the same, it was a charism that exhibited similarities and differences.

---

[27] *The Inspiration and Truth of Sacred Scriptures*, 55.

7

Five More Characteristics
of Biblical Inspiration

The last chapter examined five characteristics of biblical inspiration. But we need to push further and complete our account. This chapter will set out five more characteristics that can bring together a fuller picture of what biblical inspiration involves.

Consciousness of Being Inspired

Any version of inspiration that stresses, or at least stresses throughout the making of all the Scriptures, the *consciousness of the final authors/editors* will be deeply flawed. It is simply mistaken to demand that the inspired authors must have been aware of a special divine influence with which they cooperated in producing a sacred and authoritative text. In a few cases it is reasonable to maintain this picture. But for most scriptural books we have no way of knowing the identity of the author(s), let alone whether they were conscious of the special role of the Holy Spirit in supporting what they wrote. Sometimes such a consciousness was conspicuously lacking.

Paul and the author of the Book of Revelation belong to the few cases where we have grounds for speaking about an inspired author being conscious of the divine authority invested in his writing. In Galatians, Paul insisted on the unique authority of 'the gospel of Christ' revealed to him, which he had proclaimed, and about which he was now writing. The apostle was conscious that his letter, like his apostolic ministry, enjoyed divine authority in calling the Galatians back to accept and follow the true Gospel (Gal. 1: 1–25). What he preached and what he wrote was nothing less than 'the demonstration of the Spirit and of power' (1 Cor. 2: 5).

The author of Revelation is conscious of his God-given authority to write down what he 'has seen and what will come after this' (Rev. 1: 19). They will be 'blessed' who read and hear the divine revelation that comes through Jesus Christ and 'an angel' (Rev. 1: 1–3). At the end, the Book of Revelation introduces the same motivation for obeying this authoritative message: 'these words are trustworthy and true, for the Lord, the God of the spirits of the prophets, has sent his angel to show his servants what must take place' (Rev. 22: 6). Not only that, but 'it is I, Jesus, who sent my angel to you with this testimony for the churches' (Rev. 22: 16). The whole book is nothing less than a work of divine 'prophecy' (Rev. 1: 3; 22: 10, 19). The author remains clearly conscious of his prophetic, God-given authority (Rev. 10: 11; 22: 9). Revelation ends with a solemn warning against altering the text (Rev. 22: 18–19). Divine input and authority stand squarely behind the whole message.

In *The Testimony of the Exalted Jesus in the Book of Revelation*, Sarah Dixon argues that 'the testimony of Jesus', a phrase that occurs five times in Revelation (1: 2, 9; 12: 17; 19: 10; 20: 4), describes the book's own message.[1] To understand the message of the book as the very 'testimony of Jesus' obviously and consciously lays claim to the highest divine backing and authority.

With other biblical authors, however, even when we know something about them, we may lack evidence for concluding that they were aware of writing under special divine guidance. Let me take two examples: 2 Maccabees and the Gospel of Luke.

Writing in Greek between 124 BC and 63 BC, the anonymous author of 2 Maccabees follows current conventions to announce that he will tell the story of Judas Maccabeus, his brothers, and their battles to regain the Temple, set Jerusalem free, and re-establish Jewish law in Judaea. He discloses that he will be condensing a five-volume work (which is no longer extant) written by Jason of Cyrene (2 Macc. 2: 19–32). This preface, composed, therefore, by an epitomist (rather than a straightforward author), highlights what is to come in his work,

---

[1] S. S. U. Dixon, *The Testimony of the Exalted Jesus in the Book of Revelation* (London: T. & T. Clark, 2017).

and, like Thucydides, Tacitus, and other classical historians, aims to stir the interest of prospective readers.

An epilogue closes 2 Maccabees with an expression of conventional 'modesty' about the story that has been told: 'If it is well told and to the point, that is what I myself desired; if it is poorly done and mediocre, that was the best I could do.' The epitomist ends with the hope that 'the style of the story' will 'delight the ears of those who read the work' (2 Macc. 15: 38, 39).[2] Reactions to the story depend upon the quality achieved in the writing. There is not a word here about being aware of having collaborated with divine inspiration and so produced a work that enjoys divine authority and requires believers to read or hear it with the appropriate reverence.

Whether we should identify the author of the third Gospel with Luke, a physician who was Paul's travelling companion and co-worker (Col. 4: 1; Philem. 1: 24), is somewhat controversial. But, at least, we have from him a prologue resembling the openings of classical or Hellenistic historical works which introduced the purpose of their authors. This is what Luke explains in his address to Theophilus ('friend of God'), who could have been a particular person or symbolically meant as an ideal Christian reader:

> Since many have undertaken to set down an orderly account of the events that have been fulfilled among us, just as they were handed on to us by those who from the beginning were eyewitnesses and servants of the word, I too decided, after investigating everything carefully from the very first [or 'for a long time'], to write an orderly account for you, most excellent Theophilus, so that you may know the truth concerning the things about which you have been instructed.   (Luke 1: 1–4)

Luke recognizes previous Christian writing: 'many have undertaken to set down an orderly account of the events that have been fulfilled among us [Christians]'. One of those 'many' is, almost certainly, the

---

[2] 'The ears of those who read' reminds us that in ancient times one usually read books aloud, even to oneself. For example, on the road going down from Jerusalem to Gaza, Philip overheard an Ethiopian eunuch reading Isaiah to himself (Acts 8: 28). See L. W. Hurtado and C. Reith, 'Writing and Book Production in the Hellenistic and Roman Period', in J. C. Paget and J. Schaper (eds), *The New Cambridge History of the Bible*, i (Cambridge: Cambridge University Press, 2012), 63–80, at 77–8.

Gospel of Mark. Luke then acknowledges, in general, the sources on which he will draw: he has 'investigated everything from the very first'—the whole story of Jesus' origins, life, death, and resurrection, and what he has learned about all this from 'eyewitnesses', evangelists, and other Christian teachers ('servants of the word'). He announces the point and purpose of his work: he is writing 'an orderly account for you, most excellent Theophilus, so that you may know the truth concerning the things about which you have been instructed'.

No claim is made here of any special divine help and authority, not even the authority of being personally an eyewitness of what he will write.[3] Luke follows the normal conventions of historical writing when introducing his work. He has done his best in carrying out careful and appropriate research into the theme of his work; and now he will do his best in crafting an 'orderly account'. He presents himself as a reliable member of the guild of historians, and in no way as an inspired author who is conscious that his words are also the Word of God. As a matter of fact, the Holy Spirit is specially involved in the composition of the third Gospel, but Luke shows no awareness of that.

Luke begins his second work, traditionally known as the Acts of the Apostles, by referring to his first work (as many ancient writers did when moving to their next book) and dedicating his new work to the same person, real or symbolic: 'In the first book, Theophilus, I wrote about all that Jesus did and taught from the beginning until the day when he was taken up to heaven, after giving instructions through the Holy Spirit to the apostles whom he had chosen' (Acts 1: 1–2). In the twenty-eight chapters of Acts, when telling the story of the Church's birth and expansion across the Mediterranean world, Luke will move from the ascension of Jesus into heaven until the arrival of Paul in Rome. Luke makes no explicit reference to sources that he has used or research that he has undertaken.[4] He will note the presence and activity of the Holy Spirit at key points in the development of early Christianity (e.g. Acts 8: 29; 10: 19; 16: 6), but he makes no claim

---

[3] On the question of passages where Luke writes of 'we', see C. S. Keener, *Acts: An Exegetical Commentary*, i (Grand Rapids, MI: Baker Academic, 2012), 406–9.

[4] Through the so-called 'we passages' (Acts 16: 10–17; 20: 5–15; 21: 1–18; and 27: 1–28: 16), Acts hints at Luke's being a companion of Paul on his journeys; see Keener, *Acts*, 406–9.

that the Spirit has been the 'prime mover' in preparing and composing what we know as the Acts of the Apostles. To a degree Luke follows classical and Hellenistic practices, and not least in the speeches that make up almost one third of the text of Acts. While conveying Luke's theological understanding of what has happened in the emerging Church, the speeches resemble those which ancient historians thought appropriate for various circumstances and inserted into the narrative to enlighten and entertain their readers.[5]

To sum up: the Spirit of God can be actively present in special ways—specifically, by inspiring biblical authors—but need not make that presence and activity consciously felt. It is a matter of common experience that we may be blessed and enriched by others, without our being aware of what is happening and how we are being helped in one or other of our projects.[6] Something like that seems to have been the case with the authors of 2 Maccabees and Luke–Acts. They were blessed and enriched by the special activity of the Holy Spirit, but apparently remained unaware of that presence.

The Biblical Commission, when sketching a phenomenology of inspiration, helpfully gathers from the Scriptures 'the testimony of biblical writings to their origin in God'.[7] They state, for example, 'Luke explicitly indicates the source of his Gospel was "those who from the beginning were eyewitnesses and ministers of the word" (Luke 1: 2), suggesting, in this way, that his gospel comes from Jesus, the ultimate and supreme revealer of God the Father.' Even if Luke 'does not present the source of the Book of Acts and its divine provenance in the same explicit way', the divine provenance of the book is also 'the immediate, personal relationship' of 'the eyewitnesses and ministers of the word with Jesus'.[8]

These are useful comments on the longer prologue of Luke's Gospel and the briefer introduction to Acts. The Commission may

---

[5] On the speeches in Acts, see J. A. Fitzmyer, *The Acts of the Apostles* (New York: Doubleday, 1998), 103–13; Keener, *Acts*, 258–319.

[6] See I. U. Dalferth, *Becoming Present: An Inquiry into the Christian Sense of the Presence of God* (Leuven: Peeters, 2006).

[7] Biblical Commission, *The Inspiration and Truth of Sacred Scripture*, trans. E. Esposito and S. Gregg (Collegeville, MN: Liturgical Press, 2014), 1–68.

[8] Ibid. 33.

well be right in examining the Scriptures for signs of the inspired authors disclosing, in one way or another, a sense of the divine origin of what they were writing. Some kind of *divine provenance* for their books can be widely established. Asking about the authors' precise *consciousness of divine guidance* may be a related question, but it is not an identical question. It is much more difficult, and in many cases impossible, to establish such a consciousness.

Special Impulses

The previous chapter and, here and there, earlier chapters spoke of biblical inspiration as 'a special impulse [singular]' coming from the Holy Spirit and prompting human beings to set something down in writing. Often it would be more accurate to speak in the plural of 'special impulses' to write.

A singular word is obviously appropriate for a biblical work that could have been written in a single sitting. Paul's Letter to Philemon runs to only twenty-five verses and is easily the shortest of the certainly authentic letters of the apostle. In an hour or so, Paul could have written this text or, rather, dictated it to a secretary. What of the sixteen chapters of the apostle's longest letter, Romans, which he dictated to Tertius (Rom. 16: 22)? Composing and dictating his masterpiece presumably took weeks of work together, if not longer. Here it might be more suitable to think of divine impulses (plural) acting on and through Paul and Tertius, a secretary who could well have contributed something to the final text.

Instead of having a solo author writing with or without a secretary (as, for example, in the case of Paul's seven authentic letters, Sirach, 2 Maccabees, Matthew, Luke, Acts, and Revelation), many books of the Bible (like Genesis, the Psalter, and Isaiah) emerged from a long process, as so-called 'social theories' of inspiration have rightly insisted. On any showing, Genesis was hundreds of years in the making. The composition of all the psalms took several centuries. What was more or less the final text of Isaiah came into shape between 700 and 400 BC.[9] The community of those sharing in the charism

---

[9] See E. Ulrich, 'The Old Testament Text and its Transmission', *New Cambridge History of the Bible*, i, 84–104, at 85: 'Israel drew on the rich religious and literary

could be complex, varied, and unexpected. Witness the example of letters being taken up into the inspired texts of Ezra and 2 Maccabees (see Chapter 6 above). Inasmuch as they helped to create some part of the Scriptures, special impulses of the Holy Spirit moved all those who played a part in bringing about the final texts.

Some charism of inspiration guided all those who contributed to composing the historical books of the Old Testament, and was not restricted to the final editor(s). Likewise the same charism touched all those Christians who, as 'eyewitnesses' and/or 'ministers of the word' (Luke 1: 2), provided the stories and sayings that came to be woven into the four Gospels. We can identify some of these eyewitnesses and active agents of the Gospel traditions: for instance, the twelve apostles and female companions of Jesus like Mary Magdalene. In a similar way, even if they remain anonymous, we should recognize the inspiration received by the author(s) of hymns subsequently incorporated into New Testament letters (e.g. Phil. 2: 6–11; 1 Tim. 3: 16). All such cases from both Old and New Testament require a plural language: impulses of the Holy Spirit.

Not Modern Authors

We should not compare the authorship of biblical books too closely with the work of modern authors. Unlike many contemporary authors, the biblical writers (e.g. the authors of the historical books of the Old Testament, Matthew, and Luke) often drew on oral and written material that had already taken some shape. They were constrained by traditional witness and, in some cases (e.g. the Psalms), by traditional styles of writing (which, of course, can also affect secular writers). Their aim was consistently religious, and, with a few exceptions (e.g. 2 Maccabees), they did not aspire to win public recognition for their literary prowess, as is usual with modern authors. Some of them (e.g. Isaiah and his followers) showed a remarkable grasp of language and intensity of human feeling. But they did not wish to be

---

treasury of older, more established cultures within which it came to be and continued to live.'

judged either by their artful expression or by their capacity to articulate deep personal experience.

The key differences could be put this way. Modern poets, dramatists, and novelists normally write on their own behalf, often reflect their own personal background, and remain very much individuals in their own right and with their own creative powers. But what about Ben Sira, a scholar who identified himself and described something of his background experience—for instance, what he had learned through travel (Sir. 34: 9–13; 39: 4; 51: 13)? Nevertheless, he presented himself as a scholar of the Sacred Scriptures (Sir. 39: 1–3, 7–8), intent on retrieving the great figures of biblical history (Sir. 44–9). He was embedded in the wisdom tradition, even if, as we saw in Chapter 2, he took it up in some fresh ways. The biblical authors usually remained anonymous, drew on the traditions and experiences of other (often earlier) believers, and produced works to serve communities of faith. Even if they were more, at times ever so much more, than mere mouthpieces of their communities (e.g. Paul and the author of the Book of Revelation), we would ignore at our peril the social setting, religious responsibility, and faith function of their writings. These factors regularly set them apart from modern authors.

Church-founding Function

My previous eight points, five in the last chapter and three already in this chapter, have clarified somewhat how the special impulses of the Holy Spirit worked—or did not work—through the authors of the Bible. Provided we acknowledge the real human role of these writers (point 1), we will be able to recognize various limitations in their activity as writers (points 2 to 8). Admittedly what has been said so far about inspiration has largely attended to what the guidance of the Spirit did *not* involve. The biblical authors did not write in all possible styles; their works do not always enjoy a religious impact superior to that of non-inspired texts; they were not necessarily conscious of being inspired, and so forth.

It seems unreasonable to expect a fuller description of all the dynamics of biblical inspiration, let alone a totally clear explanation of it. Such an account will not be looked for, once we acknowledge how this charism (which makes the biblical texts both the Word of

God and the words of human beings) belongs to the total mystery of Christ, who was and is truly divine and fully human. If we cannot explain the relationship between humanity and divinity in the incarnation, we should not expect to explain the similar (but not identical) relationship between divine and human activity found in the operation of inspiration.[10]

Nevertheless, we can offer a positive, if limited, summary of inspiration's function in founding the Church, a function which also indicates what made God the 'author' of the Scriptures and why we can call the Bible 'the Word of God'.[11] The gift of inspiration belonged to the divine activity in the history of revelation and salvation that led to the founding of the Church, with all the elements (including the Scriptures) that constitute her total reality. Where the books of the Old Testament record various events, persons, and experiences that prepared the way for Christ and his Church, the books of the New Testament witness to persons (above all, Jesus himself and his apostles), events, and experiences (above all, Jesus' life, crucifixion, resurrection, and the outpouring of the Holy Spirit) that immediately fed into the founding of the Church.

Hence, God could be called the 'author' of Scriptures, inasmuch as a special divine activity formed and fashioned the Church. Creating the community of the Church also involved 'authoring' the Bible and turning human words into the Word of God.[12]

By taking such a Church-founding view of biblical inspiration, we will be better able to appreciate how the charism of inspiration was communicated primarily to the community, and to individuals in

---

[10] See G. O'Collins, 'The Incarnation: The Critical Issues', in S. T. Davis, D. Kendall, and G. O'Collins (eds), *The Incarnation: An Interdisciplinary Symposium* (Oxford: Oxford University Press, 2001), 1–27, at 6–12.

[11] See K. Rahner, *Foundations of Christian Faith*, trans. W. V. Dych (New York: Seabury Press, 1978), 369–78; Rahner, *Inspiration in the Bible*, trans. C. H. Henkey (New York: Herder & Herder, 1961).

[12] Kevin Vanhoozer has proposed the covenant-forming activity of God as the context for understanding biblical inspiration (*First Theology: God, Scripture and Hermeneutics* (Leicester: Apollos, 2002), 127–203). Covenant-forming activity coincides with Church-founding activity.

as much as they belonged to the community. This dimension of inspiration has already surfaced in our discussion, right through to the reminder that we must recognize the social function of biblical authors that sets them apart from modern authors.

Since God communicated the gift of inspiration precisely as part of the divine activity in bringing the Church into existence, we can understand why that gift did not continue beyond the apostolic age. It belonged finally to the unique, non-transferable role of the apostles and the apostolic community in (a) witnessing to Christ's resurrection from the dead and the coming of the Holy Spirit and (b) with and under Christ founding the Church. The first Christians and their leaders, acting as resurrection witnesses and Church founders, shared in the once-and-for-all quality of the Christ-event itself. The biblical authors and, specifically, the New Testament writers had a similar once-and-for-all function, whether they were apostles like Paul or simply members of the apostolic community like Luke. Since the charism of inspiration reached its highpoint with God's activity in founding the Church, it was not needed for producing further inspired texts once the Church was fully founded. Inspired writing ceased when the long period of foundational revelation, initiated in the shadowy pre-history of the Old Testament, clearly gave way to the period of post-apostolic, dependent revelation. The biblical texts were to prove richly inspiring, but the production of new biblical texts was closed.

To sum up the change: later generations of Christians bear the responsibility of proclaiming Christ's resurrection from the dead, keeping the Church in existence, and living by the Bible. But they neither 'directly' witness to the risen Christ (as did those like Peter, Paul, and Mary Magdalene, who met him gloriously alive after his death and burial), nor do they found the Church, nor do any of them continue to compose inspired Scriptures.

Through the inspired record of their foundational experiences, preaching, and activity, the members of the apostolic Church remain uniquely authoritative for all subsequent generations of Christians—a theme very dear to Karl Barth (see Chapter 1 above). Thus the priority of the apostolic Church was and remains theological and much more than a merely chronological priority.

The Inspiring Quality of the Inspired Bible

The tenth and final characteristic of inspiration must be reckoned to be its inspiring quality. Right from Chapter 2, we have noted the power of the Scriptures to inspire insights in and communicate revelation to subsequent readers or hearers. Within the Old Testament itself, later writers like Ben Sira drew inspiration from earlier books. Citations from and echoes of Old Testament texts (e.g. Isaiah, Ezekiel, and the Psalms) permeate Matthew, Paul, Revelation, and other books of the New Testament (see Chapter 3). The New Testament would be unthinkable without the inspiring power and presence of the Old Testament books.

Chapter 4 picked out areas of post-apostolic Christianity that illustrate abundantly how the inspired Scriptures have proved universally and vibrantly inspiring. There is no need to dwell again on the ways in which the Bible has guided and enlivened Christians: in the celebration of baptism, the Eucharist, and the other sacraments; in the liturgy of the hours (which would be impossible without the psalms), preaching, teaching, hymns, and sacred drama (including such popular devotions as the Stations of the Cross); and in Christian painting (including icons), sculpture, literature (including poetry down to W. H. Auden, T. S. Eliot, Kevin Hart, G. M. Hopkins, E. M. Muir, and Les Murray).

While the *causality* of the inspired Scriptures, both in their origin and continuing impact, often remains hidden in considerable mystery, their inspiring *effect* is everywhere to be seen and valued in the two thousand years of Christianity (and beyond, as we saw in the example of the impact of the Beatitudes on Mahatma Gandhi). Its inspiring impact must be recognized as the most significant characteristic of biblical inspiration, the Spirit's impulse that produced the Bible and continues to speak and sanctify through the sacred texts.

Donald Bloesch has rightly written of the need to distinguish but not separate 'the inspiring action of the Spirit in the past' (the original *cause* of the inspired Scriptures) from the Spirit's 'illuminating activity in the present' (the enduring causality of divine inspiration). The past causality continues, albeit in diverse modes, in the present.[13]

---

[13]   D. G. Bloesch, *Holy Scripture: Revelation, Inspiration & Interpretation* (Carlisle: Paternoster Press, 1994), 119.

The inspiring action of the Holy Spirit in the past (the principal cause at work in the composition of the biblical texts) directly affected a limited number of people, the sacred authors. The Spirit's illuminating and sanctifying action continues to affect innumerable persons and produce countless effects. The inspired writings functioned and continue to function as a vehicle for the Holy Spirit to touch the lives of many millions.

8

The Truth and 'Canonization' of the Scriptures

Believers expect to find in the inspired and inspiring Scriptures the truth which guides their belief, life, and worship. This was the case with the Jewish people and with the New Testament Christians. We saw earlier how Paul fashioned from Genesis (and some Jewish traditions) his teaching on Christ as the Second or Last Adam and how he made Isaiah his colleague in preaching the good news. In the second century Irenaeus of Lyons championed against Marcion and others the authoritative truth of the Old Testament, as well as drawing on the truth of the New Testament, notably the four Gospels, for his preaching and writing. For Irenaeus, the Rule of Truth (*Adversus Haereses* 2. 27. 1; 3. 2. 1), as he also called 'the rule of faith', coincided with the content of Scriptures. Over two centuries before the definitive list of canonical books was finally formed, the truth of the Scriptures provided decisive guidance. Hence it seems preferable to reflect first on scriptural truth and then move to examine the process of biblical 'canonization'.

The cause of truth seems more urgent than ever. In the past, when wars broke out, it was said that the first casualty was truth. Nowadays we do not need to be engaged in actual wars for truth to become a casualty. As political leaders know, truth may be real, but falsehood often works better. Strategic falsehoods blur the binary distinction between truth and falsehood, since distorting or even inventing reality may prove a more successful weapon than honest fidelity to basic facts. A supreme authority can turn itself into a TV reality show, which trades in alternative facts and statements that are no longer operative. While denouncing 'fake news', speakers for post-truth hypocritically trade in its production.

The Saving Truth of the Bible

Before expounding the saving truth of the Scriptures,[1] we need (a) to take a stand on terminology and (b) to set aside a common but misleading view. With regard to terminology, many Christians continue to speak of biblical 'inerrancy' or freedom from error.[2] However, it is preferable to use a positive and more scriptural term, 'truth'. Biblical truth aims positively at saving human beings integrally and not merely at keeping them free from error. It is also identified with the persons of the Trinity, as we shall see. It would be strange to characterize Father, Son, and Holy Spirit as 'Inerrancy [upper case] itself'; we can and should call each of them 'Truth itself' or 'Truth in person'. John's Gospel presents Jesus as promising that 'the Spirit of truth will guide you into all truth' (John 16: 13). To express this promise as 'the Spirit of inerrancy will guide you into all inerrancy' would seem odd.

Along with the issue of terminology, one should notice the frequent and misleading tendency to identify biblical inspiration with the truth (or inerrancy) of the Bible. Rather than being identical with inspiration, biblical truth (to be described below) is a major result or consequence of inspiration. The Bible was written under a special impulse of the Holy Spirit and, therefore, is true. Biblical inspiration enjoyed other results: for instance, it produced texts like the psalms, which over thousands of years have nourished personal prayer and

[1] See O. Loretz, *The Saving Truth of the Bible*, trans. D. J. Bourke (London: Burns & Oates, 1968); J. van Oorschot et al., 'Wahrheit/Wahrhaftigkeit', *TRE*, xxxv, 337–78, at 337–45; A. E. Padgett, 'A True Word? Scripture, Authority, and the Question of Truth', in C. P. Ruloff (ed.), *Christian Philosophy of Religion* (Notre Dame, IN: University of Notre Dame Press, 2015), 333–44; A. E. Padgett and P. R. Keifert (eds), *But Is It All True? The Bible and the Question of Truth* (Grand Rapids, MI: Eerdmans, 2006); I. de la Potterie, *La Vérité dans Saint Jean* (Rome: Biblicum Press, 1977); G. Quell et al., '*Alētheia*', in G. Kittel and G. Friedrich (eds), *Theological Dictionary of the New Testament*, trans. G. W. Bromiley, 10 vols (Grand Rapids, MI: Eerdmans, 1964–76), i, 232–51; K. J. Vanhoozer, 'The Trials of Truth', *First Theology: God, Scripture & Hermeneutics* (Downers Grove, IL: InterVarsity, 2002), 337–73.

[2] C. H. Pinnock, for instance, prefers, like many others, to speak of 'inerrancy'; 'truth' does not even feature in the index to his *Scripture Principle* (London: Hodder & Stoughton, 1985).

public worship for Jews and Christians. Expressing and encouraging truth was one such major consequence of inspiration.

In *The Inspiration and Truth of Sacred Scripture*, the Biblical Commission, while not identifying them, tied biblical truth more closely to inspiration by calling it a 'fundamental' and 'divine' *quality* (rather than a result) of inspired Scripture:

> Since it originates in God, Scripture has divine qualities. Among these is the fundamental one of attesting the truth, understood as a revelation of God himself [*sic*] and his salvific plan. The Bible, in fact, makes known the mystery of the Father's love, manifested in the Word made flesh, who, through the Spirit, leads to a perfect communion of human beings with God.[3]

This was to link the Bible's testimony to truth with the *self-revelation* of the tripersonal God and its inseparable salvific purpose. An essentially personal account of biblical truth will now be developed under seven headings.

(1) First, the central purpose of the inspired Scriptures could be called *attesting the truth* about God and attesting the truth about ourselves—a witness that leads to salvation. But that truth is not necessarily derived straight from such persons and events in which God is directly revealed as the life, death, and resurrection of Jesus Christ. The Bible, as we have seen, *also records* (under the impulse of inspiration) matters that do not seem so closely connected with God's self-manifestation. Some of what we read in Leviticus, for example, comes from human customs rather than from any special divine disclosure. To use the language of the Biblical Commission, rather than all such passages being 'perennially valid', they may merely reflect 'a culture, a civilization, or even the mentality of a specific period of time'.[4]

(2) Second, a further limit to be respected when reflecting on biblical truth derives from the nature of language used in the Scriptures and literature in general. Language may express a true judgement made by our intellect about the way things are. If what the intellect judges

---

[3] Biblical Commission, *The Inspiration and Truth of Sacred Scripture*, trans. T. Esposito and S. Gregg (Collegeville, MN: Liturgical Press, 2014), 162.

[4] Ibid. 150.

about reality (and hence causes us to say or write) actually conforms to reality (*adequatio intellectus et rei*), then we are in touch with truth.[5] This way of understanding truth highlights the individual person's intellect, emphasizing the mind and judgement of the thinking subject.[6] It may reduce 'truth' to the truth of propositions which represent reality and conform to the 'facts'.

Understanding truth along these lines risks turning the biblical texts into a series of informative propositions, whose function it is to make factual claims and state true judgements. The Bible, however, forms no such catalogue of propositions which are to be tested solely (by the correspondence theory of truth) for their truth or error. Unquestionably, the Scriptures do contain many true propositions: for instance, 'Christ died for our sins, was buried, has been raised, and appeared to Cephas and then to the Twelve' (1 Cor. 15: 3–5). But the Scriptures also use language in other ways by raising questions, issuing exhortations, conveying commands, making prayers, uttering cries of joy, and so forth.

Questions asked by God (e.g. Gen. 3: 9), Jesus (e.g. John 1: 38), Paul (e.g. Gal. 3: 1), and others in the biblical texts may be, as is the case elsewhere, clear, relevant, and meaningful. But as such, questions do not aspire to describe reality and may not be classified under the headings of truth or falsity. To pose a question does not amount to saying anything either true or false.

Exhortations delivered by the prophets, the apostle Paul, and others abound in the Bible. These exhortations may be called for, may change attitudes, and may bring about right behaviour. But in and of themselves exhortations should not be characterized as 'true' or 'false'. That would be a category mistake.

It is the same with *commands* and *laws*, like the two versions of the Decalogue cited by Exodus 20: 2–17 and Deuteronomy 5: 6–21, respectively. The first 'develops mainly a theology of creation', and

---

[5] See R. L. Kirkham, 'Truth, Correspondence Theory of', in E. Craig (ed.), *Routledge Encyclopedia of Philosophy*, ix (London: Routledge, 1998), 472–5; G. Vision, *Veritas: The Correspondence Theory and its Critics* (Cambridge, MA: MIT Press, 2004).

[6] As we shall see later in this chapter, biblical truth calls for much more than intellectual activity, and invites human beings 'to do the truth' and follow the personal Truth who is the Son of God incarnate.

the second 'insists mostly on the theology of salvation'. They summarize the Torah, and aim at constructing 'a true' or faithful community.[7] Yet it could be misleading to say that these two versions of the Decalogue 'combine the attestation of a truth concerning God (he is the *Creator* and *Saviour*) with a truth regarding the manner of a just and upright life'.[8] Other biblical passages directly attest these two truths, respectively: 'I am the Lord your Holy One, the Creator of Israel, your King' (Isa. 43: 15); 'happy are those' whose 'delight is the law of the Lord' (Ps. 1: 1–2). Such passages might be scrutinized in the light of the correspondence theory of truth: is it true that YHWH is the Lord and Creator of Israel? Is it true that those who delight in the law of the Lord are happy and blessed people? But as such, the Decalogue, in either of its two forms, is not precisely in the business of making such truth claims about the way things are, and should not be assessed as to whether such judgements correspond to the facts. Rather the Decalogue enjoins patterns of living and relating to other human beings and to God.

The *joyful cry* 'alleluia' appears in the psalms and the Book of Revelation. But as such 'alleluia' is, strictly speaking, neither true or false. It is a cry of joy uttered in the presence of God.

(3) We need to insist on aspects of biblical truth, which, while not always proving foreign to the pervasive correspondence view of truth,[9] have their particular accents as *interpersonal* and less one-sidedly intellectual. In the Old Testament, the Hebrew term *emet*, generally translated in the (Greek) Septuagint as *alētheia*, bespeaks the consistent faithfulness and firm reliability of God, revealed in word and deed. Biblical history 'seeks to show that God is faithful in his relationship with humanity [. . .] God leads his people to salvation, in and with him, through the events of history'. God is totally reliable (Deut. 32: 4), so that 'the truth of the Lord is comparable to that of a rock (Isa. 26: 4)'.[10]

[7] Biblical Commission, *Inspiration and Truth of Sacred Scripture*, 75–6.

[8] Ibid. 77.

[9] Most post-modernist thinkers seem to query the idea of language as 'referential' and so dismiss the correspondence view of truth. Hardcore common sense, however, constantly implies this theory when evaluating what witnesses in court swear to, what professors of medicine propose to their classes, and what people claim when filling in forms for government agencies.

[10] Biblical Commission, *Inspiration and Truth of Sacred Scripture*, 78, 79.

In the New Testament 'truth' features strongly in the Pauline and Johannine corpus: *alētheia* features forty-seven times in the letters attributed to Paul and forty-four times in the Gospel and Letters of John. Remaining faithful and reliable, God is 'proved true' (Rom. 3: 1–7) and is fully revealed through the person of his Son: 'the truth is in Jesus' (Eph. 4: 21).[11]

The witness of Jesus is 'true' (John 8: 14), because he has 'come from heaven' and provides testimony to what he has seen (John 3: 31–6). It is through Jesus that the fullness of 'grace and truth' have come among us (John 1: 14, 17).[12] We might sum up the divine self-revelation as the truth of salvation manifested in Christ. He himself is 'the true bread' (John 6: 32) and 'the true vine' (John 15: 1). In fact, he is the Truth (John 14: 6) who reveals the Father (John 1: 18; see also 14: 7) and who will send the Spirit of truth (John 16: 7, 13).

The powerful presence of Christ and the Holy Spirit enables believers to 'do the truth' (John 3: 21; 1 John 1: 6) and to 'belong to the truth' (John 18: 37). The truth that 'sets them free' (John 8: 32) does much more than conform their minds to reality. It transforms their entire existence by making them true or reliable persons (3 John 12; see also Rom. 9: 1) in a deep relationship with God who is Father, Son, and Holy Spirit.

(4) A personal notion of biblical truth links up with its being *progressive*, a truth not communicated once and for all at the start. Earlier scriptural authors recorded some unsatisfactory and even downright erroneous views of God: for instance, that God could order the total destruction of all the Amalecites (e.g. Deut. 25: 19). Under the impulse of the Holy Spirit, the sacred writers recorded this and other instances of *herem*. It was an image of God that the Israelites genuinely entertained. It needed to be radically purified if they were to grow towards the true image of God who loves and cherishes all

---

[11] The Book of Revelation calls Jesus 'the true one' (Rev. 3: 7); he is 'faithful and true' (Rev. 19: 11).

[12] Here the Scriptures prefigure the philosophical notion of truth developed by Martin Heidegger (1889–1976), according to which something is true when it ceases to be hidden (*a-lēthēs*) and discloses itself. In this sense truth is the unveiling or throwing open of being.

people, as we find in Second and Third Isaiah (Isa. 40–55 and Isa. 56–66, respectively), Jonah, and other later books and traditions.[13]

Unless we recognize the progressive nature of biblical truth, we may find ourselves in the company of many people and even a few scholars who attempt to justify genocidal practices by arguing that God is the Lord of life and death.[14] What the biblical authors recall at times is nothing less than an horrendous (if, historically speaking, not always a truly accurate) story: for instance, 'doing the divine will' by massacring the inhabitants of town after town when the Israelites took possession of the promised land (Deut. 2: 31–3: 7); God killing 70,000 people by sending a pestilence after David ordered a national census (2 Sam. 24: 1–16; 1 Chron. 21: 1–14); and a daughter being sacrificed in thanksgiving to God for a military victory (Judg. 11: 29–40). There is a sad truth in what these and other passages record under the impulse of divine inspiration: namely, a picture of what (at least many) Israelites thought about God and what God wanted from them. Their image of God called for massive purification. But gradually they progressed towards a fuller and more truthful view of God reflected in later books of the Bible that were also composed under the inspiration of the Holy Spirit.

(5) A progressive understanding of biblical truth leads naturally to acknowledging that biblical truth *is found in the whole Bible*. It is 'canonical truth', as the Biblical Commission puts it.[15] We may not properly speak of the truth of the Bible before all the scriptural texts have been composed and then recognized as belonging to the canon. Hence we should not look for the truth of the Scriptures primarily in one passage, in one book, or even in one Testament. The truth is in the whole.[16]

An ancient Christian conviction, still reflected in a liturgical introduction 'the Gospel according to Matthew' (or 'according to Mark,

---

[13] See G. O'Collins, *Salvation for All: God's Other Peoples* (Oxford: Oxford University Press, 2008), 64–78; and T. J. Demy, 'War', in R. L. Brawley (ed.), *The Oxford Encyclopedia of the Bible and Ethics*, ii (New York: Harvard University Press, 2014), 395–403, at 397.

[14] But see J. S. Kaminsky, 'Did Election Imply the Mistreatment of Non-Israelites?', *Harvard Theological Review* 96 (2003), 387–425.

[15] Biblical Commission, *Inspiration and Truth of Sacred Scripture*, 119–21, 163.

[16] This is not to play down the challenge involved in interpreting many individual passages of the Bible; see ibid. 123–56, and our next chapters.

Luke, or John'), conveys a sense of the full truth being found in the whole. There is only one Gospel of Jesus Christ, attested by the witness of four evangelists. The truth is found in the one, four-fold Gospel.

(6) We can state this unity more precisely and personally: the truth of the Bible is found primarily in the person of Jesus Christ. He is the truth attested prophetically in the Old Testament and apostolically in the New Testament. Ultimately the Bible does not convey a set of distinct truths but has only one truth to proclaim and practise: the personal disclosure of the tripersonal God in Jesus. 'Other' biblical truths or 'mysteries' with their distinct (but not separate) contents do nothing else than articulate this one primordial Mystery, which the apostolic generation of believers experienced and transmitted to later generations.

The twelfth-century Augustinian canon Hugh of Saint-Victor shared this Christological vision: 'all divine Scripture speaks of Christ and finds its fulfilment in Christ, because it forms only one book, the book of life which is Christ'.[17] In the sixteenth century, William Tyndale expressed a similar conviction: 'the scriptures spring out of God, and flow into Christ, and were given to lead us to Christ. Thou must therefore go along by the scripture as by a line, until thou come at Christ, which is the way's end and resting place'.[18] In the twentieth century, Pope Benedict XV had this to say in his 1920 encyclical *Spiritus Paraclitus*: 'all the pages of both [the Old and New] Testaments lead towards Christ as the centre'.[19]

(7) The Scriptures create the conditions by which God speaks to us and enables us to acknowledge and practise the truth. In the last resort, the truth of the Bible is something to be lived. The truth is known by living in it and living by it. Biblical truth is to be experienced and expressed in action as much (or even more than) it is to be seen and affirmed in intellectual judgements. Through doing and 'speaking the truth in love' (Eph. 4: 15), we will know and understand, at least partly and provisionally, what this truth is.

---

[17] *De Arca Noe Morali*, 2.8–9; *PL* 176, cols 642–3.

[18] *The Work of William Tyndale*, ed. G. E. Duffield (Philadelphia: Fortress Press, 1965), 353.

[19] *Enchiridion Biblicum*, 4th edn (Rome: Pontifical Biblical Commission 1961), 176.

The Canon of Scripture

Before directly facing the 'canonization' of the Scriptures, we need to set aside a defective analogy that has been drawn between the way texts were received into the biblical canon and the way books become authoritative classics in certain cultures. The Biblical Commission endorsed the analogy,[20] which David Tracy developed years ago.[21] Sallie McFague had also endorsed this analogy: 'the Bible is not absolute or authoritative in any sense except the way that a "classic" text is authoritative.'[22] Even earlier, John Coventry had interpreted the Scriptures as 'classic' texts.[23]

Francis Schüssler Fiorenza drew attention to a basic flaw in this 'classic' interpretation of the Scriptures and their authority. It insufficiently distinguishes the Bible from classic works of literature (and art). The classics exemplify the deepest realities of human existence; in such books (and works of art), generations of readers have recognized 'the truth of their own identity'. By way of contrast, it is 'the identity of Jesus' that forms the basis for scriptural authority rather than the power of Scriptures to elicit from one generation to the next compelling truths about the human condition. Schüssler Fiorenza recalled Krister Stendahl's observation: 'it is because of their authority as scripture that the Scriptures have become classics', and it is not that 'they have authority because they are classics'.[24]

One could add to this rebuttal by pointing out that classics, like Homer's two epic poems and Dante's *Divine Comedy*, may feature at the birth of a culture's literature, but not necessarily. The dialogues of

---

[20] *Inspiration and Truth of Sacred Scripture*, 62–3.

[21] He interpreted at length the Scripture as 'classics' in *The Analogical Imagination* (New York: Crossroad, 1981), 248–304.

[22] S. McFague, *Metaphorical Theology: Models of God in Religious Language* (Philadelphia: Fortress Press, 1982), 19. Incidentally one should challenge using 'absolute' and 'authoritative' as equivalent alternatives. The Bible is authoritative but not 'absolutely' so; its authority, as we shall see later, derives from the Holy Spirit, Christ, and his apostles. What is derivative cannot be absolute (that is to say, independent and unconditional).

[23] J. Coventry, *Christian Truth* (London: Darton, Longman & Todd, 1975), 45, 66.

[24] F. Schüssler Fiorenza, 'The Crisis of Biblical Authority: Interpretation and Reception', *Interpretation* 44 (1990), 153–65, at 360–1.

Plato and the works of Goethe, for instance, came long after Greek and German literature, respectively, were established. No 'canon' of literary classics can be declared to be closed. Outstanding writers may emerge later, in our own generation, or in the future; their works can merit 'canonization' and inclusion among a people's classic texts. The inspired Scriptures, however, were completed in the foundational period of Christianity. The biblical canon, as we shall see, is closed and cannot be enlarged.

Moreover, we should not forget what was pointed out earlier: some inspired books (e.g. the Epistle of Jude, apart from its closing doxology in vv. 24–5) and whole sections of other scriptural books (e.g. 1 Chron. 1–9) do not display the literary quality one expects from a literary classic. The Holy Spirit inspired the composition of all the books of the Bible, but such inspiration did not guarantee a 'high', classical standard of human writing.

In short, the particular kind of authority enjoyed by the sacred Scriptures, their historical provenance, and the 'failure' of some biblical books to reach a 'classical' level disqualify any easy comparison between the Scriptures and the classical literature of various cultures around the world. What then is the canon?

One can describe the canon as a closed list of foundational, sacred books, acknowledged by the Church as divinely inspired, and enjoying a normative value for Christian belief, worship, and practice.[25]

---

[25] On the canon, see J. M. Auwers and H. J. de Jonge (eds), *The Biblical Canon* (Leuven: Leuven University Press, 2003); R. T. Beckwith, *The Old Testament Canon of the New Testament Church and its Background in Early Judaism* (London: SPCK, 1985); R. F. Collins, 'Canonicity', in R. E. Brown, J. A. Fitzmyer, and R. E. Murphy (eds), *The New Jerome Biblical Commentary* (London: Geoffrey Chapman 1989), 1034–54; C. A. Evans et al., 'Canon', *Oxford Encyclopedia of the Books of the Bible*, i, 85–120; H. Y. Gamble, *The New Testament Canon: Its Making and Meaning* (Philadelphia: Fortress Press, 1985); M. Hengel, *Die vier Evangelien und das Evangelium von Jesus Christus: Studien zu ihrer Sammlung und Entstehung* (Tübingen: Mohr Siebeck, 2008); M. W. Holmes, 'The Biblical Canon', in S. A. Harvey and D. G. Hunger (eds), *The Oxford Handbook of Early Christian Studies* (Oxford: Oxford University Press, 2008), 406–26; L. M. McDonald, *The Formation of the Biblical Canon*, 2 vols (London: T. & T. Clark, 2017); B. M. Metzger, *The Canon of the New Testament: Its Origin, Development, and Significance* (Oxford: Clarendon, 1987); R. Wall, 'Canon', in S. E. Balentine (ed.), *The Oxford Encyclopedia of Bible and Theology*, i (New York: Oxford University Press, 2015), 111–21.

'Canonization' presupposed and went beyond biblical inspiration or the special guidance of the Holy Spirit in composing the Scriptures. In the Old Testament period, inspired texts came into existence before the *tripartite canon* of the Law (the Torah or Pentateuch), the prophets (including the historical books Joshua to 2 Kings), and 'the writings' (mainly wisdom books) began to form in the seventh century BC. This canon gradually emerged after the return from the Babylonian exile, and seemingly became definitive only in the second century AD. But, as John Barton remarked, 'there is a great deal we still do not know about how the Old Testament came to be canonized and arranged'.[26] The process was similar with the twenty-seven books of the New Testament. They were written under inspiration and then sooner or later recognized as such by the post-apostolic Church. Jozef Verheyden describes the Church's 'struggle to create a canon of authoritative' books which 'would regulate its liturgical and spiritual life, define its identity, and function as the source and criteria of much of its theologizing'.[27]

Roman Catholics acknowledge in a decree from the Council of Trent (DzH 1502–4; ND 211–12) a definitive act of recognition which firmly established a clear canon of inspired writings. When making this solemn definition of the canon, Trent confirmed the doctrine of the Council of Florence (DzH 1334–5; ND 208), which in its turn was based on teaching coming from local councils and Church fathers in the fourth and early fifth centuries.[28]

---

[26] J. Barton, 'The Old Testament Canons', in J. C. Paget and J. Schaper (eds), *The New Cambridge History of the Bible*, i (Cambridge: Cambridge University Press, 2012), 141–64, at 164.

[27] J. Verheyden, 'The New Testament Canon', ibid. 389–411, at 411.

[28] In this 39th festal letter (for Easter 367), Athanasius of Alexandria listed the twenty-seven books of the New Testament. The Muratorian Canon, generally dated to the late second century (see H. Bettenson and C. Maunder (eds), *Documents of the Christian Church*, 4th edn (Oxford: Oxford University Press, 2011), 30–1), included all the books of the New Testament except Hebrews, James, and 1 and 2 Peter. As regards the Old Testament canon, Athanasius recognized the twenty-two books of the Hebrew Bible, which correspond to the protocanonical books of the Christian Bible. From the late second century AD, Melito of Sardis provided the earliest Christian list of Old Testament books; it was much the same as the twenty-two books of the Hebrew Bible. See D. Brakke, 'A New Fragment of Athanasius'

We cannot be expected to trace the ins and outs of the history of (a) particular books which were initially favoured but came to be excluded from the canon (e.g. *The Epistle of Barnabas* and *The Shepherd of Hermas*), or (b) those which came to be included after initial doubts (e.g. the Letter to the Hebrews, the Book of Revelation, and the deuterocanonical books of the Old Testament). Yet we should recall three criteria used in determining the canonical books. But before spelling out these criteria, we need to clarify the terms: protocanonical, deuterocanonical, and apocrypha.

The label of 'protocanonical' (or 'first-time member of the canon') applies to the thirty-nine books of the Old Testament which Christians universally accept as inspired and canonical and which correspond to the twenty-two books of the Hebrew Bible. The label of 'deuterocanonical' (or 'second-time member of the canon') applies to seven books (plus portions of other books) found in the Greek (Septuagint) version of the Old Testament (but not in the Hebrew Bible) and printed in Catholic and Orthodox Bibles. The seven books are Judith, 1 and 2 Maccabees, Sirach, Baruch, Tobit, and Wisdom. Some of these works (Judith, 2 Maccabees, and Wisdom) were written in Greek, while 1 Maccabees, Sirach, and much of Baruch were composed originally in Hebrew. Written in Hebrew before 180 BC, Sirach was translated into Greek fifty years later; since 1900 two-thirds of the original Hebrew text has been recovered. Tobit was originally written in either Hebrew or Aramaic, but, apart from some fragments in those languages, only the Greek version remains.

Some Protestant and all ecumenical Bibles include the deuterocanonical books, but normally call them 'Apocrypha'—to be distinguished, however, from the Apocryphal Gospels (e.g. 'The Gospel of the Hebrews', 'The Gospel of Mary', 'The Gospel of Peter', and 'The Gospel of Thomas'), works from the second or third centuries that no mainline Bibles include. For Catholic scholars and such Protestant scholars as Hans Hübner, who recognize the authority of some or all of the deuterocanonical books, being 'second-time members of the canon' refers to their being written in the second or first century BC

Thirty-Ninth *Festal Letter*: Heresy, Apocrypha, and the Canon', *Harvard Theological Review* 103 (2010), 47–66.

and hence after the protocanonical books. It also refers to their being accepted into the canon of Christian Scripture after a certain hesitation that came from some Church fathers such as St Jerome, who expressed doubt about the full canonical status of deuterocanonical books.

The term 'deuterocanonical' is not intended to belittle the authority of these books. The New Testament contains numerous allusions and verbal parallels to the deuterocanonical books of the Old Testament. These books enjoyed authoritative status for the first Christians. Around the Mediterranean world, Jews who became Christians brought with them the Septuagint or Greek version of the Bible that included the deuterocanonical books which had also fed their belief and spiritual lives. The authority of the Septuagint showed through when the New Testament authors often followed the Septuagint rather than the Hebrew original when citing what came to be called the protocanonical books of the Old Testament. Chapter 3 above quoted a famous case of Matthew's preference for the Greek translation (*parthenos* or 'virgin') over the Hebrew original of Isaiah 7: 14 (*almah* or 'young woman'), because he wished to point to Jesus being conceived by a virgin (Matt. 1: 23).

Formation of the New Testament Canon

What then of the criteria at work for receiving new, Christian books into the canon and thus accepting them (along with the Old Testament) as the Sacred Scriptures in and for the Church? Surprisingly, inspiration did not seem to function directly as a criterion for early Christians when they recognized or rejected different books. They understood the inspiration of the Holy Spirit to be widely present in the Church both during the apostolic era and later. Granted such a broad recognition of inspiration, an appeal to inspiration could not easily establish the canon. Moreover, claims that a particular text was inspired could not be readily verified, either at the time of writing or, particularly, after the death of its author. How were other Christians to know that *this* writer had been specially guided by the Holy Spirit unless they referred to other, public criteria? Such public criteria were needed to counter the claims to have received revelation and inspiration made by Gnostics in the second and third centuries. Three such criteria shaped the early Church's recognition of sacred or God-inspired texts: (a) *apostolic writings* (or apostolicity), (b) *orthodox teaching* (or 'the rule of faith'), and (c) *wide and consistent usage*, particularly in the Church's liturgy and catechesis (an appeal to catholicity).

(a) First, there was the historical criterion of apostolic origin. The Christian writings, which complemented the scriptural books inherited by Jesus and his followers and were to constitute the canonical New Testament, came from the closing period of foundational revelation. It reached its apotheosis when the apostles proclaimed the resurrection and the outpouring of the Holy Spirit and completed the foundation of the Church.

To be sure, apostolic origin was often taken narrowly, so that the books which would make up the New Testament were all understood to be written by the apostles themselves or one of their close associates: Mark (connected with Peter) as author of the second Gospel, Luke (connected with Paul) as author of the third Gospel and the Book of Acts. In such a view, apostles gave their authority both to the Jewish Scriptures which they inherited and to the new sacred books which they or their associates composed for Christian communities. Such a strict version of apostolic origin no longer works. Very few scholars agree, for example, that Paul wrote Hebrews or that Peter wrote 2 Peter. Hesitations about the strict 'apostolic origin' of Hebrews and 2 Peter, as well as the Book of Revelation, were expressed in early Christianity before Athanasius and others accepted these works into the canon of sacred texts.

Nevertheless, in a broader sense, the criterion of apostolic origin still carries weight in sorting canonical from non-canonical writings. Only those works which witnessed to Christ prophetically (the Jewish Scriptures) or apostolically (the Christian Scriptures) could enter and remain in the canonical Bible. Those books constituted the inspired witness coming from believers who had experienced the *foundational* self-revelation of God that ended with the apostolic age. Only persons who shared in the events that climaxed with the crucifixion, resurrection, sending of the Holy Spirit, and full foundation of the Church were in a position to express through the inspired Scriptures their (direct or indirect) testimony to these experiences. Later writings, even those of such importance as the Nicene-Constantinopolitan Creed of 381 or the Chalcedonian Definition of 451, came from a period of *dependent* revelation. They could not as such directly witness to the experience of foundational revelation, and were composed at a time when the charism of biblical inspiration had ceased to be conferred on sacred authors. Seen in this way, the criterion of apostolic origin still works to accredit canonical writing. Canonicity implies apostolicity.

(b) Second, there is the *theological criterion* of conformity to the essential Christian message, 'the rule of faith (*regula fidei*)' or 'the rule of truth', highlighted by Irenaeus and later called 'the Catholic faith that comes to us from the apostles' (the Roman Canon). For a text to be recognized as canonical, it needed to be consonant with the orthodox tradition transmitted by the bishops of major dioceses. In particular, it would be excluded if it contradicted the apostolic rule of faith expressed in various Christological affirmations (Irenaeus, *Adversus Haereses*, 3. 4. 2). Since it failed to meet clearly the test of orthodoxy, *The Shepherd of Hermas*, which was written perhaps in the very early second century and so might have fitted the chronological criteria, was excluded from the canon. Other writings, like the Book of Revelation, were eventually included when their orthodox content came to be sufficiently recognized.

There was a certain circularity, of course, in applying 'the rule of faith'. Because certain writings fitted their understanding of Christianity, the faithful and their leaders judged those writings (e.g. the four Gospels and the letters of Paul) to be orthodox, built the canon around them, and then used them to test orthodoxy. At the same time, these Scriptures, inasmuch as they were written under the special guidance of the Holy Spirit, never simply mirrored what the Christian community was, but rather challenged believers by picturing what they should be and should believe. In leading them to a fully transformed life, the canonical Scriptures proved their worth in practice. We might express the circularity this way: just as the Christian community shaped the canon, so the community and its basic identity were shaped by the canon.

(c) Third, constant and wide use, above all in the context of *public worship*, also secured for inspired writings their place in the canon of the Christian Bible. We can spot this happening in the case of Paul: when various communities received his letters, they treasured, copied, and read them at liturgical assemblies. These texts shared the apostolic authority of Paul's oral witness and teaching. By the time of the composition of 2 Peter, the letters of Paul seem to have been already collected (and misinterpreted by some on the issue of the final judgement being delayed) (2 Pet. 3: 15–16).

When treating this third (liturgical) criterion, we should recall the case of 1 Clement. Around AD 170 it was still being read in the church of Corinth, along with Scriptures that were to belong definitively to the New Testament canon.[29] But this letter never entered the canon of the New Testament, later attested by Athanasius and others, since it failed to win lasting and widespread liturgical acceptance. That counted against the text's canonical status, even if it might have been acceptable on the basis of the first (historical) criterion and the second (theological) criterion.

The Closed Character of the Canon

We spoke above of the canon as a closed collection of sacred writings. Several reasons justify this closed nature. First, since the charism of biblical inspiration was no longer granted to sacred authors after the apostolic age, there could be no later instances of inspired writings. Being possible candidates for inclusion in the canon ended when a particular epoch of history—in this case the foundational period of revelation and salvation—closed.

Second, without it being closed and so immune to modification, the canon cannot function as a canon: that is, as a truly normative rule for Christian belief and practice from which the Church receives her identity. The canonical books are acknowledged as forming together an adequate account of Christianity. If they did not adequately reflect the basic Christian experience and identity which responds to the divine self-revelation through Christ and his Spirit, they could not serve as an authoritative norm for Christian faith and life.

Third, the closed nature of the canon belongs to the closed and normative nature of the apostolic age itself. Just as the members of the apostolic Church shared in the unique, once-and-for-all character of the Christ event, so too did their sacred writings—both those they composed and those that they took over from their Jewish heritage.

[29] See L. L. Welborn, 'Clement, First Epistle of', *ABD*, i, 1055–60.

The composition of the inspired books shared in the unrepeatable role of the apostles and their associates.

The consequences of this argument for the closed character of the canon are clear. On the one hand, to exclude some writings and thus *reduce* the canon (as Marcion did in the second century[30] and others have done since) tampers with the richness of the Church's foundational witness to the divine self-communication, reduces the diversity of the apostolic experience and witness,[31] and challenges the divine fullness of Christ's person and work (see Col. 1: 19–20). On the other hand, enlarging the canon by adding such writings as the later Gnostic 'scriptures' would also call into question the fullness and perfection of what Christ revealed through the witness of the apostolic generation.

In the second century we find Irenaeus of Lyons battling on two fronts in support of the emerging Christian canon. On one front, he defended the enduring authority of the Old Testament Scriptures against Marcion's rejection of them. On another front, he upheld the unique value of the New Testament Scriptures—especially the one, four-fold 'Gospel' according to Matthew, Mark, Luke, and John—against Gnostic attempts to add further 'gospels' and other texts. Very recently R. W. L. Moberly has taken issue with a similar attempt to sideline the Old Testament and provide an alternative New Testament by adding ten works (seven of which are Gnostic-style documents of the second or third century discovered in 1945 at Nag Hammadi in Egypt).[32]

---

[30] See J. J. Clabeaux, 'Marcion', *ABD*, iv, 514–16; R. M. Grant, 'Marcion, Gospel of', ibid. 516–10; J. M. Lieu, *Marcion and the Making of a Heretic* (Cambridge: Cambridge University Press, 2015). Some parishes have the habit of regularly omitting the first (Old Testament) reading in the Sunday liturgy; occasionally the responsorial psalm is also dropped, even though the New Testament makes the Psalter its most quoted Old Testament book. Such contemporary practices suggest a Marcionite tendency.

[31] Chapter 3 above illustrated the impact of the Old Testament Scriptures on the authors of the New Testament—not least Paul, for whom Isaiah was virtually a colleague in preaching the good news. To drop the Old Testament violates the steady conviction of the New Testament writers, for whom their inherited Scriptures were authoritative sources (see also e.g. Matthew and the Book of Revelation).

[32] R. W. L. Moberly, 'Canon and Religious Truth: An Appraisal of *A New New Testament*', in T. H. Lim (ed.), *When Texts are Canonized* (Providence, RI:

Granted the essentially closed nature of the canon, would it still be possible to entertain the possibility of adding to the collection of sacred books? What of the Jewish psalms actually discovered in a Qumran cave, or a missing letter of Paul that might be recovered by archaeologists? Such writings could satisfy the historical and theological criteria expounded above. Inasmuch as they would not substantially modify the total message expressed through the existing canon of Scriptures, they might win a place in the canon—under one condition, however. Such newly discovered texts from the period of foundational revelation would have to vindicate themselves through constant liturgical usage, a process that would take some time and has so far (in the case of several psalms from Qumran) not even begun.

The Authority of the Canon

Like some others, but unlike the Biblical Commission in its latest document,[33] I have spoken above of the normative authority of the canonical Scriptures.[34] Can we explain more fully the nature of the authority as recognized by Christians and justify its binding quality?

Brown University Press, 2017), 108–35. *A New New Testament* (Boston: Houghton, Mifflin, Harcourt, 2013) was edited with commentary by H. Taussig.

[33] The Commission's *Inspiration and Truth of Sacred Scripture* does not introduce the language of biblical 'authority', but repeatedly speaks of the 'truth' of the Scriptures. Biblical truth implies authority. It would have been good to have, at least, sketched the links between such truth and divine authority. An earlier document of the Commission, *The Jewish People and their Sacred Scriptures in the Christian Bible* (Vatican City: Libreria Editrice Vaticana, 2001) dedicates an opening section to the New Testament's recognition of the authority of the Jewish people's sacred Scriptures (art. 3–5).

[34] See W. P. Brown (ed.), *Engaging Biblical Authority* (Louisville, KY: Westminster John Knox, 2007). D. A. Carson (ed.), *The Enduring Authority of the Christian Scriptures* (Grand Rapids, MI: Eerdmans, 2016); G. R. Evans, 'Authority', in E. Cameron (ed.), *The New Cambridge History of the Bible*, iii (Cambridge: Cambridge University Press, 2012), 387–417; T. E. Fretheim and K. Froehlich (eds), *The Bible as Word of God in a Postmodern Age* (Minneapolis: Fortress Press, 1998); M. Goshen-Goldstein et al., 'Scriptural Authority', *ABD*, v, 1017–56; W. W. Klein, 'Authority of the Bible', *OEBI*, i, 52–60; W. Pannenberg and T. Schneider (eds), *Binding Testimony: Holy Scripture and Tradition*, trans. M. M. Matesich (Frankfurt: Peter Lang, 2014);

Believers give permanent allegiance to the authoritative biblical texts as promising to preserve the Church's self-identity by constantly illuminating and enlivening her faith and practice. They read and hear the Bible as the rule of life for their community. They acknowledge the authority of the Bible because it shares in the authority of Christ and his Holy Spirit, a life-giving authority that builds them up and lets them grow. Here etymology proves suggestive. The Latin nouns *auctor* (author) and *auctoritas* (authority) are related to *augeo* ('cause to grow' and 'increase in value').[35] The 'authority' exercised by Christ and the Spirit (through the Scriptures and in other ways) promises to do just that.

In other words, the Church's fidelity to the Scriptures rests on her fidelity to Jesus Christ as the Revealer and Saviour, and on her faith in the Holy Spirit who provided special guidance to those involved in producing the Scriptures. Apart from that fidelity and faith, the Bible cannot credibly claim any normative value, and becomes little else than a 'mere' historical source, the record of Israel's story and Christianity's origins, and an anthology of more or less edifying religious texts from the ancient Middle East. Through faith in Christ and his Spirit, however, believers acknowledge the Scriptures as sacred and embodying divine authority, and accept them as the authoritative account and interpretation of Israel's history and the formation of Christianity through Jesus Christ and his first followers. As the official collection of foundational books, the canonical Bible witnesses to the history of revelation and salvation that climaxed with Christ and remains the decisive point of orientation for all subsequent believers and theologians.

Faith in Jesus Christ underpinned the New Testament authors' sense of the divine status of the Old Testament Scriptures, identified by them as sharing in the authority of God. These authors disclosed the heart of their theological convictions by citing their inherited

---

H. Graf Reventlow, *The Authority of the Bible and the Rise of the Modern World*, trans. J. Bowden (London: SCM Press, 1984); S. M. Schneiders, 'Scripture as the Word of God', *Princeton Seminary Bulletin* 14 (1992), 148–61, 478–89.

[35] See P. G. W. Glare (ed.), *Oxford Latin Dictionary* (Oxford: Oxford University Press, 1982), 204–7, 212–13.

Jewish Scriptures.[36] The Letter to the Hebrews illustrates how Christians understood the Jewish Scriptures as divinely inspired and authoritative. Citing these Scriptures thirty-seven times, Hebrews attributes all the passages to God, Christ, or the Holy Spirit, mentioning only two human authors—Moses (Heb. 8: 5; 12: 21) and David (Heb. 4: 7)—and even then referring two of these three passages to the divine 'author' (Heb. 4: 7; 8: 5).

The authority at stake is the *de iure* authority of the Scriptures: the canonical Bible in and of itself constitutes the primary norm for determining the Church's faith and practice. Such authority in principle goes beyond mere *de facto* authority, or the way in which the Scriptures as a matter of fact affect the life, worship, and teaching of Christians. Such *de facto* authority functions insofar as the Scriptures 'work' for us but does not allow them an independent authority to challenge and judge us and our society. To accept their *de iure* authority, however, involves acknowledging that they legitimately invite an obedient hearing because they derive from a foundational and authoritative past rooted in the missions of the Son of God, the Holy Spirit, and (by participation) the apostles.

To put this in terms of truth: what is at stake is receiving the Scriptures not merely as true but as authoritatively true. Since they come from the Spirit of the risen Christ, they can be trusted to provide the truth, for belief and practice, that leads to salvation (the *veritas salvifica*).

This *de iure* authority of the Bible comes from its historical origins in the mission of the Holy Spirit, a mission invisible in itself but visible in its effects, and the visible mission of Christ (with the passage of authority from him to his apostolic collaborators). In short, the authority of the Scriptures is Pneumatological, Christological, and apostolic. It derives from persons: the Holy Spirit and Christ with his apostles. Through the Scriptures, as well as in other ways, Christ, the Spirit, and the apostles remain powerfully and authoritatively present.

---

[36] See H. Hübner, 'New Testament, OT quotations in the', *ABD*, iv, 1096–104.

9

Three 'Intentions' to Respect

God speaks to us not only by way of authoring (through the inspired writers) the text of the Scriptures but also by way of our reading and interpreting it. We need a vision of the biblical inspiration based on the Word of God expressed in the words of human beings that prove inspiring when read, interpreted, preached, and applied.

No text, not even an inspired text, can speak for itself; it always needs interpreting. Unquestionably, we can trust that the Holy Spirit, who was powerfully present at the writing of Scripture, continues to be present at its reading. This inspiring work of the Spirit never ends. In the words of Kevin Vanhoozer, 'the inspiration of the Scripture in the past and the illumination of the Scripture in the present are but twin moments in one continuous work of the Holy Spirit'.[1] The Spirit continues what the risen Christ is represented as doing—by opening minds and hearts to understand the Scriptures (Luke 24: 25–7, 45). Through the Spirit 'lifting the veil' (2 Cor. 3: 16) and 'enlightening the eyes of our hearts' (Eph. 1: 18), the Bible never ceases to convey the wisdom that leads to salvation. Yet understanding and interpreting the Scriptures involve a human as well as a divine agency.

The present chapter will expound what is involved when the biblical texts are interpreted *integrally*. This entails respecting not only the 'intention' of the human authors who produced the texts (the *intentio auctoris*), where and to the extent that this can be established, but also the 'intention' of the readers who take up the texts

---

[1] K. J. Vanhoozer, 'Scripture and Tradition', in K. J. Vanhoozer (ed.), *The Cambridge Companion to Postmodern Theology* (Cambridge: Cambridge University Press, 2003), 149–69, at 165.

(*intentio legentis*) and the 'intention' of the text itself (*intentio textus ipsius*).[2] As far back as 1981, I argued that the interpretation of texts—I had in mind biblical texts—should not be limited to (a) the authorial intentions, but should also attend to (b) the multiple meanings that emerge when we study the history of the texts and their reception (*intentio textus*), and to (c) the insights of readers with their different presuppositions, questions, and expectations (*intentio legentis*).[3]

Naturally I was satisfied to find the 1993 document of the Pontifical Biblical Commission, *The Interpretation of the Bible in the Church*,[4] spelling out at length the need to go beyond the intentions of the original authors. Interpreters should also approach the scriptural texts through the *history of their reception*, as well as apply methods that yield fresh

[2] See P. Bouteneff and D. Heller (eds), *Interpreting Together: Essays in Hermeneutics* (Geneva: WCC Publications, 2001); M. J. Gorman (ed.), *Scripture and its Interpretation: A Global, Ecumenical Introduction to the Bible* (Grand Rapids, MI: Baker Academic, 2017); W. G. Jeanrond, 'Interpretation, History of', *ABD*, iii, 424–43; B. C. Lategan, 'Hermeneutics', *ABD*, iii, 149–54; S. L. McKenzie et al., 'Interpretation, History of', *Encyclopedia of the Bible and its Reception*, xiii (Berlin: De Gruyter, 2016), 64–147; J. C. Paget et al. (eds), *The New Cambridge History of the Bible*, 4 vols (Cambridge: Cambridge University Press, 2012); S. E. Porter and M. Malcolm (eds), *The Future of Biblical Interpretation: Responsible Plurality in Biblical Hermeneutics* (Milton Keynes: Paternoster, 2013); B. E. Reid, *Wisdom's Feast: An Invitation to Feminist Interpretation of the Scriptures* (Grand Rapids, MI: Eerdmans, 2016); H. Graf Reventlow, *History of Biblical Interpretation*, trans. L. G. Perdue and J. O. Duke, 4 vols (Atlanta: Society of Biblical Literature, 2009–10); B. Smalley, *Study of the Bible in the Middle Ages*, 2 vols (South Bend, IN: University of Notre Dame Press, 1940–78); R. S. Sugirtharajah (ed.), *Voices from the Margin: Interpreting the Bible in the Third World* (Maryknoll, NY: Orbis, 2016); K. J. Vanhoozer, *First Theology: God, Scripture & Hermeneutics* (Downers Grove, IL: Intervarsity, 2002); F. M. Young, 'Interpretation of Scripture', in S. A. Harvey and D. G. Hunter (eds), *The Oxford Handbook of Early Christian Studies* (Oxford: Oxford University Press, 2008), 845–63.

[3] G. O'Collins, *Fundamental Theology* (New York: Paulist Press, 1981), 251–8. For those seeking the *intentio auctoris*, the text, as we shall see, operates as a window through which they look back to its historical origins. For those seeking the *intentio textus ipsius*, the text resembles a stained glass window that seizes their attention. For those seeking the *intentio legentis*, the text may operate as a mirror that reflects their questions and interests.

[4] Pontifical Biblical Commission, *The Interpretation of the Bible in the Church* (Vatican City: Libreria Editrice Vaticana, 1993).

meanings coming from the *readers* of the Bible.[5] This document noted with apparent approval what, as a philosopher and literary critic, Paul Ricœur called a certain 'distancing' or distinguishing between author and text, as well as between text and successive readers.[6]

Interpreting the Bible through Authorial Intention

In a study of literary theory that first appeared in 1967, Eric Donald Hirsch argued that a text means and continues to mean only what its author originally intended to communicate (the *intentio auctoris* alone). As he put it tersely, 'a text means what its author meant'.[7] He supposed the meaning to remain immutable, and simply resistant to historical change and reinterpretation in the ever-changing contexts of human history. For Hirsch, his predecessors, and his followers, 'meaning is unchangeable because it is always the intentional act of an individual at some particular point of time'.[8]

For this theory, valid interpretation involves meaning being conveyed from one set of minds, those of the historical authors, to another (later) set of minds, those of the readers. When reading and interpreting the biblical texts, contemporary exegetes and other readers have the task of grasping and restating what was in the minds of the sacred authors and what they consciously wished to convey.

Any pursuit of the *intentio auctoris* seeks to identify the meaning that the authors had in mind when they wrote the texts that we now read. Hirsch hammered those who disdained such pursuit and claimed that the meaning of a text is completely 'independent of the authorial will' and 'the author's control'.[9] He had no time for those who championed an 'authorial irrelevance' and 'ruthlessly' banished the author as 'the

---

[5] Even if it does not use the terminology of a triple *intentio*, what the Commission says about the historical-critical method (34–41), various approaches to the text (50–69), and methods involving readers (41–50, 86–7, 117–19) corresponds, respectively, to the *intentio auctoris*, the *intentio textus*, and the *intentio legentis*.

[6] Ibid. 74–5.

[7] H. D. Hirsch, *Validity in Interpretation* (New Haven, CT: Yale University Press, 1967), 1.

[8] T. Eagleton, *Literary Theory: An Introduction*, 2nd edn (Oxford: Blackwell, 1996), 61.

[9] Hirsch, *Validity in Interpretation*, x, 1; he obviously took aim at those classified under 'the New Criticism'.

determiner of his [!] text's meaning'.[10] Yet joining Hirsch in establishing and honouring, to the extent that we can,[11] the intention of the authors should not exclude *also* looking beyond them for further meanings in the texts they produced. We do not face an 'all or nothing' choice: *either* the only normative principle for expounding the meaning of a text is the authorial intention (Hirsch), or this *intentio auctoris* is simply irrelevant for the task of interpretation (the followers of the so-called New Criticism).

This chapter will present an integral, 'both/and' situation. Both (a) the *intentio auctoris* and (b) the *intentio legentis* and the *intentio textus ipsius* should be examined and respected.

Although he does not mention Hirsch's *Validity of Interpretation*, Nicholas Wolterstorff seems not too far from endorsing his view on authorial intention. Wolterstorff rightly criticizes the ways Jacques Derrida could ride roughshod over what authors intended to say,[12] but he presses too far the claims and responsibilities of authorial intentions. He argues, for instance, that speakers/writers must 'take expected audience reaction into account'.[13] St Paul, to be sure, needed to take into account reactions to the letters that he sent to far-flung communities. But how, in general, could he and other sacred authors be expected to anticipate audience and reader reaction down through the centuries? Could the psalmists have anticipated what the Letter to the Hebrews would do with their verses by putting them into the mouths of the Father, Son, and Holy Spirit (see Chapter 2 above)? Could Paul have anticipated Martin Luther's reading of the Letter to the Galatians (see Chapter 4 above)? At best, taking into account

[10] Ibid. 2, 5. Eagleton describes the view Hirsch defended: 'if we do not choose to respect the author's intention, then we have no "norm" of interpretation, and risk opening the floodgates to critical anarchy'. In short, we would 'open the door to complete relativism' (*Literary Theory*, 60, 61).

[11] I speak of establishing the intention of the authors 'to the extent that we can'. In the case of some or even many biblical texts (e.g. Genesis) the personal identity and many of the circumstances of the authors seem lost forever. Nevertheless, something of their intention emerges from the texts they produced.

[12] N. Wolterstorff, *Divine Discourse: Philosophical Reflections on the Claim that God Speaks* (Cambridge: Cambridge University Press, 1993), 153–70.

[13] Ibid. 199.

expected audience reaction is a limited enterprise.[14] What then should be said about the claims of the biblical authors and their world (the scriptural *intentio auctoris* examined by the work of historical-critical exegesis), an area in which since 1971 I have continued to write every now and then?[15]

The first task involves understanding and clarifying, to the degree we can do so, the historical origins of the final form of biblical texts and, above all, what their authors intended to communicate: that is to say, their original, literal meaning and message.[16] In the world in which they wrote and employing the resources of their culture and religious community, what did the sacred writers wish to communicate and 'fix' in their texts for the specific audiences for which they wrote (to the extent that we can establish the identity and nature of these audiences)? Their meaning was generated and expressed by their choice of genre (e.g. a psalm or a letter), the goals to which they directed themselves, the judgements they made, the responsibility they assumed by asserting some truth-claims, the invitations they conveyed, and the commitments in which their texts involved them (e.g. an apostle's mission).

Obviously the sacred authors' meaning did not coincide in a simplistic way with the wording they adopted. The literary and religious conventions of the thought-world of biblical times (e.g. the traditions for composing psalms), as well as what we might learn about an

---

[14] Something similar happens in the area of those who draft legislation; they cannot foresee 'every possible contingency or circumstance that might arrive' (D. C. Pearce and R. S. Geddes, *Statutory Interpretation in Australia*, 7th edn (Chatswood, NSW: LexisNexis Butterworths, 2011), 5).

[15] See, among other articles, G. O'Collins, 'Power Made Perfect in Weakness: 2 Cor. 12: 9–10', *Catholic Biblical Quarterly* 33 (1971), 185–95; G. O'Collins, 'The Appearances of the Risen Christ: A Lexical-Exegetical Examination of St Paul and other Witnesses', *Irish Theological Quarterly* 79 (2014), 128–43; G. O'Collins, 'Collaborators of the Apostles', *Irish Theological Quarterly* 82 (2017), 185–96; G. O'Collins, 'The Ecclesiology of the General Epistles (James, 1 Peter, Hebrews, Jude, and 2 Peter)', in P. D. L. Avis (ed.), *Oxford Handbook of Ecclesiology* (Oxford: Oxford University Press, forthcoming in 2018).

[16] Here 'literal' does not mean falling into the errors of fundamentalism and taking texts 'literalistically', or in a wooden fashion that 'explains' parables (e.g. the Book of Jonah) and apocalypses (e.g. the Book of Revelation) as if they were historical or predictive texts, respectively.

author's particular life-setting (e.g. that of Ben Sira and Paul), offer indispensable guides towards recovering what these writers wanted to say when they used the words they did. Here exegetes and interpreters must allow for a certain imprecision both in the 'original' intention and audience. We may not presuppose that the original meaning was always sharply defined, as if it could be precisely recovered and exactly paraphrased. This is particularly true when we face poetic and imaginative texts (e.g. in the prophetic books). Poetic images can baffle those who want to settle *the meaning* of a text. The original audience likewise was often not a single, clearly demarcated group, made up of readers and hearers of uniform convictions and needs.

We call this exegesis *historical*, because it tries to leap over the temporal and cultural gap that separates us from the authors and return imaginatively to the contexts in which the texts were formed and fashioned. Many difficulties attend this exercise. Working in the twenty-first century, how can scholars recapture the intentions of authors, often unknown or difficult to identify, who wrote twenty centuries ago or more and in a very different kind of world? Yet we should not discount (a) the basic human affinity between the biblical authors and modern interpreters and (b) that mutual understanding established by sharing in the same faith. Such a common faith can help contemporary readers enter into the world and mind-set of the authors.

We call this exegesis *critical*, because it requires professional knowledge of biblical languages and times, as well as a balanced judgement that can assess the evidence. The historical-critical method, which attempts to clarify the *intentio auctoris*, remains essential but insufficient: one should not unilaterally overstate the case for it. Many of its conclusions remain tentative and may not be proposed as 'assured results'. In fact, such conclusions range from the highly probable through the possible to the highly unlikely.

Those who continue to press one-sidedly the need to concentrate simply on the *intentio auctoris* sometimes seem to fear that otherwise interpreters will be 'free to read into a text whatever they like'.[17] But the interaction between readers and texts is constrained by practices,

---

[17] S. Fish, *Doing What Comes Naturally: Change, Rhetoric, and the Practice of Theory in Literary and Legal Studies* (Oxford: Clarendon, 1985), 97.

shared presuppositions, and a whole history of procedure. Readers who construe texts to produce meanings that prove unreasonable, 'unnatural', and who even contradict what the original authors patently intended lose credibility with their peers and the wider public. Admittedly, the precise limits of what is reasonable and 'natural' can be controversial. Yet some interpretations go so far as to disqualify themselves by appearing tortured and even absurd. I think here of Jacques Derrida's sexual 'interpretation' of Revelation 22: 17 ('the Spirit and the bride say, "Come", and let everyone who hears say "Come"').[18] It is a gross example of unchecked reader freedom that manipulates the meaning of the text and remakes the text in its own image.

intentio textus

As Hans-Georg Gadamer and other philosophers and literary critics have maintained, all written documents enjoy a potential for developments in meaning beyond what authors expressed in particular situations for specific audiences (the *intentio auctoris*).[19] Texts can communicate more than their writers ever consciously knew or meant. Thus the biblical texts gained a life of their own, a 'reception history', as they distanced themselves from their original authors and addressees, entered new contexts, and found later readers and hearers.[20] This

[18]   Sir Anthony Kenny reports this 'counterfeit' explanation: 'Derrida has written at length on the text, making great play with the double entendre that attaches, in French and English, to the word "come" [. . .] the Greek word translated "come" cannot possibly have the sense of "achieve orgasm"' (*A New History of Western Philosophy* (Oxford: Clarendon, 2010), 827–8).

[19]   Gadamer states a universally valid principle: 'not just occasionally but always, the meaning of a text goes beyond its author'. In repeating this point, he adds that texts also become independent from their addressees (e.g. Philemon to whom Paul sent a letter, and Theophilus to whom Luke dedicated his two-part work): 'the horizon of understanding cannot be limited either by what the writer originally had in mind, or by the horizon of the person to whom the text was originally addressed'. Hence Gadamer argues that 'reconstructing what the author really had in mind is at best a limited undertaking' (*Truth and Method*, trans. J. Weinsheimer and D. G. Marshall, rev. edn (New York: Crossroad, 1989), 296, 373, 395).

[20]   See M. Lieb, E. Mason, and J. Roberts (eds), *The Oxford Handbook of the Reception History of the Bible* (Oxford: Oxford University Press, 2011). We could

happened, as we saw in Chapter 3 above, when the first Christians read and reread their inherited Jewish Scriptures (e.g. Matthew, Paul, and the author of the Book of Revelation). It continued to happen when these Scriptures and the twenty-seven books that came to be known as the New Testament were read and applied to practice over nearly two thousand years in a changing church and a changing world.

To begin with, the physical form in which Christians met the Scriptures changed. Where Jewish sacred texts, like the Torah and the prophets (see Luke 4: 17–20), were copied onto scrolls (of six to eight metres length or even longer), Christians used codices, bound volumes that resemble modern books. The inspired texts were collected into one volume, first the letters of Paul and the four Gospels, and eventually the whole Bible, as in the famous biblical codices of the fourth and fifth centuries (the Codex Sinaiticus, the Codex Vaticanus, and the Codex Alexandrinus). While even those three codices were not perfectly uniform in their collection of canonical texts and in the order of arrangement, they signalled the arrival of the Bible as we know it today—a single volume containing the inspired and inspiring texts of the Old and New Testaments.[21]

After emerging 'diachronically' over many centuries, the inspired texts through being bound together invited a 'synchronic' reading. Published in a one-volume edition, the biblical texts were presented as forming a single, if diversified, canon, in which individual texts illuminated the meaning of other texts and were in turn illuminated by them. That is the way in which readers continue to meet these sacred texts, physically joined together in a mutually illuminating and

---

well prefer here the term *Wirkungsgeschichte* (effective history or history of effects), which we mentioned initially in Chapter 2; it focuses more on the inspiring power and impact of the sacred texts than on the active receptivity of the readers. *The Rubáiyát of Omar Khayyám*, in the translation by Edward Fitzgerald, classically depicts the freedom of any published text: 'The Moving Finger writes; and, having writ, / Moves on: nor all your Piety nor Wit / Shall lure it back to cancel half a Line, / Nor all your tears wash out a word of it' (quatrain LX).

[21] See L. W. Hurtado and C. Keith, 'Writing and Book Production in the Hellenistic and Roman Periods', in J. C. Paget and J. Schaper (eds), *The New Cambridge History of the Bible*, i (Cambridge: Cambridge University Press, 2012), 63–80.

enriching canon, in which previously unexpected associations and fresh meanings can catch our eyes.

Fidelity in copying the inspired texts ensured in general that they were transmitted more or less intact.[22] In the quest to establish the oldest recoverable text, however, there are difficulties with some books, for instance Jeremiah and the Acts of the Apostles. Social, theological, and other factors could affect the transmission and development of texts, which experienced a history inseparable from the history of local communities. Nevertheless, the Qumran caves (for the Old Testament) and the Bodmer Papyri, Chester Beatty Papyri, and other sources for the New Testament, which go back to AD 200 or even earlier, yield a wealth of early witnesses incomparably older and richer than those for the Latin and Greek classics.

It was regularly in new cultural and historical *contexts*, which left behind the foundational, first century of Christianity, that the texts (either singly or collectively) were read and their message interpreted. Around AD 100, a history of reception began, which not only discovered latent meanings in the biblical texts but also gave them new meanings, never anticipated by the authors and their original audiences in their particular religious, social, and historical conditions. Once published, the inspired texts began a 'decontextualized' history and opened themselves to unlimited readers and an unlimited series of readings in innumerably different contexts.

This history of textual reception of the Bible may concern even a single word and can remind us that every word is latently rich in meaning. Chapter 2 cited the example of a word found twenty-four times in the Psalms, 'Alleluia' or 'Hallelujah', which has enjoyed a remarkable 'history of effects'. We can also recall the example of the very name of 'Jesus', used 993 times in the New Testament and having a unique impact in the post-apostolic Church. Another, much lesser, example comes from the Book of Revelation, which places the inaugural vision of John the divine on Patmos (Rev. 1: 9), the only time this

---

[22] See B. M. Metzger, *The Text of the New Testament: Its Transmission, Corruption, and Restoration*, 4th edn (New York: Oxford University Press, 2005); B. M. Metzger, *A Textual Commentary on the Greek New Testament* (Stuttgart: United Bible Societies, 1994); D. C. Parker, 'The New Testament Texts and Versions', *New Cambridge History of the Bible*, i, 412–54.

island is mentioned in the New Testament. A recent study has brilliantly traced the reception of 'Patmos' in the history of Christian literature and art, a reception that both found meaning in and gave meaning to this one word.[23]

No less than other texts, the books of the Bible illustrate the truth of what Paul Ricœur wrote: 'the meaning of what has been written down is henceforth separate from the possible intentions of the authors [...] What we call the semantic autonomy of the text means that the text unfolds a history distinct from that of the authors'.[24] In short, 'what the text signifies no longer coincides with what the author[s] meant'.[25] Ricœur cited the view of Hirsch (see above) and firmly rejected it: 'the problem of the right understanding [of a text] can no longer be solved by a simple return to the alleged intention of an author'.[26] Even where we can establish to our satisfaction what an author (e.g. Luke or Paul) intended, their intentions do not enjoy a one-sided privilege, let alone an exclusive role, when interpreting the texts they composed.

Add too that, unlike the interpretation of purely literary texts but like the interpretation of legal statutes, the interpretation of biblical texts does not remain a merely mental exercise but leads to application and action. To put this in more solemn terms, understanding and interpreting the Scriptures call for 'decisional' hermeneutics and not merely 'speculative' ones. Interpreting biblical texts involves allowing oneself to be interpreted by the texts. Appropriate interpretation cannot take place if readers refuse to allow their self-understanding to be challenged and changed by these texts. Being grasped by the meaning of the sacred texts takes precedence over grasping their meaning.

When, after many centuries of Christianity and world history, we try to understand biblical texts, the 'effective history' of these texts always influences us, whether we are aware of this or not. Interpreting,

---

[23] K. Boxall, *Patmos in the Reception History of the Apocalypse* (Oxford: Oxford University Press, 2013).

[24] P. Ricœur, *Hermeneutics*, trans. D. Pellauer (Cambridge: Polity, 2013), 12.

[25] P. Ricœur, *Hermeneutics and the Human Sciences: Essays on Language, Action, Interpretation*, ed. and trans. J. B. Thompson (Cambridge: Cambridge University Press, 1981), 139.

[26] Ibid. 211.

for instance, the meeting between Christ and Mary Magdalene (John 20: 11–18) will be affected by the celebration of her feast (22 July), by artistic representations of the scene (e.g. by Cranach, El Greco, Beato Angelico, Grünewald, Perugino, Titian, Veronese, and Rogier van der Weyden), by legends about her, by churches and colleges that bear her name, and, not least at times, by the misguided identification of her with 'the woman who was a sinner' and anointed Christ's feet in Luke 7: 37.

Originally graced in their composition by an effective input from the Holy Spirit, the Scriptures proved richly *graced* as bearers of later illumination and redemption, mediated through their use in the liturgy, preaching, catechesis, theology, and the whole life of the Church. Despite the sin, corruption, and ineptitude that has disfigured the post-New Testament, dependent phase of revelation, the Holy Spirit has continued to guide the interpretation and use of the Scriptures. It is the same Spirit who once and for all inspired the original writing of those Scriptures, a composition period that closed with the time of Christ and the apostolic Church.

Two thousand years of biblical reflection and interpretation have been marred by neglect, decadent formalism, and the misinterpretation of the Scriptures in bad causes. Yet the patristic witnesses, the followers of St Benedict and St Scholastica, the best of the medieval theologians, the *devotio moderna* of Thomas à Kempis, the Reformers' return to the Scriptures, mystics of every age, and the impact of the Bible on Christian liturgy, hymns, and art reveal the enduring and pluriform vitality of the inspired texts (see Chapter 4 above). The history of the Church, East and West, and her tradition are to be evaluated through her attention to and interpretation of those texts. We might even describe tradition as the Church's collective experience of the Bible.

Above I spoke of challenges and changes happening when readers allow the biblical texts to exercise some control over their response. This brings us to the third major theme in my view of interpretation.

intentio legentis

Any text remains incomplete, un-interpreted, and unrealized until it is read and read closely. Texts need readers and readers need texts.

There is reciprocal relationship between texts and readers. Texts do not 'have' meaning before they are read and interpreted. Meaning emerges when texts are reflected upon, discussed, and applied. For meaning to happen, readers are just as necessary as authors. Hence any adequate view of interpretation, biblical or otherwise, must also attend to the 'intention' of successive readers. Faced with scriptural texts, this 'intention' (*intentio legentis*) comes into play through activating potential meanings of the texts, produced by the sacred writers (*intentio auctoris*) and interpreted during many centuries of reception history (*intentio textus*). Meaning occurs as readers discover, liberate, and recreate the sense of the text in (and to some extent from) their own contexts. Thus the Scriptures do not remain imprisoned in the past but engage with the present.

What do I expect from contemporary readers of the Scriptures? In seeking to appropriate biblical texts by establishing their meaning and truth, they should do so in the spirit of 'faith seeking understanding'.[27] They carry on their interpreting within the faith community and out of faith in the Holy Spirit, who guided the writing of the Scriptures and, despite human limitations and failures, has guided their interpretation through the living tradition of the Church. As St Jerome taught, the Sacred Scripture is to be read and interpreted in the same Spirit through whom it was written.[28] The Holy Spirit, who was at work in forming the biblical texts, continues to work in arousing faith through them. Those texts expressed and interpreted various religious experiences 'then', and will generate similar religious experiences 'now'. The Bible is truly what it is only when readers and hearers open themselves to its impact and let its consequences work themselves out in their worship and practice. The self-manifestation of the tripersonal God, effected through the inspiring work of the Holy

---

[27] This appropriation should also be done in the spirit of 'worship seeking understanding' and 'justice seeking understanding'; see G. O'Collins, *Rethinking Fundamental Theology: Toward a New Fundamental Theology* (Oxford: Oxford University Press, 2011), 323–9.

[28] *In Epistolam ad Galatas*, 5. 19–21; *PL* 26, 445A. The Second Vatican Council's Constitution on Divine Revelation (*Dei Verbum*, art. 12, n. 9) refers to this passage in Jerome, but inaccurately gives the reference as *PL* 26, 417A.

Spirit, takes precedence over any readerly activity. The biblical text shapes the reader more than the reader shapes the text.

Exegesis apart from the faith community means exegesis apart from the Spirit who gave the community those Scriptures, dwells with and in that community, and facilitates the never-ending and life-giving appropriation of the Scriptures. Numerous biblical commentators, however, distance themselves from any such confessional approach. They aspire to an objectivity that would eliminate the subjective dimension. They do their work in the name of a descriptive, impartial, independent, and scholarly research proper to allegedly disengaged reason. Their ideal practitioners are free, rational, and enlightened spectators who, emancipated from all authority and open to an 'objective' grasp of things, promise to provide the public with 'the assured results' of scholarship. What are their results like?

Let me take one example: *Five Gospels: The Search for the Authentic Words of Jesus*, edited by R. W. Funk, R. W. Hoover, and the Jesus Seminar.[29] This volume in collaboration purports to take an unbiased and 'properly' sceptical stance when treating the four Gospels and one non-canonical Gospel (the so-called Gospel of Thomas, of which the Greek original probably dates to around AD 150). It presupposes that a religiously neutral, independent, and non-traditional interpretation of the Scriptures will provide a more reliable guide to Jesus and the biblical origins of Christianity than any interpretations coming from those who are religiously committed and interpret the Gospels within a living tradition. Many leading exegetes, like Hans-Dieter Betz, Raymond Brown, James Dunn, and John Meier, have convincingly disputed detail after detail in the results of the Jesus Seminar. Theologians and others find much more reliable guides to the Gospels in the commentaries by Ulrich Luz and John Nolland (Matthew), Joel Marcus and Francis Moloney (Mark), John Nolland and Robert Tannehill (Luke), and Brendan Byrne and Andrew Lincoln (John), as well as in recent books about the historical Jesus (by Richard Bauckham, James Dunn, Paul Eddy with Gregory Boyd, Craig Keener, and Tom Wright). The central difficulty with the work of

---

[29] (New York: Macmillan, 1993). See reviews by R. B. Hays, *First Things* 43 (May 1994), 43–8; G. O'Collins, *The Tablet* (17 September 1994), 1170.

the Jesus Seminar is that their methodology expected far too much from merely 'objective' procedures. Such procedures might yield some specific results but hardly any valuable insights into the life of the Gospel texts as a whole.

Let us introduce an analogy from another, somewhat similar discipline: literary criticism. An allegedly 'scientifically objective', disengaged approach could establish the date of the composition of *Macbeth* and various sources used by Shakespeare. But only a responsive, imaginative, and participatory approach that invests us in taking over the text will give some true perspectives on the whole play, and an appropriate insight into the heart of the tragedy. Those who study great dramas in libraries but steadily refuse to attend the theatre and share in the living tradition of acting and production are hardly likely to become valuable critics of drama. Without a love for literature and a living affinity with it, we cannot expect to relate to the great texts and expound them in any truly meaningful way. It is precisely a loving affinity that provides the proper and privileged condition for understanding and assessing great works of literature.

In a similar fashion, a merely 'objective' method chokes the voice of the biblical texts, and declines to face them for what they are: extraordinary religious, ecclesial, and theological works. To ignore as an irrelevance the spiritual message of the Scriptures is a little like reading Shakespeare while sedulously ignoring the poetry and drama. This inappropriate method reminds me of scholars who used Homer's *Iliad* as a guide to the archaeology and history of ancient Troy and steadfastly refused to face and read the first and perhaps greatest epic poem of Western literature for what it primarily was/is: a richly illuminating masterpiece on the enduring human themes of life, love, breakdown in relationships, violence, and death. Likewise a religiously neutral, disinterested, and 'objective' interpretation misuses the Scriptures by taking them as presenting mere historical problems and puzzles rather than as setting us in front of the supreme interpersonal mystery: the encounter between God and human readers. True and life-giving knowledge of God and ourselves is available only by personal participation. The Scriptures are in the business of furthering such self-knowledge and knowledge of God (and not merely knowledge about God).

Nothing of what I have just written should be construed as attacking the historical-critical method as such; it rightly concerns itself with the genesis and authorial meaning of our biblical texts. To limit oneself, however, to making historical judgements from a merely 'scientific' perspective is not only a technique for avoiding the real thrust of texts but is also an illusion. Whether they like it or not, biblical scholars are always doing more than simply stating what some texts meant and then paraphrasing them. After the work of Albert Einstein, Werner Heisenberg, Max Planck, and others, natural scientists have come to terms with the fact that observers (along with the instruments they choose) belong to the process of investigation. All human knowledge, including the knowledge of physics, chemistry, and the biological sciences, remains participatory and personal.[30] There is an inevitable relationship between the observer and the observed. Even more so in historical study, including the study of Scriptures, the subject is necessarily and properly involved—with his or her questions, beliefs, values, inherited traditions, and presuppositions.[31] Historical understanding and interpretation always remain subjective, even when (or especially when?) historians and biblical scholars deny that this is so. Any search for the meaning of biblical and other texts is essentially conditioned by the situation of the one doing the searching.

This chapter has aimed at upholding the claims of (a) the *intentio auctoris* against those who flatly ignore the intentions of the original authors, of (b) the *intentio textus* against those who deny the control that the texts should exercise over readers, and of (c) the *intentio legentis* against those who play down subjectivity and allege an illusory, 'scientific' objectivity. Readers of the Bible should listen and 'correspond' to the texts, through which they can hear the voices of the original authors, the voices of Church interpretation down through the ages, and, above all, the inspiring voice of the Holy Spirit speaking

[30] See the work of a natural scientist turned philosopher, Michael Polanyi (1891–1976), *Personal Knowledge* (London: Routledge, 1962).

[31] See two classical studies of this issue: R. Bultmann, 'Is Exegesis without Presuppositions Possible?', *Existence and Faith: Shorter Writings of Rudolf Bultmann*, trans. S. M. Ogden (London: Hodder & Stoughton, 1961), 289–96; G. Ebeling, 'The Significance of the Critical Historical Method for Church and Theology in Protestantism', *Word and Faith*, trans. J. W. Leitch (London: SCM Press, 1963), 17–61.

today. Letting themselves be encountered by the Bible and expecting that the Bible will speak to them with authority, theologians and other readers allow the scriptural texts in all their 'otherness' to convey meaning, disclose truth, and authoritatively transform ideas, interest, and practices. In the words of St Ambrose of Milan, 'when we pray we address God; when we read the divine words we listen to him' (*De Officiis Ministrorum*, 1. 20. 88).

10

Ten Principles for Theologians
Interpreting the Scriptures

In the recent and present state of theology it is painfully obvious that the Scriptures have often been used incoherently or at least inconsistently and inaccurately. Some theologians claim to enlist support from biblical scholars, but in fact limit themselves to reading one or two authors. That practice risks taking over into theology the adventurous and even maverick opinions advanced by an individual biblical scholar or by a small group with its own particular agenda. To some extent Edward Schillebeeckx did just that in his work on Christology.[1] The same regrettable tendency of some theologians to consult only one or two biblical scholars and naively adopt their views was detailed in a study by Nunzio Capizzi of the use of Philippians 2: 6–11 in some modern works in Christology.[2] This chapter aims to help theologians to avoid misinterpreting the Scriptures, and to improve the passage from the Bible to systematic theology, a passage that has not always been negotiated skilfully. Admitting that the Scriptures are not always readily

---

[1] E. Schillebeeckx, *Jesus: An Experiment in Christology*, trans. H. Hoskins (New York: Seabury, 1979). In a review (*Catholic Biblical Quarterly* 42 (1980), 421–3), R. E. Brown regretted Schillebeeckx's one-sided reliance on N. Perrin, S. Schulz, T. J. Weeden, and others—that is to say, a reliance on what F. Kerr (*New Blackfriars* 60 (1979), 549–52) called 'the extremely fragile and arguable hypotheses of his [Schillebeeckx's] favourite exegetes'. In their reviews, R. H. Fuller (*Interpretation* 34 (1980), 293–6) and A. E. Harvey (*Journal of Theological Studies* 51 (1980), 598–60) also noted the way in which Schillebeeckx, even if claiming to do his own exegesis, in fact followed the quite dubious views of a few other exegetes.

[2] N. Capizzi, *L'uso di Fil. 2, 6–11 nella cristologia contemporanea (1965–93)* (Rome: Gregorian University Press, 1997).

intelligible, I will suggest ten principles that should guide any theological appropriation of them.[3]

1. The Principle of Faithful Hearing

Theologians are called to be *faithful hearers of the Word*, oriented primarily towards the scriptural texts (rather than towards themselves), and responsive primarily to the meaning they discover and receive rather than the meaning they construct and create for themselves. They read the whole Bible with consent (and not with suspicion) and with the expectation that, being imbued with the true, good, and beautiful God, it can say something to them that they have never heard before. Aware of the immense spiritual richness of the Scriptures, they expectantly engage with the Bible and its inexhaustible meaning. They come face to face with the biblical text and are 'answerable' to that text. St Augustine of North Africa exemplifies the exposure to the Scriptures all theologians need: in his extant writings he quotes or echoes over half of the verses in the Bible. His example invites theologians to hear again the voice crying out '*tolle et lege* (take and read)'.[4]

This first principle moves close to a practice launched by Origen in the third century, central to the Benedictine tradition, and widely revived in modern times: *lectio divina* or *lectio sacra* (divine reading or sacred reading).[5] This spiritual practice involves quietly reading the Sacred Scriptures for transformation rather than information, surrendering ourselves to what we read, and allowing ourselves to be guided or 'inspired' by the Holy Spirit. Letting the Scriptures question us will shape us. The practice of *lectio divina* overlaps with the requirements of my first principle.

[3] See A. Paddison (ed.), *Theologians on Scripture* (New York: Bloomsbury, 2016). Some of the material on these principles will be adapted from G. O'Collins and D. Kendall, *The Bible for Theology* (Mahwah, NJ: Paulist Press, 1997).

[4] St Augustine, *The Confessions*, 8. 29; trans. M. Boulding (Hyde Park, NY: New City Press, 1997), 206–7. In *Saint Augustine on the Resurrection of Christ* (Oxford: Oxford University Press, 2017), I have expounded Augustine's use of the Gospels, Paul, and the other Scriptures that witness to and illuminate the resurrection of Jesus.

[5] See J. Rousse et al., 'Lectio divina et lecture spirituelle', *Dictionnaire de Spiritualité*, ix (Paris: Beauchesne, 1976), col. 470–510.

My first principle opposes the practice of theologians and other writers who take little notice of the Scriptures, force them into their closed 'orthodoxies',[6] or make them mean just about anything they want them to endorse. Such theologians draw from the Bible what they have already decided to say. Thus Robert Funk enlisted Jesus in support of recreational sex, or what he called 'responsible, protected recreational sex between consenting adults'.[7] This risks turning the Scriptures into a series of Rorschach inkblots that call up merely individual, purely projective interpretations. Should one raise here the question of ethics in biblical reception—moral rules that should guide our meeting with the Bible? May we remake the text and invent its meaning in our own image? Sadly, leading publishing houses are not averse to putting out books that 'remake' what the biblical texts have to say.[8]

Some build such practice into theory, claiming that authors have no rights, texts belong absolutely to readers, and texts may be used (or misused?) in whatever ways readers choose. In the name of excavating for the hidden subtext, some critics dismantle biblical and other texts, let meanings proliferate, and come up with an uncheckable range of

---

[6] In a lecture given recently in London, a well-known cardinal explained that Matthew 22: 14 ('many are called but few are chosen') supported his view that, according to Jesus, many people will in fact be condemned forever to the pains of hell. But this conclusion to the parable of the wedding feast (Matt. 22: 1–14) is a *apocalyptic warning* rather than a prediction of what will happen. Jonah announced that in forty days Nineveh would be destroyed—a divine threat that in fact was not carried out, since the Ninevites repented en masse; see G. O'Collins, *Salvation for All: God's other Peoples* (Oxford: Oxford University Press, 2008), 36–41; U. Luz, *Matthew 21–28*, trans. J. E. Crouch (Minneapolis: Fortress Press, 2005), 57. A conservative exegete, John Nolland expounds the enigmatic verse as saying: 'not all those who are "called" will turn out to be "chosen"' (*The Gospel of Matthew: A Commentary on the Greek Text* (Grand Rapids, MI: Eerdmans, 2005), 894–5, at 895.

[7] R. W. Funk, *Honest to Jesus: Jesus for a New Millennium* (San Francisco: Harper San Francisco, 1996), 314.

[8] See G. Vermes, *The Resurrection* (New York: Doubleday, 2008); and R. Aslan, *Zealot: The Life and Times of Jesus of Nazareth* (New York: Random House, 2013). On Vermes' book, see G. O'Collins, *Believing in the Resurrection: The Meaning and Promise of the Risen Jesus* (Mahwah, NJ: Paulist Press, 2012), 20–2; on Aslan's book, see the Appendix below.

alternative explanations.[9] Such total reader-freedom dominates the texts and turns interpretation into mere reflections of a particular community or of an individual's interests and experiences. It espouses an extreme form of reader-response that constructs meaning without being in any way rooted in the texts read; meaning is simply what the reader makes of the texts. This approach not only worried such a secular literary critic as Umberto Eco,[10] but can also be turned against those who espouse such freedom. If we may interpret the meaning of texts quite independently of those who produced them, and if meaning in no sense inheres in the texts themselves, we readers can give free rein to our projective interpretations of *these modern critics* and make *their texts mean whatever fits our purposes*. Pure reader-freedom is a self-destructing theory, as well as an unethical one. We should neither arbitrarily manipulate the meaning of texts (the *intentio textus*) nor do violence to what the authors originally intended to communicate (the *intentio auctoris*), to the extent that we can establish it.

Theories of reader-oriented and reader-created meaning, where texts almost inevitably become reader-manipulated, are even less appropriate in the case of the Scriptures. There, if anywhere, readers should be listening and 'corresponding' to the texts, through which they can hear the voices of the sacred authors, the voices of tradition down through the centuries, and, above all, the voice of the Holy Spirit. Letting themselves be encountered by the Bible and expecting something new from their reading, and especially from those sections which have the closest relationship to God's self-revelation, theologians allow the scriptural texts in all their otherness and strangeness to convey meaning, disclose truth, and authoritatively transform theological ideas, interests, and practice.

Only those who let themselves be addressed and judged by the Bible will notice, for instance, where their routine appeals to certain scriptural texts enjoy little more validity than ingrained habits, fostered

---

[9] See the anonymous editorial 'What's Wrong with Deconstructionism', *American Philosophical Quarterly* 29 (1992), 193–5; and A. C. Thiselton's critical evaluation of Jacques Derrida in *New Horizons in Hermeneutics* (London: HarperCollins, 1992), 103–32, 472–4, 582–92.

[10] U. Eco, *Interpretation and Overinterpretation* (Cambridge: Cambridge University Press, 1992), 23.

perhaps by some merely doctrinaire and inadequate tradition. Only those theologians consistently open to revelatory encounters effected by the Bible will cherish their work as a process in which their interpretation can never enjoy final, still less definitive, status (see principle seven below).

2. The Principle of Active Hearing

Along with an obedient openness, theologians should also be active, responsive, and 'answerable' interpreters of the Scriptures, and not merely passive, purely receptive hearers of the Word, who woodenly repeat biblical texts in a formal way and do not 'give' them anything or 'complete' them in any way. Hearing the Scriptures lets these inspired texts preserve the identity of Christian theology; yet these same texts must be constantly and freshly reappropriated as the living Word of God for today.[11]

This second principle calls for choice, creativity, coherence, and a self-awareness about one's experiences, presuppositions, questions, and interpretative framework. Theology, like art, dies in the hands of those who are content to do little more than turn out the motifs already crafted by their predecessors. Inventiveness let Albrecht Dürer (1471–1528) break through to something new in the history of Western art. His innovative woodcuts depicting Christ's birth, life, death, and resurrection gave him an honourable place in the story of Christian spirituality and theology. With his genius Dürer illustrated admirably another aspect of great innovation, be it artistic or theological: developing individual themes, he set out a coherent whole. When drawing on the Scriptures, theologians must inevitably attend to specific texts and themes. But brilliant creativity shows through when the particular biblical items are coherently related to the whole.

Theological activity requires appropriate choices among the methods suited to the different texts of the Bible. Narrative criticism can illuminate, for instance, historical books of the Old Testament;

---

[11] Thomas Aquinas proved an outstanding example of such 'active hearing'; on the need to read his biblical commentaries as well as his systematic works, see J.-P. Torrell, *Saint Thomas Aquinas*, i: *The Person and his Work*, trans. R. Royal (Washington, DC: Catholic University of America Press, 2005), 54–9.

rhetorical criticism has its value in interpreting the Pauline letters.[12] The divergent nature of parables, hymns, prophetic texts, apocalyptic literature, and wisdom texts—to cite some major examples—must obviously affect the methods used for interpreting and appropriating them in theology. Some texts, like the kerygmatic passages about Christ's death and resurrection (e.g. 1 Cor. 15: 3–5), convey a meaningful message that calls for the response of faith. Other texts, like parables and apocalypses, aim at generating meaning by partly stimulating their readers and hearers to react. We interact with these texts to create fresh meaning, which, while not unconnected with the texts, is not simply 'there' waiting to be encountered. Active interpretation of the Scriptures by theologians also entails critical awareness of three items: their *interests*, *audiences*, and *contexts*.

Various interests activate theological practice. The reading purposes of theologians will vary according to their particular specialization in fundamental, historical, systematic, moral, pastoral, and spiritual theology.

Their audiences form an interpretative community who can relate the biblical texts to the changing realities of current Christian and world history and contemporary culture. Meaning is always, at least in part, a cultural and social phenomenon. Any cultural tradition will persistently help to shape a community's perception and interpretation of reality. This is not, however, to accept that the criteria of theologians' own culture and audiences should have sole, or even decisive, authority in appropriating the Scriptures.

[12] See Y. Amit and D. R. Bauer, 'Narrative Literature', in K. D. Sakenfeld (ed.), *The New Interpreter's Dictionary of the Bible*, iv (Nashville: Abingdon Press, 2009), 223–7; D. D. de Silva, 'Rhetorical Criticism', *OEBI*, ii, 273–83; D. N. Fewell and D. M. Gunn, 'Narrative, Hebrew', *ABD*, iv, 45; R. Majercik et al., 'Rhetoric and Rhetorical Criticism', ibid., v, 710–19; R. Rhoads, 'Narrative Criticism', *New Interpreter's Dictionary of the Bible*, iv, 222–3; R. C. Tannehill, 'Narrative Criticism', in R. J. Coggins and J. L. Houlden (eds), *A Dictionary of Biblical Interpretation* (London: SCM Press, 1990), 488–9; C. J. Sharp, 'Hebrew Biblical Narrative', *OEBA*, i, 406–17; P. K. Tull, 'Narrative Criticism and Narrative Hermeneutics', *OEBI*, ii, 37–46. For an excellent example of rhetorical criticism, see J.-N. Aletti, 'God Made Christ to be Sin (2 Corinthians 5: 21): Reflections on a Pauline Paradox', in S. T. Davis, D. Kendall, and G. O'Collins (eds), *The Redemption: An Interdisciplinary Symposium on Christ as Redeemer* (Oxford: Oxford University Press, 2004), 100–20.

The contexts for theologically interpreting the Scriptures move beyond (a) the chapel or church of the worshipping community[13] and (b) the study, the library, and the lecture hall. Theologians also discover the meaning and truth of biblical texts in (c) hospitals, prisons, refugee camps, countries ravaged by war, and scenes of mass hunger and starvation. Changes of context strikingly reveal how texts can express further ranges of meaning. We will make something different of Matthew 26: 52 ('all who take the sword will perish by the sword') if we study it at the Biblical Institute in Rome, or proclaim it in one of the enormous military cemeteries where the dead from the 1916 Battle of Verdun lie buried.[14]

An incident featuring a friend of mine exemplifies this point. One Saturday in 1968 several trade-union leaders in his parish were arrested for holding an illegal meeting. At the time his country was still ruled by a very right-wing government. The following day my friend used no words of his own in his sermon preached at the main parish Mass, but simply quoted such appropriate passages as these from the Old Testament:

> Then the Lord said, 'I have seen the affliction of my people who are in Egypt, and have heard their cry because of their taskmasters; I know their sufferings, and I have come down to deliver them out of the hands of the Egyptians' (Exod. 3: 7–8). Then the Lord said to Moses, 'Go in to Pharaoh and say to him: "Thus says the Lord, 'Let my people go'"'' (Exod. 8: 1). Woe to him who builds a town with blood and founds a city on iniquity (Hab. 2: 12).

On the following Monday morning, a police officer arrived with an order for the priest to present himself before a judge. After a preliminary hearing, my friend was charged with the tendentious use of the Scriptures. Eventually the case was dropped. One thing came through loud and clear. The government recognized the message of powerful

---

[13] The daily and Sunday readings at the Eucharist offer constant examples of contexts that affect meaning. By being inserted between the first reading and the Gospel (daily scheme) or between the Old Testament reading and the second reading (Sunday scheme), the psalms can receive fresh and even unexpected meanings.

[14] On the sword saying, see Luz, *Mathew 21–28*, 419–20; and Nolland, *Gospel of Matthew*, 1112–14.

protest those biblical texts carried in a specific context—the days following the arrest of trade-union leaders in a working-class suburb. The meaning conveyed in that context went far beyond anything envisaged by those who composed the passages from Exodus and Habakkuk well over two thousand years ago.

The Sacred Scriptures should be allowed to promote not only (a) the holiness of people gathered in liturgy to praise God and join Christ the High Priest in interceding for the world, and (b) a holy integrity of mind that shapes what theologians teach and write, but also (c) the practical holiness of those whose faith 'does justice' and strives to eliminate oppression and alleviate human suffering. Like musical scores the Scriptures remain incomplete if they are merely studied and not performed in liturgy and life, which can break open their multiple meanings.

Theologians encounter and interpret the vital potential of the Bible in three ways: (a) adoring on their knees and standing to sing hymns to God; (b) maintaining religious and intellectual honesty at the desks where they sit; and (c) being committed to serve in the mud of camps for asylum seekers and the overcrowded slums of mega-cities. Theologians' interpretation of scriptural texts constitutes both academic theory and prayerful and socially effective practice. The biblical texts make truth claims about reality—a truth to be, respectively, (a) prayed over (or worshipped as the divine Truth), (b) explored and understood, and (c) practised with steady commitment. These truth claims need to be pondered in the light of experiences of (a) worship, (b) an intellectual concern for truth, and (c) commitment to alleviate suffering and injustice. They will not yield their meaning to a closed community of interpreters who indulge vested interests by (i) manipulating biblical texts to illuminate their own experiences, legitimate their own programmes, and further their own ambitions, and by (ii) steadily ignoring the hopes and dreams of the young, the sufferings of exploited women and children, and the voices of those everywhere marginalized.

3. The Principle of the Community and its Creed

The Christian public as a worshipping, studying, and acting/suffering community brings to mind my third principle for the theological use of

the Scriptures: they are read and interpreted within the living community of faith[15] and in continuity with undivided Christianity's
creed. Primarily and indeed almost exclusively inspired by the Scriptures, the Apostles' Creed and the Nicene-Constantinopolitan Creed
normatively summarized the history of salvation and illuminated the
biblical texts by highlighting central truths about the tripersonal God
and human destiny. St Irenaeus (d. around AD 200) had insisted that
valid theological understanding is possible only within the hearing-
and reading-community of faith, guided by the rule of faith or the rule
of truth (*Adversus Haereses* 2. 27. 1; 3. 2. 1; 3. 15. 1).[16] Creeds emerged
and were taken not as substitutes for the Scriptures but as essential and
normative frames of reference guiding theological understanding and
interpretation within the mainline tradition.[17]

In his *Catecheses*, St Cyril of Jerusalem (d. 386) explained to his
baptismal candidates the creedal faith: 'the faith which the Church
hands down to you has all the authority of the Scriptures behind it
[. . .] This summary of our faith is not a merely human composition;
the more striking sayings of the Scriptures have been assembled
together to form the comprehensive statement' (5. 12–13). The
creedal faith of the community clarifies the Scriptures, and in its
turn is clarified by the Scriptures.

Having already been widely used during the Eucharist and at baptism for well over one thousand years, the Nicene-Constantinopolitan
Creed of AD 381 was adopted at the foundation of the World Council
of Churches in 1948. That creed, along with a common listening to the

---

[15] See the sixth thesis of E. E. Davis and R. B. Hays (eds), *The Art of Reading Scripture* (Grand Rapids, MI: Eerdmans, 2003), 3: 'Faithful interpretation of the Scripture invites and presupposes participation in the community brought into being by God's redemptive action—the Church.'

[16] This rule or truth of faith was the saving revelation of the Father, Son, and Holy Spirit in creation and redemption. To this truth, baptismal confession, the Scriptures, and orthodox preaching bore witness. For Irenaeus, the rule of faith coincided with the content of Scriptures, since God had ordered the biblical texts towards the divine self-manifestation.

[17] See F. E. Vokes et al., 'Apostolisches Glaubensbekenntnis', *TRE*, iii, 528–71; E. Lanczkowski et al., 'Glaubensbekenntnis(se)', *TRE*, xiii, 384–446; J. N. D. Kelly, *Early Christian Creeds*, 3rd edn (London: Longman, 1972). For very early creeds, see DzH 2, 10, 13, 16, 30, and 40; ND 1–6.

Scriptures, has worked towards healing divergences between Christian communities and ending their separation.

4. The Principle of Biblical Convergence

We come now to our fourth principle, that of convergence. Far from endorsing a biblical positivism that is content to pile up allegedly clear 'proof' texts, the principle of convergence involves letting the broadest and most varied array of scriptural witnesses bear on the theological question at issue. The opposite approach would be content to build a position out of one or two isolated biblical texts.

The principle of convergence emphasizes the unity of the canonical Scriptures more than their diversity, that unity effected by the Holy Spirit over against the diversity due to the human authors and the complex differences between the Old and New Testaments. To expect convergent biblical testimony presupposes that one takes the Bible to exhibit, in and through its diverse witnesses and the tension between their perspectives, much more unity than a mere anthology of ancient, religious writings held together by the covers of the one book. Ultimately it is the divine authorship that forges the Christological unity of the Bible in the convergence of its many witnesses. To quote Rupert of Deutz (d. 1129 or 1130), whose work reveals the interaction between the older monastic style of theology and the new, scholastic mode of thinking, 'the many words' of the Scriptures are really 'only one Word', Christ himself (*In Ioannnem*, 2. 7).

5. The Principle of Contemporary Consensus

By 'contemporary consensus' I intend the willingness of theologians to prefer, all things being equal, the line taken by widely respected, centrist biblical scholars or at least the majority of them. In reflecting on the Scriptures, theologians should not plunge forward by themselves and ignore what professional exegetes have to say. However, they cannot remain stuck on major questions waiting for a universal consensus to emerge in biblical studies about such matters as the empty tomb of Jesus.[18] Experience shows that such a consensus may

[18] On the empty tomb, see O'Collins, *Believing in the Resurrection*, 80–99.

never emerge. It is also ill-advised to adopt theses advanced by isolated biblical scholars or groups.[19] One might dub this practice 'rushing to apply in theology the latest thesis from the banks of the Neckar [the river that flows through Tübingen]'. (A lively centre of theology, the faculties at Tübingen have produced some adventurous theses that, though bold, are yet pretty unlikely.) At the same time, theologians need to know whether certain interpretations have come to win or lose a broad spectrum of support in biblical circles. James Barr and others have put an end, for instance, to Joachim Jeremias' original proposal to interpret 'Abba' (Mark 14: 36; Rom. 8: 15; Gal. 4: 6) as 'Daddy' or baby talk.[20] Theologians should respect the work of their professional colleagues in biblical studies. They may not maintain interpretations that exegetical arguments have shown to be implausible or even false. In the spirit of '*caveat emptor* (let the buyer beware)', they must learn to adjudicate between competing explanations and choose carefully what they buy on the exegetical market. The call for creativity in theology (principle two above) does not exclude testing the material taken on board from the distinct, if closely related, field of exegesis.

Furthermore, theologians need to be alert to four factors that affect the making of any biblical consensus and what they can draw from it.

(1) In their pursuit of the 'literal' meaning of Scriptures those who practice the historical-critical method may at times presuppose that in all cases there is *only one* meaning to be established: what Paul, Luke, or some other biblical author intended to communicate in a given text addressed to a specific audience (the *intentio auctoris*). But the intended meaning need not have always been single and solitary. Especially in hymnic and poetic passages (e.g. Phil. 2: 6–11), the intended meaning

---

[19] See Pheme Perkins's review (*Theological Studies* 78 (2017), 229–31) of John P. Meier, *Rethinking the Historical Jesus*, v: *Probing the Authenticity of the Parables* (New Haven, CT: Yale University Press, 2016). In a volume that is ultimately disappointing, Meier allows only four parables to be 'authentic'. Unlike the majority of scholars, Meier disqualifies as clearly authentic such parables as the Good Samaritan and the Prodigal Son, and allows only a marginal role for the parables in reconstructing the ministry and teaching of Jesus.

[20] See J. Ashton, 'Abba', *ABD*, i, 7–8; J. A. Fitzmyer, *Romans* (New York: Doubleday, 1993), 498–9, 501; J. Marcus, *Mark 9–16* (New Haven, CT: Yale University Press, 2009), 977–8; J. L. Martyn, *Galatians* (New York: Doubleday, 1997), 392.

cannot always be precisely paraphrased, as if Paul and other inspired writers meant 'just this' and nothing else. Right from their historical origins at the hands of a given author, some texts could bear different shades or even different levels of meaning. In such cases it is folly to expect only one correct answer to the question: what did the author intend? What did Paul (and the source he might well have drawn on) mean, for instance, by being 'in the form of God' and 'equality with God' (Phil. 2: 6)? Straight divine status, pre-existence as a heavenly being (Dan. 7: 14), or the immortality which belonged originally to Adam (Wis. 2: 23–4) and which Jesus Christ renounced by 'humbling himself' and becoming subject to death (Phil. 2: 8)? Could the *intentio auctoris* of Paul (and/or his sources) have allowed for two or even three of these possible meanings?

(2) Not all exegetes have made their peace with the fact that, while necessary and valuable, the historical-critical method needs to be supplemented with further methods and approaches. Texts will bear meanings that go beyond the original authorial intentions. Once composed, texts begin to enjoy a life of their own and yield further meanings, particularly as they are read in different and later contexts. Chapter 2 above cited the meaning the Letter to the Hebrews gave to some psalms (as utterances of Father, Son, and Holy Spirit), and Chapter 3 cited Paul's enlisting of Second Isaiah as his colleague in a worldwide missionary activity. Theologians need to be on the lookout for what exegetes envisage themselves as doing: (a) merely clarifying the original authorial intent, or (b) also allowing for more than such literal meaning. The example of New Testament authors reading their inherited Scriptures in new settings and taking their meaning beyond their original meaning decisively supports being open to (b).

(3) About fundamental matters (e.g. the value of Jesus' death) some measure of biblical consensus is clearly more important than would be the case with less fundamental issues, such as the 'best' title or image to use when summing up the earthly ministry of Jesus (e.g. 'Prophet' or 'Son of man'). But theologians should listen to exegetes about all significant matters. This leads to my fourth and final observation on consensus.

(4) Even on fundamental issues theologians may at times have to allow for considerable differences between exegetes—a kind of

'differentiated' consensus, if you will. We have an example of this situation in the debate from the 1970s and 1980s about the intentions of Jesus when faced with death. Among the numerous biblical scholars (e.g. Martin Hengel, Xavier Léon-Dufour, C. F. D. Moule, E. P. Sanders, and Heinz Schürmann) who contributed to the discussion, some (e.g. Anton Vögtle) argued for a rather minimalist interpretation, while others (e.g. Rudolf Pesch) argued for a stronger, even maximalist, interpretation of Jesus' pre-crucifixion intentions and expectations. Nevertheless, the exegetical community in the seventies and eighties broadly agreed that Jesus anticipated a violent death and somehow prepared himself for it.[21] Systematic theologians have to be content with this differentiated consensus. The redemptive value of Jesus' death should never be alleged to depend simply on his conscious intentions when faced with a violent end. His death drew its meaning also from what came before (his utter dedication to the preaching of the kingdom and the service of those in need) and from what came later (the resurrection and the outpouring of the Spirit).[22]

6. The Principle of Metathemes and Metanarratives

Metathemes and metanarratives provide a sixth principle for guiding theological appropriation of the Scriptures. These are, respectively, single themes and extended narratives that rise above their original settings and recur, with appropriate developments and modifications, in new contexts.[23]

We can measure a given theology by its success in incorporating *metathemes* that pervade the Bible: for instance, covenant, creation,

---

[21] On this exegetical debate as it developed from 1970 to 1993, see W. M. Becker, *The Historical Jesus in the Face of his Death* (Rome: Gregorian University Dissertation, 1994), 105–60.

[22] See G. O'Collins, *Christology: A Biblical, Historical, and Systematic Study of Jesus*, 2nd edn (Oxford: Oxford University Press, 2009), 67–8.

[23] Such postmodern thinkers as Jean-François Lyotard and Jacques Derrida have questioned metanarratives and metathemes as being mere social constructs. Who then is to say what is true or false? But, thanks to such philosophers as Umberto Eco and Maurizio Ferraris, a school of New Realists has brought fresh courage to the quest for evidence and truth; see M. Ancona, *Post Truth: The New War on Truth and How to Fight Back* (London: Ebury Press, 2017).

faith, law/gospel, liberation, life, love, mercy, prophecy, sin (in particular, idolatry), and wisdom.[24] Love as *agapē* already surfaces in the Greek Septuagint and then appears in the New Testament with overwhelming frequency.[25] God's liberating and transforming love found prophetic expression as spousal love for Israel and, specifically, Jerusalem (e.g. Jer. 2: 2; Hos. 2: 14). This nuptial language and imagery fed into the New Testament's presentation of Christ's redemptive work (e.g. Mark 2: 18–21; Eph. 5: 21–32), right through to the closing vision of the new Jerusalem adorned as a bride for her loving Redeemer who is to come (Rev. 21: 1–22: 21).

Such a *metanarrative* as the exodus from Egypt, celebrated yearly at the Passover feast and then re-enacted once and for all in the resurrection of the crucified Jesus, provides an overarching theme for theological interpretation. The story of the first Good Friday and Easter Sunday, conclusively and once and for all (Heb. 1: 3; 5: 9; 6: 19–20), condemns all idolatry (1 Cor. 8: 4–6) through the 'spiritual' wisdom of the cross (1 Cor. 1: 18–2: 16), reveals God as the effective God of resurrected life (1 Cor. 15: 15), relativizes all 'normal' human differences (Gal. 3: 26–8), and reinterprets the history not only of Israel but also of the whole world. As the central metanarrative of the whole Bible, the resurrection of the crucified Jesus binds the Scriptures into one and holds theology together for all those who consciously align themselves with the Easter mystery. They acknowledge that the crucifixion and resurrection stand in judgement on all historical efforts and achievements.

These metathemes and metanarratives make the Bible into one cumulative story. Respect for them allows us to satisfy something of

[24] These themes are often well treated in such standard reference works as *The Anchor Bible Dictionary*, *The New Interpreter's Dictionary of the Bible*, *The Oxford Encyclopedia of Bible and Theology*, *The Oxford Encyclopedia of the Books of the Bible*, *The Theological Dictionary of the New Testament*, and *Theologische Realencyclopädie*. *The Encyclopedia of the Bible and its Reception* (Berlin: De Gruyter, 2009–) already includes the following entries on the metathemes listed above: C. Koch et al. 'Covenant', v, 897–933; B. Pongratz-Leisten et al., 'Creation and Cosmogony', v, 963–1012; A. Klein et al., 'Faith', viii, 690–732; D. C. Allison et al., 'Gospel', x, 673–7; M. D. Dick et al., 'Idols, Idolatry', xii, 806–38.

[25] Every book of the New Testament contains at least one occurrence of *agapē* or of the corresponding verb 'to love (*agapaō*)', or of the adjective 'beloved (*agapētos*)'.

the desire expressed in the Reformation's call to interpret the Scriptures in the light of the Scriptures: 'the infallible rule of interpretation of Scripture is the Scripture itself'.[26] Earlier themes and narratives in the Bible recur (in new and modified ways) to illuminate what comes later: for instance, the yearly ceremony of the Day of Atonement (Lev. 16: 1–34) interprets something greater and definitive that occurred in the once-and-for-all sacrifice of Christ (Heb. 9: 1–10: 18). This sixth principle aims at noting patterns of divine activity and promise that recur in the Scriptures, yield an overall picture, evoke varying human responses, and throw light on Jesus' activity and identity. Any adequate theology will be sustained by the biblical metathemes and metanarratives.

This sixth principle, like the fourth, is not intended to arrest the momentum of the new, which the Scriptures constantly attest. Talk of convergence and metathemes/narratives is not to be dismissed as a mental straight-jacket that tries to make everything biblical count in the same way, as if after all there was nothing new under the biblical sun. My fourth and sixth principles are to be understood flexibly, as allowing for discontinuity within continuity, my seventh principle.

7. The Principle of Discontinuity within Continuity

This seventh principle may be happily exemplified by the classic shift from Jesus to Paul.[27] If we lay the Synoptic Gospels alongside Paul's

---

[26] On the rule of 'scriptura sui ipsius interpres', see the 1643 *Westminster Confession of Faith*, in H. Bettenson and C. Maunder, *Documents of the Christian Church*, 4th edn (Oxford: Oxford University Press, 2011), 306.

[27] See the seminal study by J. Blank, *Jesus und Paulus* (Munich: Kösel Verlag, 1968); J. D. G. Dunn, 'From Jesus' Proclamation to Paul's Gospel', *Jesus, Paul, and the Gospels* (Grand Rapids, MI: Eerdmans, 2011), 95–115; D. Wenham, *Paul: Follower of Jesus or Founder of Christianity?* (Grand Rapids, MI: Eerdmans, 1995). In what follows we attribute to Jesus what seems to go back historically to stage one (his earthly ministry) and not merely to stage two (the transmission of accounts of Jesus' life and work) or stage three (the redactional work of Mark and the other evangelists). At every stage the witness to Jesus was interpreted; that is simply the nature of human knowledge and experience. There never was a non-interpreted Jesus; Peter, Mary Magdalene, and the other early disciples started interpreting Jesus from the first moment they met him.

letters, it may seem that nothing is changed—except for two facts:
Paul's rhetorical, theological, and autobiographical style has replaced
Jesus' unique, storytelling style, and Paul does not include (or deliberately leaves to others) the teaching of the earthly Jesus, even if at
times his parenesis echoes Jesus' words. Both are deeply Jewish, even if
they express that Jewishness in different ways and through different
concerns. Both accept their inherited Scriptures (our Old Testament)
as normative literature that enjoys divine authority. Both clearly
uphold monotheism (Mark 12: 29; Rom. 12: 29–30).

Jesus calls God 'Abba (Father dear)'. The apostle not only maintains this distinctive usage, especially in his opening greetings, but also
cites 'Abba' as entering into Christian prayer (Rom. 8: 15; Gal. 4: 6).
By drawing together Deuteronomy 6: 4–5 and Leviticus 19: 18, Jesus
teaches that the whole Mosaic law should be understood in terms of
love (Mark 12: 28–31). He extends love for one's neighbour to include
love for one's enemies (Matt. 5: 43–8; Luke 6: 27–36). Paul likewise
sees love as the 'fulfilment' of the Law (Rom. 13: 8–10; Gal. 5: 14), and
urges his fellow Christians to show love towards their enemies (Rom.
12: 14, 20–1). Jesus denies any absolute religious significance of food
laws (Mark 7: 14–23), and so too does Paul (Rom. 14: 13–23). The
apostle flatly declares: 'the kingdom of God is not food and drink, but
righteousness and peace and joy in the Holy Spirit' (Rom. 14: 17).

This example brings to mind a change that goes beyond mere
habits of speech. Unlike Jesus, Paul rarely speaks of the (present
and future) kingdom—only eight times in the seven letters generally
recognized as authentic (Romans, 1 and 2 Corinthians, Galatians,
Philippians, 1 Thessalonians, and Philemon). These eight occurrences
come in 1 Corinthians (five) and one each in Romans, Galatians, and
1 Thessalonians. Jesus presents his exorcisms and miracles as signs of
God's powerful rule breaking into the world to deliver men and
women from the spirit of evil (Luke 11: 20; see also 10: 18; 13: 16).
Paul associates his own mighty works with his apostolic ministry (Rom.
15: 18–19; 2 Cor. 12: 12) in the service of 'the Gospel'. Replacing
'kingdom' talk, 'the Gospel' runs as a leitmotif right through Paul's
masterpiece (from Rom. 1: 1 to 16: 25). Behind the different terminology, both Jesus and Paul are substantially saying the same thing.
For Jesus, the kingdom or reign of God has entered the world
(e.g. Luke 11: 20) and is to be received as sheer gift with childlike

simplicity (e.g. Mark 10: 20) and with great joy (e.g. Matt. 13: 44–6). Paul agrees that there is no self-redemption: we cannot reach the goal of life through our own efforts. For the apostle, faith 'comes' (Gal. 3: 23, 25). God's justice is revealed and imparted (e.g. Rom. 1: 16–17; 3: 24), and the apostolic ministry itself is a gift of God's grace (e.g. 1 Cor. 15: 10; Gal. 1: 15–16). Jesus' language about his being 'sent' (e.g. Mark 9: 37; 12: 6) or having 'come' (e.g. Mark 2: 17; Matt. 11: 19) is mirrored by Paul's talk about the Son being 'sent' (Gal. 4: 4) or having taken the initiative in assuming the human condition (Phil. 2: 7–8). The case seems similar with the 'Son of man' language Jesus uses. It drops out in Paul's writing, but a major function of that self-description (his role as the judge to come) is maintained (e.g. 1 Thess. 2: 19; 3: 13).

One could press also the similarity between the 'already' (Luke 11: 20; see Matt. 12: 28) and the 'not yet' (Matt. 6: 10 = Luke 11: 2) in Jesus' preaching of the kingdom and Paul's message of an adoption that has already taken place (Rom. 8: 14–17) and is yet to be completed in the future (Rom. 8: 18–25). The perspective remains the same, even if thematized differently. Paul's teaching about inheriting the kingdom (1 Cor. 6: 9–10) displays the 'time frame' found in Jesus' language about the future kingdom. Likewise the apostle's assurance that believers can experience here and now some of the kingdom's benefits (Rom. 14: 17) matches Jesus' proclamation of the kingdom's present power.

In a sense nothing seems changed, as we move from Jesus to Paul, and yet with the resurrection of the crucified Jesus nothing is the same. Revelation and salvation are now thoroughly personalized in the Easter proclamation (1 Cor. 1: 23; 15: 1–11); redemption has come through Christ's sacrificial death (Rom. 3: 24–5; 1 Cor. 5: 7; 11: 23–6). The 'Lord' Jesus, who now stands with 'God our Father' as the source of 'grace and peace' (e.g. Rom. 1: 7) is announced, *and worshipped* as Messiah (Christ), Lord, and Son of God (e.g. 1 Cor. 8: 6; Phil. 2: 9–11).[28] The fullness of salvation history, summed up in terms of grace, love, and fellowship (2 Cor. 13: 13), has been enacted through the Father, the Son, and the Holy Spirit.

---

[28] See L. W. Hurtado, *Lord Jesus Christ: Devotion to Jesus in Earliest Christianity* (Grand Rapids, MI: Eerdmans, 2003).

Jesus had called for conversion, offered forgiveness of sins, and invited his audience to participate through love in the coming reign of God. Now Paul proclaims the liberating and reconciling love released through the saving events of Christ's crucifixion and resurrection from the dead. This Easter mystery, together with the associated gift of the Holy Spirit, forms the most crucial watershed in the whole history of revelation and salvation, being the instance par excellence of discontinuity in continuity.

Some writers deny the resurrection, push discontinuity to the extreme of a complete break with Jesus' ministry, and misrepresent Paul as the real (and misguided) founder of historic Christianity. But those who accept that Jesus rose from the dead face an Easter mystery, which neither replaces *tout court* all that went before nor is to be reduced to the situation of Jesus' ministry. The uniquely new event that has taken place does not invalidate what has preceded it, but it does entail freshly interpreting everything prior to it and recognizing the great Easter gift (the Holy Spirit), the new family created by Christ's resurrection, and the power of divine love at work in the Church. Thus the Easter-event, with the move it brought from the situation of the earthly Jesus to that of Paul, stands out as the classic exemplification of my seventh principle.

R. W. L. Moberly's 'discernment' of what Paul says about his apostolic ministry in 2 Corinthians brings out nicely the presence of discontinuity within continuity.[29] Where the historical Jesus calls others to follow him in a discipleship that would involve suffering and loss (Matt. 16: 24–6 parr.), the very pattern of the new life of the crucified Jesus is now made visible through the ministry of his apostle. Paul not only follows a persecuted Jesus but also reveals and communicates to others the risen life of the crucified One (2 Cor. 4: 7–12).

8. The Principle of Eschatological Provisionality

A sense of discontinuity within continuity characterizes the theological appropriation of the Scriptures, above all in handling the shifts from

---

[29] R. W. L. Moberly, *Prophecy and Discernment* (Cambridge: Cambridge University Press, 2006), 186–8.

the Old Testament to the New Testament and from the situation of Jesus to that of Paul. In close association with this seventh principle, I introduce an eighth: the eschatological provisionality of everything the biblical texts yield for theology. The future-oriented nature of God's self-revelation has impressed a similar characteristic on its biblical record and interpretation. The divine promise controls the way we understand the present; we dare not let everything revolve around the contemporary state of the Church and the world. The promised consummation of all things has not yet arrived. First-order biblical words and second-order theological words can give only the faintest idea of the shape of things to come.

As I observed above (principle two), theological interests, contexts, and audiences can be classified in a threefold fashion: in terms of worship, knowledge, and action. At the end of all things, action will blend with worship and knowledge to bring the vision of God in a transformed universe. The mysterious fullness of future glory invites us to acknowledge the partial, provisional, and anticipatory nature of even the best insights to be drawn from the Scriptures about the tripersonal God and the world of grace in which we live today. When appropriating the biblical evidence, theologians enjoy no special exemption from the never-ending search for understanding that characterizes their discipline. Reflecting in faith on the meaning and message of the inspired Scriptures, they pursue a goal that will be fully realized only in the final vision. Here and now they know only 'in part' (1 Cor. 13: 12).

9. The Principle of Philosophical Assistance

Principles three through eight, which elucidate various aspects of the active hearing of the Scriptures (principle two), call for the fine-tuning and use of *historical* reason. My ninth principle states that theology will lack clarity and substance unless it puts the Scriptures into dialogue with *philosophical* reason. To be more explicit and orderly, theologians need philosophy, albeit not necessarily any *particular* philosophy.[30]

---

[30] Studies at the University of Melbourne, the University of Cambridge, and the University of Tübingen made me familiar with the Western philosophy

From the time of St Justin Martyr (d. around AD 165), philosophical views of God, the created world, and the divine interaction with the world have assisted the interpretation of the Bible. Philosophical reason sharpens the questions to be asked, helps to organize the methods and material, illuminates the condition of human beings and their world, and brings conceptual clarity to bear on the biblical texts, which by and large are pre-philosophical.[31] Beyond question, philosophical hermeneutics or principles for interpreting texts are needed,[32] but philosophy has more to contribute than that.

The debate about Jesus' intentions when faced with death (reported above in my discussion of principle five) would, for instance, have been sharpened by introducing the philosophical distinction between event and act: that is to say, by distinguishing between the language of *causality* (which asks *how* the agent contributed to some occurrence) and the language of *intention* (which asks *why* the agent acted in this

---

discussed by A. Kenny, *A New History of Western Philosophy* (Oxford: Clarendon Press, 2010). R. Audi (ed.), *The Cambridge Dictionary of Philosophy* (Cambridge: Cambridge University Press, 1995) includes many entries on non-Western philosophies and philosophers.

[31] On the relationship between theology and philosophy, see I. Dalferth, *Theology and Philosophy* (Oxford: Blackwell, 1988); Pope John Paul II, *Fides et Ratio: On the Relationship between Faith and Reason* (Boston: Pauline Books, 1998); T. V. Morris (ed.), *God and the Philosophers: The Reconciliation of Faith and Reason* (Oxford: Oxford University Press, 1994); G. O'Collins, *Fundamental Theology* (New York: Paulist Press, 1981), 24–31; E. F. Osborn, *The Beginning of Christian Philosophy* (Cambridge: Cambridge University Press, 1981); K. Rahner, 'Philosophy and Theology', *Theological Investigations*, vi, trans. K.-H. Kruger and B. Kruger (London: Darton, Longman & Todd, 1969), 71–81; K. Rahner, 'The Current Relationship between Philosophy and Theology', *Theological Investigations*, xiii, trans. D. Bourke (London: Darton, Longman & Todd, 1975), 61–79; C. Stead, *Philosophy in Christian Antiquity* (Cambridge: Cambridge University Press, 1994). On difficulties that arise between biblical scholars and philosophers, see T. P. Flint and E. Stump (eds), *Hermes and Athena* (South Bend, IN: University of Notre Dame Press, 1993), and the review of that book by H. Meynell in *New Blackfriars* 76 (1995), 127–39.

[32] On the role of such hermeneutics, see the Pontifical Biblical Commission's *The Interpretation of the Bible in the Church* (Vatican City: Libreria Editrice Vaticana, 1993), 73–7.

way). By developing such insights, philosophy affects our reading and hearing of the Scriptures.

Philosophy also copes with questions about the status of *religious language*. Does such language merely reflect and express our inner experience? Or can both literal and metaphorical statements about God yield true knowledge? If we agree that God's being is too mysterious to be caught in a net of descriptive language, are we necessarily condemned to Neo-Kantian agnosticism? St Augustine's thinking about biblical interpretation and preaching (e.g. in *De Doctrina Christiana*) involved reflecting philosophically on texts, language, signs, and truth.[33] He wrestled with such questions as: How do words in the Bible and elsewhere relate to things they purport to describe? Here philosophy has something to contribute to the kind of knowledge and even certainty that we should expect from interpreting biblical texts.

In modern times epistemology (or the theory of knowledge concerned with distinguishing between justified belief and mere opinion) has widely displaced metaphysics (or the study of first principles). Epistemology tackles religious experience and asks: What probative value does such experience enjoy? What counts as evidence that such experience puts us in touch with ultimate reality? Epistemology also asks such questions about the religious experience of the Old Testament prophets, Jesus, Paul, the author of the Book of Revelation, and other persons who feature in the biblical narratives.

In short, over the centuries the best of its contributions to theology and exegesis have shown that philosophy does not 'leave everything as it is'.[34] To be sure, we should distinguish faith and *philosophical* reason (principle nine), just as we distinguish faith and *historical* reason (principles two through eight). But in neither case is there a separation: reason, whether philosophical or historical, should work in, with, and through faith and a faithful hearing of the inspired, biblical word (principle one).

---

[33] See C. Harrison, 'Augustine', in J. C. Paget and J. Schaper (eds), *The New Cambridge History of the Bible*, i (Cambridge: Cambridge University Press, 2012), 676–96.

[34] L. Wittgenstein, *Philosophical Investigations*, n. 124, trans. G. E. M. Anscombe, 3rd edn (New York: Macmillan, 1969), 49e.

Such valid collaboration becomes, however, impossible when philosophy replaces the voice of revelation, assumes control, and allows dubious convictions to take over. We have already noted this problem in the case of Derrida. Let me add three further modern examples: John Hick, Maurice F. Wiles, and Gordon D. Kaufman.

In *The Metaphor of God Incarnate*[35] Hick allowed questionable philosophical presuppositions about God and our world to take over the meaning that he was ready to find in the New Testament witness. For instance, the 'incarnation' did not mean what for Hick is an impossibility, a divine person assuming the human condition, but simply that Jesus lived a life of unselfish love that 'incarnated' the ideal human response to the divine reality.[36] A special, personal self-communication of God in Christ would be 'incompatible with a universal divine love'.[37]

A deist-style cosmology that rejects a priori any special divine interactions with the world dictates, for example, the way Wiles interpreted the New Testament texts about Christ's pre-existence, incarnation, and virginal conception. Instead of being 'particular divine acts ensuring the birth of the particular person, Jesus', he (mis)understood all three beliefs 'as a retrospective way of expressing the totality of his [Jesus'] commitment to and fulfilment of the will of God for the world'.[38]

A similar deist philosophy firmly controlled the way Gordon Kaufman interpreted New Testament texts about the virginal conception of Jesus: 'It is not possible for us to think of an "event" as simply, supernaturally caused.'[39] The debate here concerns the validity of 'our' preconceived notions of what could or could not have occurred. Those who maintain a 'higher' view of divine activity, on the one hand, and acknowledge the incompleteness of scientific explanations, on the other, leave open the possibility of thinking and speaking literally

[35] John Hick, *The Metaphor of God Incarnate* (London: SCM Press, 1993).

[36] Ibid. 105, 152.

[37] Ibid. 159. For further criticism of Hick's interpretation of the Scriptures, see G. O'Collins and D. Kendall, *Focus on Jesus: Essays in Christology and Soteriology* (Leominster, UK: Gracewing, 1996), 30–46.

[38] M. F. Wiles, *God's Action in the World* (London: SCM Press, 1986), 89.

[39] G. D. Kaufman, 'On the Meaning of "Act of God"', *Harvard Theological Review* 61 (1968), 175–201 at 185, n. 10.

of such a divine action as the virginal conception. Modern science does not, as Kaufman would have it, render such divine actions impossible. After the insights and discoveries of Einstein, Planck, Bohr, Heisenberg, and others, the clockwork universe is dead. Even if the closed, Newtonian model of the natural order had still prevailed, the impossibility of such events as the virginal conception of Jesus would be, 'at most, an impossibility within the natural order, not an unqualified impossibility'.[40]

10. The Principle of Inculturation

Tenth and lastly, theologians need not only some philosophical expertise but also the intellectual and spiritual courage to inculturate the biblical testimony and let their theology become enriched by different cultures—in traditionally Christian countries, in lands where for centuries Christians have remained a tiny minority, in lands where Christian majorities became minorities centuries ago, and in recently evangelized lands. There is one Christ and one Bible, but there are many cultures.[41]

Translating scriptural teaching into contemporary languages and cultures (so that every generation can appropriate and 'inhabit' the biblical narratives) calls for a deep knowledge of cultural experiences and for innovative fidelity. Inculturation could have been listed with my second principle; in fact, I noted under that principle how

[40] W. P. Alston, *Divine Nature and Human Language: Essays in Philosophical Theology* (Ithaca and London: Cornell University Press, 1989), 211; see 208–13 for further criticisms of Kaufman's position.

[41] See *Studia Missionalia* 44 (1995), an issue dedicated to 'Inculturation: Gospel and Culture'; K. Blaser, 'Culture and Christianity', in E. Fahlbusch et al. (eds), *The Encyclopedia of Christianity*, i (Grand Rapids, MI: Eerdmans, 1999), 749–53; G. O. Lang, 'Culture', in *New Catholic Encyclopedia*, iv, new edn (Washington, DC: Catholic University of America, 2003), 426–36; H. R. Niebuhr, *Christ and Culture* (London: Faber, 1952); F. Rodi et al., 'Kultur', *TRE*, xx, 176–209; A. Smith, 'Cultural Studies', *OEBI*, i, 179–88; H. Zdarzil et al., 'Culture', *Encyclopedia of Christianity*, i, 746–9. Experts in cultural anthropology and sociology (e.g. Robert Bellah, Peter Berger, Clifford Geertz, Anthony Giddens, Thomas Luckman, Talcott Parsons, and their successors) have much to say or at least to suggest about culture and inculturation.

meaning is always, in part, a *cultural phenomenon*. But the task is so important that it deserves to be named separately and, preferably, in close proximity to philosophy. Through its dialogue and debate with contemporary thought, philosophy offers invaluable help both towards understanding the spiritual experiences, ethical values, theological perspectives, and symbolic expressions of other religions (including indigenous religions that do not have written traditions), and towards articulating and spreading the biblical message through all cultures.

Let me insist that I understand 'culture' to include but not to be limited to the explicitly religious sectors and dimensions of human existence; culture expresses the totality of life. Hence culture (and with it the task of inculturation) does not merely concern language and differences in language. It spans a whole complex of secular, ethical, and religious value-systems, modes of thinking, orientations towards God, and traditional lifestyles and ways of celebration. The fact that some cultures involve such subcultures as those formed by the urban proletariat, the younger generation, and the farming community reminds us of further complexities in the reality and notion of culture. Nor should we ignore multicultural and multiracial societies like Australia, where one nation embraces and fosters many cultures. What is it to inculturate the Scriptures in such a society? Finally, we should recall two further items. Each culture, experiencing as it does one and the same human nature, enjoys a potential universality. But not every inherited culture is sufficiently open and dynamic to develop and even be transformed when it encounters fresh knowledge and experience.

A thorough inculturation of the biblical message depends, at least in part, on the success or failure of theologians in discerning the potential of their own culture (including literature and the visual arts) to be illuminated by the Scriptures and to serve as vehicles for expressing the great metanarratives and metathemes of the Bible. This capacity to discern requires a mastery of what one's own culture and biblical faith within that culture mean. Such mastery grasps how the scriptural message has been or at least could be embodied in a particular culture. Attention to inculturation implies both faith and reason: both (1) a faith that, as the Word and Wisdom of God, Christ is present at least seminally and anonymously in all human cultures and that, as centred on him, the Bible is a book for all cultures, and (2) a sensitive mind to discern and fashion the way inculturation should function for any given period, people, and the values and meanings that shape particular ways of life.

Asia summons theologians to reflect deeply on its ancient religions (with their sacred writings, ways of life, and forms of worship), so as to enable the Jewish-Christian Scriptures to be appropriated not only theologically but also pastorally and liturgically. A respectful dialogue with Asia's cultures will mean seeking and finding God in the religious traditions of its peoples—a mutual teaching and learning that can shed fresh light on the Christian Scriptures and on the whole Christian message.[42] Such an inculturating dialogue, if it is going to be integral, involves the three contexts we expounded above (principle two).

First, it calls for a theological exchange that attempts to know and understand 'the others' (in their culture and religion) as they wish to be known and understood. Such an academic dialogue calls for (a) the courage to hear painful truth about our Christian theology and lives, and (b) a love that is open to find God and Christ everywhere and, not least, in the dialogue itself. Apropos of (a), it may take 'others' to show us how conditioned, parochial, or ideologically captive our theology and use of Scriptures can become.

Second, such dialogue also requires common action with those of other religious traditions, in order to overcome racism, sexism, genocidal intolerance, irrational fundamentalism, and cultural prejudices of all kinds. Every continent suffers from ideologies of hatred that arouse economic, nationalist, racial, and sexual violence. Any inter-religious, inculturating dialogue remains empty unless and until it brings a shared commitment to transform cultural and social life through promoting truth, human rights, the transmission of spiritual values to the rising generation, harmony among all, and our common responsibilities for the poor, the disabled, the sick, the old, the defenceless, and God's created world.

---

[42] Federation of Asian Bishops' Conferences (FABC), *Theses on Interreligious Dialogue, FABC Papers* 48 (Hong Kong: FABC, 1987); Catholic Bishops' Conference of India (CBCI), *Guidelines for Interreligious Dialogue*, 2nd edn (New Delhi: CBCI Centre, 1989).

Third, any inculturating dialogue involves encountering and experiencing each other's practices of prayer and worship. The Secretariat for Non-Christians (as it was then called) explained that, along with 'the intellectual dialogue' (nos 33–4) and 'the dialogue of a common commitment to works of justice and human commitment' (nos 31–2), 'there is the sharing of religious experiences and contemplation, in a common search for the Absolute' (no. 35).[43]

In short, inter-religious dialogue in the service of inculturation demands worship and practice, as well as theological thinking and sharing. For such a dialogue the Scriptures are to be celebrated and practised, and not merely interpreted academically.

The Western world—and, increasingly, other 'worlds'—presents its theologians with a special challenge. Its writing, reading, and visual culture is now deeply affected by the communications revolution. It has drawn people further and further into a world of virtual reality, which suppresses authentic human connecting and sharing. Video games of war blur the difference between imaginary and real killing. In some countries, internet addiction already affects 40 per cent of the population. 39 per cent of American children open a social-media account at eleven years of age. Along with the enormous benefits they bring, are digital technologies exercising a social and emotional impact that should be described as pathological?[44]

Social media, some or many would claim, have created a space for rapid and widespread human communication. But is much of that so-called 'communication' real interpersonal communication? Or is it 'fake' communication that is also steadily ruining language and authentic human interchange?

Inculturation, whether in the West or elsewhere, calls for fidelity to the Bible, not a capitulation that interprets the Scriptures simply according to the standards and the passing features of contemporary society. Sometimes a cultural heritage can illuminate the Scriptures;

---

[43] *Dialogue and Mission*, Bulletin 19 (1984), 126–41.

[44] M. Aiken, *The Cyber Effect: A Pioneering Cyberpsychologist Explains how Human Behaviour Changes Online* (London: John Murray, 2016); A. Alter, *Irresistible: Why We Can't Stop Checking, Scrolling, Clicking, and Watching* (London: Bodley Head, 2017); J. Taplin, *Move Fast and Break Things: How Facebook, Google and Amazon Have Cornered Culture and What It Means for All of Us* (London: Macmillan, 2017).

at other times we find the Scriptures in collision with aspects of our culture. What is it to inculturate the Scriptures in a society marked by growing biblical illiteracy and scarred by an obsession with material possessions, abortion, easy divorce, and euthanasia? How might the parables of the Good Samaritan (Luke 10: 29–37) and the Rich Man and Lazarus (Luke 16: 19–31) and the picture of the Final Judgement (Matt. 25: 31–46) be inculturated in Western countries? Internally some nations can exhibit shocking levels of educational and economic disparity. Externally they can pursue an unchecked, free-market capitalism that deprives millions of economic justice and refuses to respect the needs of the global, human community.

Finally, the task of inculturating the scriptural witness entails relating to each other the Bible's metanarratives, metathemes, and images (in particular, key metaphors) and paraphrasing them in terms that are accurate and communicative. It belongs to theology's work to seek fresh understanding and a new, lively, and experiential language which makes the biblical message intelligible and convincing. To call such organizing and restating of the Scriptures 'translating' them does not presuppose that there is consistently only one meaning to be transferred relatively simply from a biblical to a theological text. The 'reception history' of the Bible bears ample witness to the rich polyvalence of its texts.[45] Moreover, 'translating' may play down the ways in which the inculturating work of theologians also serves to proclaim the good news, rouse faith, encourage discipleship, inspire worship, and effectively criticize social and political injustice. The work of inculturation should not only enrich the identity and welfare of the entire Christian community but also spread the biblical message into the whole world.

11. The Principles Summarized

My ten principles require listening faithfully to the Scriptures (principle one), doing so creatively (principle two), within the framework of tradition and the rule of faith (principle three), looking for convergence in the biblical witness (principle four) and consensus among

---

[45] See M. Lieb, E. Mason, and J. Roberts (eds), *The Oxford Handbook of the Reception History of the Bible* (Oxford: Oxford University Press, 2011).

the exegetes (principle five), and respecting central metathemes and metanarratives—above all, the critical role of the Easter mystery—(principle six), continuity in discontinuity (principle seven), the eschatological provisionality of all theological interpretations (principle eight), the contribution of philosophical reason (principle nine), and the broad task of inculturation (principle ten). Like a golden thread, Christocentrism binds together all these ten principles.

The principles invite theologians to be faithful and active hearers (principles one and two) of the Scriptures, which converge on Christ (principle four) and have their enduring frame of reference in the historic creeds built around Christ's incarnation, life, death, resurrection, and the gift of the Holy Spirit (principle three). The classic metathemes and metanarratives of the Bible (principle six), illuminated by exegetical consensus (principle five), find their heart in the radical discontinuity-in-continuity of the Easter mystery (principle seven). The eschatological provisionality of the Scriptures refers us to the final consummation of all things in Christ (principle eight). Inculturation (principle ten) proceeds from (a) the faith that as divine Word and Wisdom Christ is present through his Spirit in all cultures, and (b) the conviction that philosophical reason (principle nine) can support a biblical message about Christ, the light of all nations.

Martin Luther encourages this Christocentrism: 'Think of the Scriptures as [. . .] the richest of mines which can never be sufficiently explored, in order that you may find that divine wisdom which God here lays before you in such simple guise as to quench all pride.' Luther echoes here what the Book of Job says about the rich minerals that human miners seek out and the uniquely precious wisdom to which only God knows the way (Job 28: 1–28). Luther then explains how this treasured wisdom is to be identified amazingly with the Christ Child: 'here you will find the swaddling clothes and the manger in which Christ lies [. . .] Simple and lowly are these swaddling cloths, but dear is the treasure, Christ, who lies in them.'[46]

By drawing his central image from the birth of Christ, Luther suggests the need to maintain steadily the historical reference when appropriating

---

[46] 'Prefaces to the Old Testament', trans. C. M. Jacobs, *Luther's Works*, xxv (Philadelphia: Muhlenberg Press, 1960), 236.

the Scriptures theologically. While I argue that philosophical reason (principle nine) and inculturation (principle ten) are to be brought into play, I would rule out any one-sided suppression of the historical origins and reference of the Scriptures, which the traditional creeds (principle three) and the central metanarratives (principle six) properly maintain. A concern for inculturating Trinitarian belief through Hindu philosophy could recommend, for example, professing faith in the tripersonal God as 'Being, Consciousness of Being, and Enjoyment of Being'.[47] But such a non-historical translation of Trinitarian belief should not be allowed to take over in an exclusive way. The more historically oriented principles (one through eight) indicate otherwise and should be respected.

This example from Hindu thought recalls the role of inter-religious learning. Let me explain. This book has treated biblical inspiration in the light of Christian faith. But we could take a further step and also learn about the Christian Scriptures by doing so 'inter-religiously' or 'comparatively'—that is to say, in conversation on their sacred texts with those of other faiths.[48] A Christian theology of inspiration might lead us on to a 'comparative theology' of inspiration, which could prove enlightening for both 'sides'.[49] Yet such 'comparative' work would call for an appropriate examination of what the followers of some 'other', specific religion held about divine revelation, responding human faith, and the religious tradition(s) stemming from the religious experiences of their founding figures. Only then would we be in a position to understand and interpret responsibly what they believe to be the case about the inspiration of their sacred texts. Thus any such inter-religious study of biblical inspiration, if it is to prove significant and valuable, would call for a book-length treatment.

[47] For details, see J. Dupuis, *Toward a Christian Theology of Religious Pluralism* (Maryknoll, NY: Orbis, 1997), 274–9.

[48] See F. X. Clooney, *How to Do Comparative Theology* (New York: Fordham University Press, 2017); F. X. Clooney, *The Future of Hindu–Christian Studies: A Theological Inquiry* (New York: Routledge, 2017); F. X. Clooney, *Comparative Theology: Deep Learning across Religious Borders* (Malden, MA: Wiley-Blackwell, 2010).

[49] See I. Vempeny, *Inspiration in Non-biblical Scriptures* (Bangalore: Theological Publications in India, 1971).

Epilogue

On rereading this manuscript, I hope that it can contribute to two valuable causes. May it help to deliver Christians from false interpretations of the Bible, the book that is essential for creating and sustaining their religious identity! May it also enrich their vision of what the Holy Spirit has achieved and continues to achieve in the arena of biblical inspiration!

This work has set itself to distinguish (not separate) (a) biblical *inspiration*, a special impulse from the Holy Spirit to set things down in writing, (b) divine *self-revelation*, the major 'source material' for the inspired record, and (c) one of the major consequences of inspiration, the *truth* of the Bible. Carefully distinguishing (a), (b), and (c) delivers readers of the Scriptures from false problems. The Books of Joshua and Judges, for example, faithfully record harsh and even false ideas about God, but such a vision of God is progressively purified in Isaiah, Hosea, and the Gospels themselves. True ideas about God, human beings, and their world are to be found in the whole Bible, which converges on Jesus, the Way, the Truth, and the Life.

This work has also set itself to distinguish inspiration as a *cause*, the activity of the Holy Spirit (in the original writing of the texts that together make up the Bible and their subsequent impact on the readers and hearers of Scriptures), from the *effects* of this activity, the *Wirkungsgeschichte* or results stemming from the Spirit's gift of inspiration. We have only a limited knowledge of how inspiration as a cause has worked and continues to work, but we have considerable information about the impact of earlier biblical texts upon later sacred writers (above all, the authors of the New Testament), and superabundant information about the inspiring effect of the Holy Spirit, working through the Scriptures, on the worship, belief, and life of innumerable believers. An account of such effects of inspiration was offered in Chapter 4 above. But a full account of this *Inspirationsgeschichte* (inspiring history) of the Bible would call for many volumes. In short, any adequate study of biblical inspiration should examine inspiration both as a cause *and as an effect,* or rather a very rich series of effects, which will continue to the end of human history.

May distinguishing (not separating) inspiration as cause and effect seriously redefine approaches to the topic of biblical inspiration. It is through that distinction that I hope that this book will prove its value.

Finally, through prayerful reading and hearing of the Scriptures, the Holy Spirit opens up fresh understanding of our relationship with God, other human beings, and the created universe. The inspired texts come alive and become the living Word of God. In this way the Spirit continues to use the Scriptures as a privileged channel for the ongoing divine self-communication. Thus the impact of the sacred texts belongs integrally to what I have called dependent revelation. The Holy Spirit remains forever 'the Lord and Giver of Life' (Nicene-Constantinopolitan Creed), or, in other words, the ever-present Lord and Giver of Inspiration, which brings Light and Life.

The powerful presence of the Spirit is more than ever necessary to change the hearts of human beings everywhere (Ezek. 11: 19–20). The future of our race has been put at risk by innumerable atomic weapons, trafficking in arms, drugs, and human beings, a widespread addiction to war that is fuelled by fear, greed, and a lust to control and dominate, and the uncontrolled wrecking of our environment. Driven by profit and indifferent to the common good, predatory capitalism has exploited the failure of ethical regulations to safeguard our planet. May the Spirit, at work through the Scriptures and in other ways, help the human race to reimagine and embrace other ways of living that are deeply just, peaceful, and beautiful.[1]

[1] See J. P. Lederach, *The Moral Imagination: The Art and Soul of Building Peace* (Oxford: Oxford University Press, 2005).

An Appendix: Critiquing the Sensational

How should theologians and exegetes react to those writers on the Bible who, far from treating the Scriptures as sacred and inspired texts, ignore mainstream scholarship[1] and misuse historical evidence to produce sensational books that may create a big splash but normally hardly leave a ripple? In his classical *The Quest of the Historical Jesus* (German orig. 1906), Albert Schweitzer thought it worth his while to dedicate a chapter to Heinrich Venturini and others who had fabricated theories of Jesus surviving his crucifixion and enjoying a subsequent career.[2]

Some of the later writers who followed Venturini despatched the post-crucifixion Jesus (often with Mary Magdalene as his partner) to France or Rome, others to India and even to Japan. They did exactly what Schweitzer observed and predicted: they reissued Venturini under another name.[3] Schweitzer's example encouraged me to follow suit. With Daniel Kendall, I published a critical study of post-Venturini authors who have pictured Jesus as somehow surviving crucifixion and living on for some or even many years.[4]

To much fanfare and in time for Easter 2010, Philip Pullman published *The Good Man Jesus and the Scoundrel Christ*.[5] He presented Jesus as a wonderful idealist crushed by human power, who never rose from the dead but whose memory power-hungry Church leaders manipulated through his twin brother, Christ. In *Philip*

---

[1] See principle five in Chapter 10 above.

[2] A. Schweitzer, *The Quest of the Historical Jesus*, trans. W. Montgomery (New York: Macmillan, 1961), 38–47.

[3] Ibid. 47, 326–9.

[4] 'On Reissuing Venturini', *Gregorianum* 75 (1994), 241–65; reprinted in G. O'Collins and D. Kendall, *Focus on Jesus: Essays in Christology and Soteriology* (Leominster, UK: Gracewing, 1996), 153–75. For significant reflections on issues raised by Schweitzer, Kendall, and myself, see T. Burke (ed.), *Fakes, Forgeries and Fictions: Writing Ancient and Modern Christian Apocrypha* (Eugene, OR: Cascade Books, 2017).

[5] (Edinburgh: Canongate, 2010).

Pullman's Jesus,[6] I argued that this essay in historical fiction told its readers much more about Pullman and his mind-set than about the history of Jesus himself.

Another sample of the literature Schweitzer warned us against has come along in Reza Aslan's *Zealot: The Life and Times of Jesus of Nazareth*.[7] What should we make of this latest retelling of Jesus' history? Aslan writes in a vivid, imaginative, and popular style. The short chapters, uncluttered by footnotes, make the book a quick and easy read. But has it any real worth? Does it pose a serious challenge to faith in the resurrection of Jesus? What is the scholarly status of its author?[8]

After securing a doctorate in the sociology of religions and a master of fine arts in fiction, Aslan became an associate professor of creative writing at the University of California. While he has read widely in biblical scholarship, his book is riddled with significant and damaging gaps. If he had studied Raymond Brown's classic and carefully argued *The Birth of the Messiah*, he might have been saved from facile judgements about the infancy narratives in Matthew and Luke.

Currently the outstanding commentary on Mark's Gospel (in two volumes) is by Joel Marcus. If Aslan had read that commentary, he could hardly have described Mark as simply 'uninterested' in the resurrection of Jesus (29). Even without help from Marcus, Aslan should have noticed in Mark's Gospel three predictions of Jesus' resurrection (in Chs 8, 9, and 10) and the repeated promise of a rendezvous in Galilee between the risen Jesus and his disciples (14: 28; 16: 7). In effect, Aslan rejects the resurrection by ignoring it.

Aslan reads some Greek and tells readers that he can work out the rest with the help of dictionaries. But he appears serenely unaware of Bauer-Danker's standard dictionary of New Testament Greek, used by scholars everywhere.

Retrieving the nineteenth-century theory of F. C. Baur, Aslan pictures a violent clash between Paul and his followers, on the one hand, and James and Peter, on the other. It was Paul who 'transformed Jesus from a revolutionary zealot into a Romanized demigod' (171).

---

[6] (London: Darton, Longman and Todd, 2010).

[7] (New York: Random House, 2013). For a review, see D. Senior, *America* magazine, 23–30 December 2013, 30–2.

[8] I will refer to Aslan's book within my text.

Some knowledge of recent scholarly writing on the pre-Pauline worship of the risen Jesus (e.g. by Larry Hurtado) and relations between Paul, Peter, and James (e.g. from Markus Bockmuehl and Martin Hengel) might have checked Aslan's enthusiasm for retrieving Baur's interpretation of Christian origins.

Moreover, the claim that Paul thought of himself not merely as equal to the other apostles but even as 'the *first* apostle' (186; emphasis original) flies in the face of what Paul writes in 1 Corinthians 15: 8–9, verses about which Aslan has nothing to say. Aslan calls Luke (the author of Acts) 'Paul's sycophant' (185), and slides over the fact that the Book of Acts would be accurately called 'the Acts of Peter and Paul'.

Here and there Aslan is ready to invent 'facts': for instance, that Peter had come to Rome some years before Paul arrived (196). When telling the story of crucifixion, Aslan informs us, quite gratuitously, that 'dozens died with Jesus that day' (172).

Inevitably Aslan wants to date all four Gospels later, even much later, than most New Testament scholars do. Despite Luke 1: 2 (a text he passes over in silence), Aslan excludes any talk of eyewitness testimony (xxvi). He rightly defends the priority of Mark, but describes the evangelist as simply 'adding a chronological narrative' to a 'jumble of traditions' (xxvi). Has Aslan ever heard of Richard Bauckham's recent and strong argument in support of the ancient tradition that Mark drew much from the eyewitness testimony of Peter?

Although he shows some acquaintance with the work on Jesus produced by John Meier, Aslan seems to be innocent about the various criteria that Meier and other scholars have proposed for identifying sayings and doings that reach back to the historical Jesus. Too often Aslan decides issues on the grounds that he personally finds a particular position or conclusion more attractive.

Aslan initially maintains that 'there are *only* two hard historical facts about Jesus': he was a Jew who led a popular movement, and Pilate crucified him for doing so (xxviii; emphasis added). But then he presses on to propose confidently (and sometimes correctly) a number of other conclusions—for instance, that Jesus chose a core group of twelve from among the wider ranks of his followers (97–8, 246–7), and that Jesus called himself 'the Son of Man' (136–44). In presenting Jesus as 'a revolutionary Jewish nationalist' (xxx), Aslan relies, in particular, on three further 'hard historical facts': that Jesus entered triumphantly into Jerusalem, that he 'cleansed' the Temple, and that Aslan's political interpretation of what Jesus meant by paying tribute to Caesar correctly reads what Jesus originally intended (73–8).

Aslan indulges in some careless generalizations and statements: for instance, that 'there are *numerous* passages in the gospels in which Jesus is accused of consorting with "loose women"' (246; emphasis added). But apart from Luke 7: 29, where does Aslan find possible evidence for this generalization? Even there, Simon the Pharisee did not make a public accusation of that kind, but merely 'said this to himself'. Aslan tells us that the parables of Jesus are 'riddled' with 'anticlerical sentiments' (100). But, apart from the story of the Good Samaritan, where do we find such anticlerical sentiments in other parables, such as the prodigal son, the treasure in the field, the lost sheep, or the sower sowing his crop? Aslan states that 'in the letters of Paul Jesus is repeatedly described as "of the seed of David"' (227), and refers to Romans 1: 3 and 2 Timothy 2: 8. But he agrees that 2 Timothy is not a letter of Paul. So 'repeatedly' means 'only once'. Aslan asserts that the letters of Paul 'make up the bulk of the New Testament' (29). But, even if we go beyond the seven letters that scholars normally acknowledge as authentic, Paul's letters make up considerably less than one third of the New Testament.

We are assured that '*all* of Jesus' miracle stories were embellished with the passage of time' (104; emphasis added). Certainly here and there we find minor embellishments. Where Mark 6: 44 writes of Jesus miraculously feeding five thousand men, Matthew 14: 21 adds, 'not to mention the women and children.' But where is the embellishment when Matthew 8: 28–34 and Luke 8: 26–39 abbreviate the story of Jesus delivering a possessed man in Gerasa (Mark 5: 1–20)? Matthew and Luke, far from embellishing Mark's story of the healing of a blind man at Bethsaida (Mark 8: 22–6), simply omit it.

Aslan remarks that 'to the modern mind, the stories of Jesus' healings and exorcisms seem implausible, to say the least' (104). What are we to say then about millions of Christians who today accept these stories? Do they fail to count as 'modern' people? Is 'the modern mind' monopolized by Aslan and those whom he approves?

The publishers claim that this book is 'meticulously researched' and the product of 'rigorous academic research'. Reputable New Testament scholars would not agree. Significantly, none of them is cited in praise of the book. Is this another deplorable example of pseudo-scholarship exploiting the gullible public's taste for novelty and controversy?

By 'sifting through centuries of mythmaking', Aslan is supposed to have 'uncovered' the truth that has been obscured or lost, and so 'shed new light' on the real, historical life of Jesus. Aslan calls the historian's work 'uncovering *facts*', or—more fully—'a critical analysis of observable and verifiable events in the past' (30–1; emphasis original). This long-discredited, nineteenth-century notion of history as simply uncovering facts and verifying events fails, of course, to describe what Aslan has himself done. His own presuppositions and subjective convictions constantly colour what he is ready to admit as 'facts' and 'verifiable events' and how he interprets them. Give me rather Paul's 'sycophant', Luke, a much more credible guide to the life and meaning of Jesus.

Schweitzer rightly set himself to refute Venturini's rewriting of history. A century later, Umberto Eco would quote a saying from G. K. Chesterton: 'when a man [*sic*] ceases to believe in God, he doesn't believe in nothing. He believes in anything.' Eco often expressed his agreement: 'we are supposed to live in a sceptical age. In fact, we live in an age of outrageous credulity.'

Aslan and others remain worlds apart from the belief that the Holy Spirit inspired the writing of the Sacred Scriptures. They disdain the major consequence of inspiration, the truth that the Bible conveys for thinking and living. But what they offer in place of Christian faith and the Bible looks very much like post-truth and fake news.

Select Bibliography

Abraham, W. J., *Canon and Criterion in Christian Theology* (Oxford: Clarendon Press, 1998).

Achtemeier, P. J., *Inspiration and Authority: Nature and Function of Christian Scripture* (Peabody, MA: Hendrickson, 1999), a rev. edn of *The Inspiration of Scripture* (Philadelphia: Fortress Press, 1980).

Alonso Schökel, L., *The Inspired Word: Scripture in the Light of Language and Literature*, trans. F. Martin (New York: Herder & Herder, 1965).

Barr, J., *Holy Scripture: Canon, Authority, Criticism* (Philadelphia: Westminster, 1983).

Barrett, M. M., *God's Word Alone: The Authority of Scripture* (Grand Rapids, MI: Zondervan, 2016).

Barth, K., *Church Dogmatics: The Doctrine of the Word of God*, I/2, trans. G. T. Thomson and H. Knight (Edinburgh: T. & T. Clark, 1956).

Barth, K., *Church Dogmatics: The Doctrine of the Word of God*, I/1, trans. G. W. Bromiley (Edinburgh: T. & T. Clark, 1975).

Beinhauer-Köhler, B., et al., 'Inspiration', in H.-D. Betz et al. (eds), *Religion in Geschichte und Gegenwart*, 4th edn, iv (Tübingen: Mohr Siebeck, 2001), 167–75.

Bloesch, D. G., *Holy Scripture: Revelation, Inspiration & Interpretation* (Carlisle: Paternoster Press, 1994).

Boersma, H., *Scripture as Real Presence: Sacramental Exegesis and the Early Church* (Grand Rapids, MI: Baker Academic, 2017).

Bürkle, H., et al., 'Inspiration', in W. Kasper et al. (eds), *Lexikon für Theologie und Kirche*, 3rd edn, v (Freiburg im Breisgau: Herder, 1996), 333–42.

Carpenter, D., 'Inspiration', in M. Eliade (ed.), *The Encyclopedia of Religion*, vii (New York: Macmillan, 1987), 256–9.

Carson, D. A. (ed.), *The Enduring Authority of the Christian Scriptures* (Grand Rapids, MI: Eerdmans, 2016).

Collins, R. F., 'Inspiration', in R. E. Brown, J. A. Fitzmyer, and R. E. Murphy (eds), *The New Jerome Biblical Commentary* (London: Geoffrey Chapman, 1989), 1023–33.

Copier, L., and C. Van der Stichele (eds), *Close Encounters between Bible and Film: An Interdisciplinary Engagement* (Atlanta, GA: SBL Press, 2016).

Crisp, T. M., 'On Believing that the Scriptures are Divinely Inspired', in O. D. Crisp and M. C. Rea (eds), *Analytic Theology: New Essays in the Philosophy of Theology* (Oxford: Oxford University Press, 2009), 187–213.

Davies, O., 'Hermeneutics', in J. Webster, K. Tanner, and I. Torrance (eds), *The Oxford Handbook of Systematic Theology* (Oxford: Oxford University Press, 2007), 494–510.

Davis, S. T., 'Revelation and Inspiration', in T. P. Flint and M. C. Rea (eds.), *The Oxford Handbook of Philosophical Theology* (Oxford: Oxford University Press, 2009), 30–53.

Ernst, J., and H. Gabel, 'Inspiration', in W. Kasper (ed.), *Lexikon für Theologie und Kirche*, 3rd edn, v (Freiburg im Breisgau: Herder, 1996), 533–41.

Farkasfalvy, D. M., *Inspiration and Interpretation: A Theological Introduction to Sacred Scripture* (Washington, DC: Catholic University of America Press, 2010).

Filippi, A., and E. Lora (eds), *Enchiridion Biblicum: documenti della Chiesa sulla sacra scrittura* (Bologna: Edizioni Dehoniane, 1993); an English translation is available online, Catholicscripture.net.

Fowl, S. E., *Engaging Scripture: A Model for Theological Interpretation* (Malden, MA: Blackwell, 1998).

Fowl, S. E., 'Scripture', in J. Webster, K. Tanner, and I. Torrance (eds), *The Oxford Handbook of Systematic Theology* (Oxford: Oxford University Press, 2007), 345–64.

Gabel, H., *Inspiriert und Inspirierend: Die Bibel* (Würzburg: Echter, 2011).

Goheen, M. W. (ed.), *Reading the Bible Missionally: The Gospel and our Culture* (Grand Rapids, MI: Eerdmans, 2016).

Goldingay, J., *Models of the Interpretation of Scripture* (Grand Rapids, MI: Eerdmans, 1995).

Goldingay, J., 'Scripture', in S. E. Balentine (ed.), *The Oxford Encyclopedia of the Bible and Theology*, ii (New York: Oxford University Press, 2015), 267–79.

Gorman, M. J. (ed.), *Scripture and Its Interpretation* (Grand Rapids, MI: Baker Academic, 2017).

Hays, R. B., *Echoes of Scripture in the Gospels* (Waco, TX: Baylor University Press, 2016).

Keener, C. S., *Spirit Hermeneutics: Reading Scripture in Light of Pentecost* (Grand Rapids, MI: Eerdmans, 2016).

Körtner, U. H. J., *Der inspirierter Leser. Zentrale Aspekte biblischer Hermeneutik* (Göttingen: Vandenhoeck & Ruprecht, 1994).

Lefebure, L. D., *True and Holy: Christian Scripture and other Religions* (Maryknoll, NY: Orbis, 2014).

Lieb, M., E. Mason, and J. Roberts (eds), *The Oxford Handbook of the Reception History of the Bible* (Oxford: Oxford University Press, 2011).

Limbeck, M., 'Die heilige Schrift', in W. Kern, H. J. Pottmeyer, and M. Seckler (eds), *Handbuch der Fundamentaltheologie*, iv (Freiburg im Breisgau: Herder, 1988), 37–64.

Loretz, O., *Das Ende der Inspirations-Theologie: Chancen eines Neubeginns*, 2 vols (Stuttgart: Katholisches Bibelwerk, 1974–6).

Mangenot, E., 'Inspiration de l'Écriture', *Dictionnaire de Théologie Catholique*, vii, 2nd part (Paris: Letouzy et Ane, 1927), cols 2067–266.

Marshall, I. H., *Biblical Inspiration* (London: Hodder & Stoughton, 1982).

Martin, D. B., *Biblical Truths: The Meaning of the Scripture in the Twenty-First Century* (New Haven, CT: Yale University Press, 2017).

McCall, T. M., 'Scripture as the Word of God', in O. D. Crisp and M. C. Rea (eds), *Analytic Theology* (Oxford: Oxford University Press, 2009), 171–86.

McKendrick, S., and K. Doyle, *The Art of the Bible: Illuminated Manuscripts for the Medieval World* (London: Thames & Hudson, 2016).

Moller, P. J., 'What should they be Saying about Biblical Inspiration?', *Theological Studies* 74 (2013), 605–31.

Paddison, A. (ed.), *Theologians on Scripture* (New York: Bloomsbury, 2016).

Paget, J. C., et al. (eds), *The New Cambridge History of the Bible*, 4 vols (Cambridge: Cambridge University Press 2012).

Pontifical Biblical Commission, *The Inspiration and Truth of Sacred Scripture*, trans. T. Esposito and S. Gregg (Collegeville, MN: Liturgical Press, 2014).

Pontifical Biblical Commission, *The Interpretation of the Bible in the Church* (Rome: Libreria Editrice Vaticana, 1993).

Porter, S. E., and M. Malcolm (eds), *The Future of Biblical Interpretation: Responsible Plurality in Biblical Hermeneutics* (Milton Keynes: Paternoster, 2013).

Rahner, K., *Inspiration in the Bible* (New York: Herder & Herder, 1961).

Rahner, K., 'Book of God—Book of Human Beings', *Theological Investigations* xxii, trans. J. Donceel (London: Darton, Longman & Todd, 1991), 214–24.

Reid, B. E., *Wisdom's Feast: An Invitation to Feminist Interpretation of the Scriptures* (Grand Rapids, MI: Eerdmans, 2016).

Reventlow, H. Graf, *History of Biblical Interpretation*, trans. L. G. Perdue and J. O. Duke, 4 vols (Atlanta: Society of Biblical Literature, 2009–10).

Robbins, V. K., W. S. Melion, and R. R. Jeal (eds), *The Art of Visual Exegesis: Rhetoric, Text, Images* (Atlanta, GA: SBL Press, 2017).

Rogers, P. M., 'Pierre Benoit's "Ecclesial Inspiration": A Thomistic Notion at the Heart of Twentieth-Century Debates on Biblical Inspiration', *Thomist* 80 (2016), 521–62.

Schneiders, S. M., 'Inspiration and Revelation', in K. D. Sakenfeld (ed.), *The New Interpreter's Dictionary of the Bible*, iii (Nashville: Abingdon Press, 2008), 57–63.

Smalley, B., *Study of the Bible in the Middle Ages*, 2 vols (South Bend, IN: University of Notre Dame Press, 1940–78).

Sokolowski, R., 'God's Word and Human Speech', *Nova et Vetera* 11 (2013), 187–210.

Stroumsa, G. G., *The Scriptural Universe of Ancient Christianity* (Cambridge, MA: Harvard University Press, 2016).

Sugirtharajah, R. S. (ed.), *Voices from the Margin: Interpreting the Bible in the Third World* (Maryknoll, NY: Orbis, 2016).

Vanhoozer, K. J., 'Scripture and Tradition', in K. J. Vanhoozer (ed.), *The Cambridge Companion to Postmodern Theology* (Cambridge: Cambridge University Press, 2003), 149–69.

Vawter, B., *Biblical Inspiration* (London/Philadelphia: Hutchinson/Westminster, 1972).

Ward, T., *Word and Supplement: Speech Acts, Biblical Texts, and the Sufficiency of Scripture* (Oxford: Oxford University Press, 2002).

Webster, J., *Holy Scripture: A Dogmatic Sketch* (Cambridge: Cambridge University Press, 2003).

Work, T., *Living and Active: Scripture in the Economy of Salvation* (Grand Rapids, MI: Eerdmans, 2002).

Index of Names

Biblical Index

Printed and bound by CPI Group (UK) Ltd, Croydon, CR0 4YY